Think Possible

Chicken Soup for the Soul: Think Possible
101 Stories about Using a Positive Attitude to Improve Your Life
Amy Newmark and Deborah Norville

Published by Chicken Soup for the Soul Publishing, LLC www.chickensoup.com
Copyright © 2015 by Chicken Soup for the Soul Publishing, LLC. All Rights Reserved.

The publisher gratefully acknowledges the many publishers and individuals who
granted Chicken Soup for the Soul permission to reprint the cited material.

Front cover cat photo courtesy of iStockphoto.com/oksun70 (© oksun70).
Front cover tiger photo courtesy of iStockphoto.com/GlobalP (© GlobalP).
Front cover mirror photo courtesy of iStockphoto.com/tiler84 (© tiler84).
Interior photo courtesy of iStockphoto.com/gregepperson (© gregepperson).
Photo of Amy Newmark courtesy of Susan Morrow at SwickPix.
Photo of Deborah Norville courtesy of Timothy White.

Cover and Interior by Daniel Zaccari

Distributed to the booktrade by Simon & Schuster. SAN: 200-2442

Publisher's Cataloging-In-Publication Data
(Prepared by The Donohue Group, Inc.)

Chicken soup for the soul : think possible : 101 stories about using a
   positive attitude to improve your life / [compiled by] Amy Newmark
   [and] Deborah Norville.

     pages ; cm

   ISBN: 978-1-61159-952-7

   1. Self-actualization (Psychology)--Literary collections. 2. Self-actualization
(Psychology)--Anecdotes. 3. Optimism--Literary collections. 4. Optimism--Anecdotes.
5. Goal (Psychology)--Literary collections. 6. Goal (Psychology)--Anecdotes. 7.
Attitude (Psychology)--Literary collections. 8. Attitude (Psychology)--Anecdotes. 9.
Conduct of life--Literary collections. 10. Conduct of life--Anecdotes. 11. Anecdotes.
I. Newmark, Amy. II. Norville, Deborah. III. Title: Think possible : 101 stories about
using a positive attitude to improve your life

BF637.S4 C45 2015
158.1/02   2015946941

PRINTED IN THE UNITED STATES OF AMERICA
on acid∞free paper

25 24 23 22 21 20 19 18 17 16 15   01 02 03 04 05 06 07 08 09 10 11

101 Stories about Using
a Positive Attitude
to Improve Your Life

Amy Newmark
Deborah Norville

CSS

Chicken Soup for the Soul Publishing, LLC
Cos Cob, CT

Chicken Soup for the Soul

Changing the world one story at a time®

www.chickensoup.com

Contents

❸

~Overcoming Adversity~

❹

~Proving that Persistence Pays~

❺
~Facing Your Fears~

❻
~Rising to the Challenge~

❼

~Getting on with Life~

❽

~The Wonders of a Positive Attitude~

~Recognizing Role Models~

Introduction

What if? It's a question that, when asked through life's rearview mirror, is usually answered with regrets. Conversations not had, opportunities not taken.

Now, turn your glance and look ahead toward your future. "What if?" is a question as filled with promise and potential as any you will ever hear. And there is only one way to answer it: Find out!

Everyone has times in their life when they don't try for something they could have. You didn't chat up the cute girl across the room. You didn't put yourself in the running for a promotion. You let the naysayers convince you your idea was a bad one. You didn't visit that friend who was ailing. And now — it's too late.

How much better would life be if lived with possibility? This book is filled with the stories of people who didn't heed the negative voice in their heads, who proved the experts wrong, who dug deep and as a result celebrated victories — some monumental, some small.

In some cases, it was a mantra repeated over and again: "I can and I am. I can do it and I am doing it." Jenna Glatzer's life slammed to a halt in her twenties when she suffered a panic disorder. An overwhelming case of agoraphobia took over her life — her house became her prison; the prospect of leaving it was terrifying. She couldn't even leave her room to greet friends who dropped by to check on her. "I can and I am" were words she repeated to herself as she re-engaged with the world. And did she reconnect! Jenna went on to build a successful writing career, working with such luminaries as Celine Dion!

Michael Whary isn't supposed to be an Eagle Scout or play in the school band or participate in ROTC. That's because he's autistic. Most people would consider the diagnosis a lamentable burden — Michael considers it his "superpower." He aspires to get his MBA and with his "anything is possible" attitude, I wouldn't bet against him.

Laura Snell turned her little boy's dream of visiting Disney World into a teaching experiment. At the end of the day, it was *she* who got an education in making goals a reality — and Laura shares her wisdom with the rest of us.

As for me, I've been humming a song from *Cinderella* since I was a little girl: "And because of all these daft and dewy eyed folks … impossible things are happening every day." After all, aerodynamically speaking a bumblebee should *not* be able to fly. Guess no one told the bee!

To some, the inspiration of others or a helpful phrase we repeat to ourselves is all it takes to summon up the courage or strength to keep trying. Others need proof. Some would use the term skeptic and I guess I am part of that group. I will confess to you, I have bought only one bumper sticker in my life. It read, "If your mother says she loves you, check it out." (This is the sort of stuff they sold at the journalism convention I attended during college!)

Here's a news flash if you suspect "thinking possible" is a waste of brain power: You are wrong!

I got into journalism because I have always been a bit of a research freak — or data geek, as you'd call it today. I actually *enjoy* reading the research published in academic journals. The research I've discovered reveals that when you've decided you are *going* to do something, you not only increase your chances of being successful by priming your brain to make the right choices to achieve your goal, you also make yourself less susceptible to the impediments that might crop up along the way. It's as though you've supercharged your mind and put on body armor to ward off the naysayers.

Here's how it works: Researchers have found that when you are in a deliberative mindset, that is, trying to figure out how you're going to deal with a situation, there is a tendency to see yourself as somewhat vulnerable to various negative events. But once you've decided to act— after the deliberative process — that sense of vulnerability is reduced and your cognitive powers are somewhat enhanced. The research also indicates people tend to put on "rose-colored glasses" when asked to evaluate their likelihood of success, but they say that's not necessarily a bad thing. On the contrary, it acts as "mind fuel" to help you reach your goal. What this means is that when you've decided to act, especially after considering all your options, you're less likely to be derailed by doubts because you've decided in *your* mind that you *are* going to do it! Some researchers even believe that *irrevocable commitments* are formed when people actually act on their goals. Maybe that's why Nike is so successful. After all, their slogan is "Just do it!"

This book is filled with proof. Deborah J. was told she didn't stand a chance of finishing college when the track star found herself single and pregnant. Her scholarship money hinged on her staying on the team and competing. Along with caring for an infant on her own, she not only got back on the track, she improved her times in her event *and* completed her studies, graduating *summa cum laude*. She says that "nearly impossible" are words she doesn't allow in her vocabulary.

Of course, not every dream comes true. Some of these stories don't end with "happily ever after," and yet the authors share with us the wisdom that can come from that. Carole Brody Fleet lost her husband and father within four months of one another. Her grief was unimaginable, and it was hard to find resources to help her deal with the practical side of being suddenly widowed. Then one day she realized the notes she was taking as she dealt with financial and other matters might be helpful to others. The realization led to her founding an online support group for widows and writing three books—so far.

Even thinking there was some good to come from her pain probably helped Carole get through the difficult times. Again, let's take a look at the data. Researchers have found that just believing something is possible has protective psychological benefits. They call it "positive illusions," and while most of us probably don't like thinking we might be "fooling ourselves," doing just that has been found to boost our emotional state, which in turn can have a positive impact on our health and the quality of our relationships. Thinking something is *possible* — though it might not happen — can help one cope. There's even one study that found "unrealistically optimistic beliefs" might be linked to "greater longevity." The jury may still be out on that one, but it's clear the research is telling us that there is nothing to lose by "thinking possible," and perhaps much to gain.

So settle down with a nice cup of tea and take a journey with us of wishes and hopes and dreams realized — and see if in your own life, what others say is impossible becomes reality for you.

~Deborah Norville

Chapter 1

Think
Possible

Following Your Heart

Impossible

Nothing is impossible, the word itself says
"I'm possible."
~Audrey Hepburn

It was one of my favorite nights of the year: the night *Cinderella* came on TV. My mom would make chocolate fudge and my three sisters and I were given the very rare treat of getting to eat the snack in the family room. We gathered around the TV — much too close to the screen — and marveled at how Lesley Ann Warren was transformed from the ash-covered girl in the garret to the glittering princess who stole Prince Charming's heart. We watched it in black and white — but to our young eyes, it was the most beautiful show in the world.

"Impossible," we sang along with the Fairy Godmother, " ...for a plain yellow pumpkin to become a golden carriage." We knew *all* the words. "Impossible. For a plain country bumpkin and a prince to join in marriage." Decades later, I am not at all surprised I still know the words. The Norville girls had them committed to memory and for me, at least, those lyrics became an anthem that I would later sing to myself every time an obstacle presented itself.

Of *course* it was impossible for a pumpkin to turn into a carriage or mice to be transformed into white horses. Everyone knew that! But who was to say that a person of common background couldn't marry the heir to a throne? Look how many non-royals now have titles!

For me the dream wasn't to marry a handsome prince, but to

get a job in television — something just as farfetched for a kid who grew up in a town that barely had a radio station. "Impossible..." the song played in my head, "for a no one from Georgia to become a news reporter. Impossible." The idea *was* ridiculous. Who was I kidding? How could someone with no connections, no important family, no fancy education even *think* she had a shot at a job on television? I wasn't the kid who acted in high school plays or was a cheerleader. I had always been solidly planted in that group of students who were just "there." On top of that, I was blond and the only blondes on television in those days were the "weather bunnies" — the buxom blondes who forecast the weather, though it always seemed their hiring had more to do with their appearance than any discernible meteorological skills. I might be hirable thanks to my hair color, but by that measure my figure was a deal breaker!

Still I dreamed. After all, the Fairy Godmother pointed out to Cinderella that the world was filled with people who didn't follow the rules. Filled with people who, because they barreled along seemingly deaf to all the naysayers, made "impossible things" happen every day.

So I pursued my dream while my friends had sensible ambitions. This guy's major would land him a job in insurance. That gal was headed to law school. Another was an education major — teachers always land a job. I kept my grades up and my head down — either in my books or in the TV industry magazines in the journalism school's library. "How bad could it be to live in Pocatello, Idaho?" I asked myself when spotting a job opening at a station there. "Where *was* Pocatello, Idaho?" was the follow-up question! If that's where I had to start my career, I figured I could manage Pocatello for a year or so.

But first, I needed some practical experience — an internship. Being buried in my books happily resulted in my GPA remaining a perfect 4.0. I applied for a position at WSB-TV, the long dominant television station in Atlanta. On paper I looked great: grades — spot on. Activities — lots of 'em, important ones too. Writing — good enough, I guess. But the one category I couldn't control is the one that tripped me up: my age. I was a year younger than all the other applicants, having tested out of my freshman year so I could enter college as a sophomore. "Come apply next year when you are a year older," the station's representative had suggested. It was as though the ugly stepsisters had just stared at my tattered dress and laughed, "You'll never go to the ball in *that!*"

Then my Fairy Godmother appeared in the form of an Executive Producer at Georgia Public Television. He had no sparkle dust or magic wand, but what he did have was an internship. He produced a daily one-hour show recapping the activities of the Georgia General Assembly. My home state was one of the first to allow cameras inside the legislative chambers and his show captured all the action — if you can call it "action" to watch the debate about which firm gets the state contract to make the reflective stuff for license plates. He had four positions and three slots were filled. The first three interns were all women attending the University of Georgia, as was I. He was under great pressure to choose a male from another institution. Nonetheless, I was granted an interview. This time my age didn't matter. He was impressed with the fact that despite my many campus activities I was carrying a perfect grade point average. Cinderella *was* going to the ball! I got the internship. And — a guy from Georgia State University got it too. He was tasked with reporting the weekend version of the show. It's possible!

Perhaps that is why in the years since my Fairy Godmother gave me my television break I have always gravitated toward the stories of people who refused to accept someone else's lowered expectations for their lives. I wrote about some of them in my book, *Back on Track*: people like the parents of Marisa Thomas, who entered this world as a breathtakingly beautiful baby. As the Thomases were about to leave the hospital they were told their daughter had a rare condition called microcephaly — an abnormally small brain. The couple's world fell to pieces as the doctors predicted their daughter would be blind and would never walk or talk. "She probably won't know you're her parents," one said. A nurse suggested they put her in an institution.

Marisa's parents refused. They took their profoundly handicapped baby home and agonized over how to find something their daughter could do. Then they noticed that when music was played in Marisa's room, she brightened. Her dad would dance around with Marisa in his arms and her face would fill with unbridled joy. Perhaps *music* was the key that would unlock the door to this little girl. That's when Marisa's parents found their Fairy Godmother: Clive Robbins, the founder of the Nordoff-Robbins Center for Music Therapy, which helps physically and mentally handicapped children who are unresponsive to other programs. Sessions proceeded at a snail's pace — but they *were* moving forward. Two years after starting music therapy, Marisa was able to hold a cup and feed herself. Four years after beginning the program she began to talk! Eventually she "graduated" from music therapy and was enrolled in a school program for multiply handicapped children. It's possible!

The German writer Johann Wolfgang von Goethe said, "Magic is believing in yourself — If you can do that, you can make anything happen." I have come to believe that this is true. And the best part of all — you don't have to have a Fairy Godmother.

~Deborah Norville

Until My Dying Breath

*A hero is an ordinary person who finds the strength
to persevere and bless others, in spite of
overwhelming obstacles.*
~Christopher Reeve

Do you remember the lyrics from a song on *Hee Haw* that lamented, "If it weren't for bad luck, I'd have no luck at all?" Well, that could have been the theme song of Barbara Brown. Despite enduring enough trials to compose a Grammy-winning country ballad, Barbara was the most inspiring patient I ever doctored.

The seventh of eight children, Barbara was born to an alcoholic mom and a marginally employed, abusive dad. Her mother chugged whiskey at the neighborhood bar most nights and then zonked out on the couch, hung over, the next day. Her father clobbered his wife and kids for the slightest infraction — a charred burger, a minor sibling squabble. In short, Barbara had every excuse to resort to drugs and alcohol — anything to escape the hellish place she was forced to call home. Instead, she found respite at her local church, where the pastor's wife and several other ladies ensured she had school clothes, encouragement, and plenty of warm hugs.

To survive the abuse at home, Barbara's siblings stuck together like a school of guppies. "How could I become bitter when my older sisters worked so hard after school to buy peanut butter, bread, and milk for me? God blessed me with wonderful sisters and a supportive church family, so I had much to be grateful for," Barbara insisted.

When a handsome classmate took an interest in her and proposed marriage after high school graduation, he didn't have to ask twice! A road out of Dysfunction Junction? Hand me the car keys! "When Roger held me in his arms and told me he loved me and would always take care of me, I couldn't believe my luck. I'd always wanted to be a wife and mother, and thanks to Roger that dream came true."

Over the next twelve years, Barbara bore six children who kept her running from baseball to football to piano lessons. At forty-two, she delivered a baby girl with Down syndrome. While many women would feel devastated or overwhelmed by the demands of a mentally challenged child, Barbara adored her baby girl. "You couldn't find a more loving child than my Alice. Her hugs and sweet smiles light up my day."

Life was good until the dreadful day Roger revealed that while he loved her and didn't want to break up their family, he now realized he was gay. "I can no longer deny who I really am," he fearfully confessed. Barbara was devastated — she loved Roger deeply and didn't want to destroy their loving family.

She had a choice: divorce, or tolerate a husband who caroused at gay bars on Saturday nights. Deeply religious, she didn't believe in divorce. "He's a great father, a good provider, he doesn't drink or beat me. He's kind and gentle, and we've been through so much together. How can I throw all that away because he has this one issue?"

Tears rolled down her cheeks as she disclosed her secret to me. I handed her a tissue, and she wiped her eyes and blew her nose. "What do I do, Dr. Burbank? He says he loves me and doesn't want a divorce. I don't either." She wrung her tissue between her fingers. "I love Roger, but it kills me every time he leaves on Saturday night — I know where he's going and what he's up to."

Right or wrong, Barbara chose to stay, and she developed a cordial, co-parenting partnership with her husband. Despite the pain and betrayal, she insisted, "I'm choosing to focus on what's good in Roger, and there's a lot that's good."

Instead of nursing her hurt or growing bitter, Barbara channeled her energy into a quilting group that raised money for African orphanages. Some of the quilts she designed were so exquisite they fetched $1200 apiece. "I might not have a college degree, but I know how to quilt, and God can use any talent we have for His glory," she said.

If a rotten childhood, handicapped child, and gay husband weren't challenging enough, Barbara's health nosedived. First, she developed breast cancer necessitating surgery, chemotherapy, and radiation. Then she got diabetes brittle enough to require insulin injections with every meal. A year later, her heart and neck arteries clogged, requiring extensive vascular surgery. With time, her vision deteriorated from macular degeneration. Sadly, she could no longer stitch the intricate quilts upon which she'd built her reputation.

Did she complain? Give up? Not Barbara! She started a new ministry — a cooking class for all the newlyweds at her church, saying, "Some of these girls can barely boil water. Don't they teach Home Economics anymore?"

Her class was a hit. Some weeks, more than a dozen women learned to roll a piecrust, baste a roast, and steam vegetables al dente. The women graced the tables with red plaid tablecloths, cleverly folded napkins, and vases teeming with cheery daisies. The young wives giggled and glowed as they served home-cooked feasts to a roomful of hungry — and grateful — husbands.

Unfortunately, Barbara's health declined even further. She suffered such severe lumbar disc disease and arthritis in her knees that she could only get around in a wheelchair. Worse still, her kidneys failed, requiring thrice-weekly hemodialysis. She was now too weak to cook for herself, let alone teach a class.

To his credit, her husband kept his promise to always take care of her, and he took over the cooking, cleaning, shopping, banking, and nursing care. He drove her to lengthy dialysis treatments every Monday, Wednesday, and Friday, and he carefully divvied out her medications at the proper time. He prepared a strict diabetic, renal, low-salt diet.

Eventually, Roger's strength waned as well. They hired a homemaker to help with cooking and cleaning. Only problem? The woman couldn't cook! Roger wanted to fire her. "She's useless," he sputtered. "She burned the toast and the eggs were raw!"

Barbara would have none of it! "We can't fire her, Roger. She's a single mother and she needs this job. If she can't cook, she'll be fired everywhere she goes. What will happen to her two little girls?"

You guessed it! Barbara, while sitting in her wheelchair, nearly blind, riddled with back pain and requiring thrice-weekly dialysis, taught the "homemaker" how to prepare chicken and dumplings, beef stew, quiche, and meatloaf. "God put this girl in my life so I could teach her to cook. I can improve her job skills. I may not be able to walk or read fine print anymore, but even in a wheelchair I can teach her to sift flour and baste a chicken. Until my dying breath, I will bless others any way I can."

I will never forget Barbara's make-the-best-of-what-you've-got-left attitude. She looked for ways to bless others with whatever strength and ability she had. She found joy, humor, and purpose in life, despite her many setbacks. She chose to focus on the good qualities in a husband, handicapped child, and hired homemaker whom others might condemn or write off as a burden. Barbara was my hero.

~Sally Willard Burbank

Hiccups

*Anger makes you smaller, while forgiveness forces you
to grow beyond what you were.*
~Chérie Carter-Scott

zzzzz… Bzzzzzz… Groggy, I reached for my cell. Caller ID answered my first question: Jim. Glancing at the clock answered my second: 3 a.m. Not a surprise. Jim and I had been dating for about a year and I was used to his late night texts and impromptu calls. I yawned my hello.

"Annie, I have to tell you something."

"All right…?"

"I haven't been completely honest with you," Jim stammered. "I'm not the man you think I am."

My stomach lurched as goose bumps chilled my skin. "What are you talking about? What do you mean you're not the man I think you are?"

Alternate identities swirled through my mind — Married, Money Launderer, Ex-Con — none of which seemed remotely possible. When I tiptoed into the dating scene after my divorce, I quickly discovered that there was a world of liars out there. But I couldn't fathom that Jim was one of them.

"There was somebody else," he faltered. "I was unfaithful to you."

Of all the "who could he be" tumbling around my head, "Cheater" was the last thing I expected. Jim had pursued me relentlessly since the day we met. His early declarations of love emboldened me to risk loving him in return. Jim's kindness and devotion restored my faith that good guys were out there — that maybe he was the good guy for me. Another woman? Who was she? How long had this been going on? How could I not have noticed?

Jim's voice pulled me back. "It was only once… a few months ago… she's an old friend… I am so sorry. I never meant to hurt you. The guilt of this has been eating me up — I had to tell you. I couldn't stand for you not to know. I couldn't…"

"Do you — do you love her?" I choked out the question.

"Oh my God — no. Annie, you're the love of my life. I've loved you since the day we met and I'll continue to love you until the day I die. I'm so sorry for betraying everything we have — I just… I hope you can forgive me. But if you can't, I understand, because I'm not sure I can forgive myself."

"Do you know how much I want to hate you?" I asked as I hung up the phone.

A flurry of text messages came next, and as the morning sun filtered into the corners of my bedroom, we agreed to get together that evening to talk.

I slogged through the day, replaying our conversation and obsessing over when this "one time thing" could have happened. I vacillated between relief that Jim wasn't an ax murderer and rage that he cheated on me. I desperately rationalized that he didn't really cheat since we weren't married or even engaged. I finally called Liz, my best friend, so she could share my misery. She was in more of a state of disbelief than I.

"But this is Jim," Liz repeated. "Jim. He's adored you since the day you met. He loves you. I really think this is forgivable. Don't you?"

Forgivable? Not a concept I was eager to consider — especially since my divorce. My ex-husband was a bitter and controlling man and throughout our marriage I doled out more than my fair share of forgiveness. I was not about to endure another relationship where "It's-okay-I-know-you-didn't-mean-to" was the dialogue *du jour*. On the other hand, everyone makes mistakes, right? Was one slip in what was otherwise an incredibly solid and loving relationship reason enough to walk away? Was it possible to forgive an infidelity that I could not forget? Did I love Jim enough to risk trusting him again?

When Jim knocked on my door that evening, slumped in remorse and defeat, my plan to smack him across the face or pound on his chest in fury dissolved. "I am so, so, so sorry," he sobbed as he pulled me into his arms. "Can you please forgive me? Please?" In his embrace, despite my hurt and anger, the overwhelming emotion I felt was surprisingly, hope — hope that I could get past this. The thought of bidding a permanent goodbye to Jim pained me more than his indiscretion. I wanted nothing more than to be able to do what he was pleading with me to do — forgive.

I realized I had to decide: was this moment a hiccup or a heart attack? Was this something I could put behind me so our relationship could heal or was it a deadly blow? The fact that Jim had come clean about his unfaithfulness of his own accord, when in all likelihood I would have never found out on my own, gave me some peace of mind. He had admitted his disloyalty without being caught, which helped me accept that his apology was sincere. Instead of perpetuating the betrayal by keeping it secret, Jim had confessed. I wanted to believe I could trust him now even more than before. "I want to find a way to trust you again," I told Jim as he got ready to go home for the night. "It's going to take time, and patience on your part, for me to work through this, but I want to work through this. I still love you."

Jim clung to me. "I love you too," he replied. " I'm so scared to go home. I'm scared I'll wake up tomorrow and you'll have changed your mind."

"I'm scared of that too," I admitted.

It took many months to put the "hiccup" behind me: months when I spontaneously grabbed Jim's phone to check his text messages, months when I showed up unannounced at his apartment, months when I demanded proof that he was really traveling on business when he went out of town. But Jim gave me what I needed — honest answers to very pointed questions about "that night," reassurance through his words and actions that he respected me, and understanding when I fell back into "where-were-you-really?" mode. Eventually, I stopped trying to catch Jim in another lie and trusted that he was the steadfast, honest, faithful man I had fallen in love with. It was a relief finally to forgive him, and with my forgiveness, Jim was able to forgive himself as well.

Four years and many proposals after the hiccup, I finally said yes. Marrying Jim is one the best decisions I have made. Forgiving him is the other. Our relationship isn't perfect, but neither are we — neither of us is immune to some variety of hiccups now and then. But Jim and I have learned that asking for and granting forgiveness is essential to our commitment to one another. Loving again after my divorce was risky and forgiving Jim when he faltered was tough. But both have allowed me to find real love — love grounded in a trust that forgiveness is a gift we are willing to give one another.

~Annie Thibodeaux

Doctor's Orders

Desire is transformed into drive when a dream creates
a passion for action.
~Dr. Robert Anthony

I was sitting in the lobby of a doctor's office waiting for my annual check-up. I was impatiently applying my favorite apple-scented lotion to my hands when the nurse called me back to see the doctor.

I plopped myself down in the examining room chair, annoyed that my mom had even scheduled the appointment to begin with. As doctors so often do, when he arrived he dove right in to the basic small talk about my health history. But then he threw in a question that took me off guard.

"So Robin, what are you going to do after high school?" he asked while scribbling away on the file in front of him.

What was I going to do after high school? Was he kidding me? He wasn't. He continued scribbling away at his notes, with not even a glance in my direction.

"Uh... I don't know," I mumbled. I didn't know. I was seventeen. I didn't have any idea what I was going to do after high school. I had just had a meeting with my high school guidance counselor about this very subject. A meeting in which she told me in no uncertain terms that I wasn't "college material" — and I believed her. My grades were sub-par. Education wasn't exactly emphasized in my family. "You don't know? Well, why don't you go to college to become a doctor like me?" He smiled as he glanced at his watch.

Go to college to become a doctor? Who was this man kidding? I thought he was crazy for even suggesting it. I was the youngest of five children and no one in my family had even graduated from college, let alone become a doctor. And I wasn't college material.

Yet, none of this mattered. He remained silent, awaiting my response. I looked up and noticed his gaze remained focused on his file, still scribbling away.

Rattled by his question, I blurted out what I believed to be true. "I'm not smart enough to be a doctor."

Time seemed to stand still. The doctor immediately stopped writing; he capped his pen and turned toward me. He moved any and all distractions aside; he looked me straight in the eyes when he very seriously said, "Let me tell you something; you don't have to be smart to be a doctor. You just have to be persistent."

Just as quickly as time seemed to stop, it abruptly picked back up again. The doctor hurriedly gathered his things and rushed off to his next appointment. I never saw him again. On the ride home I found myself thinking about what he had said. I continued to think about it when I was at school. What *would* I do after high school?

Even though I wasn't college material, that doctor made an impression on me. I applied to a college close to home and soon found myself walking the campus as a new student.

I felt completely out of place. I was going through the motions but I often questioned what I was doing there. Had I set myself up to fail? Then I would think back to that doctor's appointment. Maybe I wasn't smart enough for college, but I *could* be persistent.

So, I began breaking down anything that seemed daunting into steps. For example, I didn't think I could pass the statistics course that was required for my program. While I didn't think it was possible to pass the course, I did think it was possible to get a passing grade on the first assignment. "After all, anything is at least possible, right?" I found myself thinking. "Surely, stranger things have happened," I would tell myself.

I put all my energy toward passing the first assignment and when

I did, I put all my energy into passing the next assignment. Then I put my all into passing the first exam and so on. Viewing each assignment individually didn't seem so overwhelming. Individually, it seemed maybe possible.

I used this approach for each task and sure enough, the sum of each individual achievement got me through the course and then I started all over again with the next. I discovered that when I was persistent, I could achieve things I never believed possible. I was pleasantly surprised to find that with each individual achievement came newfound confidence in myself.

I became the first in my family to graduate with a bachelor's degree. I began to dream bigger.

If I could graduate with a bachelor's degree, I wondered if it was possible to earn a master's degree. For the longest time I had convinced myself that I shouldn't press my luck but the question of "What if?" remained. Ten years later I gave in to the "What if?" and I enrolled in a master's degree program.

I honestly thought I was crazy for even trying. I was working full-time when I enrolled. Then I got married and then I got pregnant. It wasn't easy juggling work, a marriage, becoming a new parent and the seemingly endless and lengthy assignments. But, I persisted. I had grit. I thought possible. I graduated with a master's degree in September 2014, two decades after that conversation with my doctor. I only wish I could remember his name. I still think of him often and wish I could shake his hand and tell him "thank you." Sometimes even the smallest moments in time can have a life-changing impact.

Even if you're told you don't have what it takes to succeed, it's important that you never stop dreaming. Don't let anyone tell you what you can't do. Sometimes even the "experts" are wrong: get a second opinion. And then get a third opinion, or better yet, don't even ask them — find out the answer for yourself.

Think possible.

~Robin L. Reynolds

The Little Voice Inside My Heart

You have to leave the city of your comfort and go into
the wilderness of your intuition. What you'll discover
will be wonderful. What you'll discover is yourself.
~Alan Alda

I thought about a lot of things as I sat in that room. I thought about everything that had happened. I thought about the baby I had lost and what that meant for me and for everyone else. I thought about the trouble I had been getting myself into and why. I thought about how I had become someone that I didn't even recognize. I thought about how it had taken ten years for me to come to that realization. What on earth happened?

I knew that I could end it all right then. I knew that it was what I wanted and the only way that I would ever be happy again. All I had to do was get up, walk out of the room, and say two words. Two little words... And yet, even knowing all of that, I just sat there, absolutely paralyzed with fear.

There was still the part of me that wanted to fix everything. By "fix" I meant "keep things the same." That would have been the easy thing to do. And deep down inside, I knew things were different. They would never be the same again.

I walked out of the room and found him sitting in the living room. My heart was pounding and I was holding back tears. I couldn't bear to look him in the eye so I stared at the floor. I opened my mouth to speak, to say, "I'm done," but he spoke instead.

"I want a divorce."

There was that uncontrollable urge to stop him again… to "fix" things. It took every ounce of strength that I had to stop myself from doing it. I took a deep breath and managed to say, "Okay." Then I turned around, calmly walked back to the bedroom, and completely broke down.

We had been together for nine years and married for half that time. This hurt. It felt like someone was tearing my heart from my chest.

Our relationship had seen all kinds of turmoil over the years: family tragedies, addiction and alcoholism, depression, secrets, lies, miscarriage. It was no wonder neither of us could find it in ourselves to hold on any longer. We both hurt so much because of all that had happened that all we could do was hurt each other. It had been this way for as long as I could remember. We didn't want to be mean to each other; it just happened.

I sat in that room for another couple of hours, envisioning my whole world crumbling around me. I ended up leaving him that night.

We talked a week later and came to the conclusion that we couldn't work things out. We parted ways. I moved out. I slept on friends' and family's couches for about a month. I rented a condo that I couldn't afford. I went to work at my boring office job. I spent my nights in bars and in the arms of men who couldn't offer me any more than I could offer them. I was hopelessly lost. I felt empty.

I tried to keep my friends around me but only succeeded in pushing them away. I burned countless bridges. I couldn't seem to keep my head above water long enough to catch my breath. I felt like I was drowning. And I was giving into it. After reading through fifteen years of my journals, I came to the sad realization that I didn't know who I was or what I wanted. But, thankfully, there was a little voice inside my heart that wanted to know.

A year and a half later, I finally built up the courage to listen. I wanted a better life. I didn't want to drink anymore. I wanted to be active and adventurous. I wanted a job that I could be passionate about. I wanted to feel true happiness. Toronto had become, for me, a breeding ground for negativity. I felt like I wouldn't be able to break my cycle of self-destruction if I stayed there any longer... I felt an incredible force urging me to run.

So I listened to the little voice inside my heart and I made the huge decision to move to Winnipeg. I needed to make a change and I knew it was the right choice. I could feel it in my bones. For the first time in over a decade, I felt positive energy flowing through my body. I felt free.

It was incredibly emotional saying goodbye to my friends and family. But my sadness was outweighed by my excitement about what was to come. I stayed with my cousin when I got to Winnipeg, and I spent as much time as possible by myself, writing. I wrote about my hopes and my dreams and everything that I wanted. I finally took the time to get to know myself at age thirty-one.

Along with all that self-reflection came a lot of anger. I was mad at my ex for not being what I wanted him to be. I was mad at my friends for expecting too much from me. Over time though, I discovered that the person who I was truly mad at was myself. I had let myself down! I had put everyone else's lives and needs above my own and it had left me broken.

Sometimes I wanted to give up. I had sad days when I wanted to run back to Toronto, to the comfort of my friends and my local bar and to everything else that was familiar. But I resisted. I listened to that little voice that told me to keep moving forward. I tried new things. I met new people. I became more comfortable and more confident. I was pleasantly surprised.

I made time for myself. I continued to write and spent time embracing my thoughts instead of running from them. I surrounded myself with positive people and positive activities and life became so much bigger and so much brighter. I found a job helping troubled youth. I love having the opportunity to help other people overcome their negativity like I was able to.

I fell in love with a kind and empathetic man. We go on all kinds of excellent adventures together, traveling all over the world, which is both incredible and inspiring. I moved to Saskatchewan to be with him three years ago. For me, the prairies are the most beautiful place on the planet. I love being surrounded by open air and endless sky. It makes me feel at peace.

I was driving the other day and I actually pulled over to take in the most glorious sunrise. It's so important to appreciate these moments. I am overwhelmingly thankful for the path that I was finally able to follow once I listened to that little voice inside my heart. I am exactly where I was meant to be.

~Jen Gulka

Safari for One

Don't ask what the world needs. Ask what makes you come alive, and go do it. Because what the world needs is people who have come alive.
~Howard Thurman

"Hey Mom! Having a great time in South Africa! We sent you three pictures Dad took on his Blackberry. The animals are so cool! We've seen big ones and small ones and yellow ones and gray ones and more ones! Wish you were here!"

But I wasn't there — I was home recovering from the mumps. The mumps, of all things!

My husband had been invited to speak at a conference in South Africa during a time that coincided with a milestone birthday for each of us, and we had decided to seize the opportunity and celebrate on safari. But my body wasn't cooperating. In a period of five months, I had contracted severe asthma and anemia, undergone surgery, contracted shingles, and then the mumps. My body was waving a white flag, and I needed to take notice.

I'd been a good friend to my body most of my life. It told me when I needed to de-stress and get a good massage, when I needed to eat less sugar and drink more water, when I needed to chill out and get a good night's sleep. It told me when I needed to get help. My body had been telling me for the last few years, in not-so-subtle ways, that I needed to take better care of myself. When did I start ignoring it? Finally, it grabbed my attention by succumbing to that series of illnesses that slammed into each other like dominoes.

The date of departure for South Africa loomed closer, and I was not ready. But I hated to give up the trip of a lifetime. I was trying to will myself better in time to travel. I believed it was possible for me to make that double-milestone birthday celebration with my husband. And I was trying to listen to my body — was it telling me that the trip would be good for me, that I needed to get away from it all? I wrestled with the decision; it consumed me.

Then my dad came over. It was mid-afternoon, and I had been in bed all day. I didn't have the energy to water a plant, much less make dinner, and he was bringing me soup that my mother had made. He stood at the doorway of my bedroom and shook his head. "Robin, don't go on this trip. Let the twins go instead. It'll be a wonderful father-son bonding trip for them, and you can have ten days without taking care of anyone. You need the break. Africa will be there when you're better. It's really a no-brainer."

A no-brainer. Africa will be there. My dad had such a way of taking a tough decision and making it seem simple.

Besides, there was a different opportunity: if I stayed home, I could attend a writers' conference. I had discovered it on the Internet, a local conference that would take place during the last weekend of the South Africa trip. I began to think about it. Instead of spending twenty-three hours on an airplane, I could sleep for another week and then drive down the road to the writers' event. The funny thing was, the prospect of going to this conference became more exciting to me than the prospect of going on a safari. Suddenly, my heart was speaking to me with a booming, "Yes! This is what I want to do!"

I always did like to write. Ironically enough, I had begun to dabble in it a bit when my youngest — my twins — were infants. I would sit on the couch, balance my laptop on the armrest, and nurse a baby in one arm while typing with the other. I had gotten an article published and started a book. I was pried away from the writing, however, when the twins began to move on their own. Then time blurred as my children grew. I had been raising kids and volunteering, running from after-school functions to family gatherings, for twenty years. With fourteen-year-old twin boys at home, I was still in the proverbial tunnel. But, I could see a light… it was a tiny pinprick of light, but it was a light. And maybe there was something at the end of the tunnel for me.

The day of departure arrived. I kissed everyone goodbye and went back to bed. The house was quiet and I slept for ten-hour stretches each night. Yet as I thought about the conference, I became more energized. I went there refreshed and returned home elated. I had met writers, editors, and agents; I had gotten feedback on my writing and my book idea. I had a new direction. I could call myself a writer.

Then I saw the message on my laptop from my boys — "wish you were here" — and felt a pang of regret. It would have been a romantic journey to share with my husband, to go on a safari with him and see all that exotic wildlife — the big ones and small ones and yellow ones and gray ones and more ones. I read the message again and smiled at the adventure that the three of them were experiencing, and I was glad of it.

They came home sharing photos and stories. An elephant almost overturned their Jeep; they saw a cheetah on the hunt; the food was delicious; my husband's presentation went well.

And I started writing.

I had a renewed focus. It was time for me to gently decline the many volunteer requests that came my way and to answer another calling. I was still a mother, a wife, a sister, a daughter, a neighbor, a friend; I was still an everything-in-law; but I was also giving myself permission to take care of myself. Every so often, I had to say "no" to everyone else in order to say "yes" to myself. Otherwise, that trickle of creative juice inside me would be sucked dry again, my health and spirit withering with it.

I began to write columns. I was published in my local newspaper. I joined a writers' club and a critique group. I worked on my book. I was hired as a regular columnist. I stayed home from coffee meetings and dinner gatherings, and wrote instead. And gradually, my body strengthened.

Two years after the safari trip, my father was diagnosed with lymphoma. He fought it with all of his strength and wit and good humor; he did everything the doctors told him to do. But the disease crossed into his brain and it took him.

With every piece of writing that I publish I think of my father, of how he helped me start on the path that brought me back to myself and to better health. Like someone who took me by the hand and led me to a mirror, he helped me see what I already knew.

I think of my father all the time. I tell him about the pieces I am writing — the big ones and small ones and sad ones and funny ones and more ones.

And then I say, "Dad, I wish you were here."

~Robin Conte

The Red Chair

Passion is energy. Feel the power that comes from
focusing on what excites you.
~Oprah Winfrey

There are dreams. And then there are dreams. I learned that from Oprah Winfrey. As a teenager, I would race home after school to watch her on TV. I often began my sentences with, "Oprah says…" I "joined" her book club. But more than anything, I wanted to sit in those red audience chairs. How lucky those people were! One day, I told myself, I would be as lucky as them. I didn't know how I would get there; I just prayed that I would.

"Send her a postcard," my friend Evette said. "That's how they pick you. It worked for me — twice!"

"Yeah, right," I sulked. "My parents will never let me go."

The problem was, I'd never even asked my parents if I could go. I just pictured them shaking their heads so I pushed the thought away.

I was an Oprah student, not just a fan. The naysayers in my life considered her teachings "luxuries." Money, degrees, marriage — those were tangible things that they valued. Self-esteem and following one's life purpose came afterwards and only if you had time after the "real" stuff was accomplished.

Still, Oprah remained my Dream Advocate. Whenever adults told me to do something — apply to university, get a job, find a husband — Oprah showed me how to be someone. My parents and teachers had my best interests at heart and they knew how indecisive I could be. I knew I was zoning out when Calculus began to look like Japanese but I couldn't figure out how to be my authentic self. I buried my nose in my books. In my dreams I flew like Icarus towards the sun, turned into a super sleuth and became the next Nancy Drew. In my dreams I was invincible.

But, of course, life intruded and by the time I was twenty-five I was equipped with two degrees, married to my high school sweetheart and had purchased my first new car. I should've been happy. Perhaps I was, for a bit. But I slowly lost focus and became obsessed with having more instead of being more. I hated my data entry job and I longed to start a family of my own. My dreams of sitting in the plush red chair were drowned out by resentment of getting what I thought I wanted. Instead, I grew increasingly hostile. It was never enough. Soon the red chair faded from memory.

Seven years later my husband and I owned a home, had three beautiful children, and I was able to stay at home full-time. Everything I ever wanted, right? Nope. The only thing that was getting stronger was my denial.

"Request *Oprah* tickets online," Evette said. "Just fill out the form."

"I don't think so," I said. "I can't afford to go."

"You can't afford not to go," Evette stressed. "Just try. It can't hurt."

But it would. If I applied for the tickets and didn't get them I'd never get over the rejection. It was so close to my heart. However, if I got tickets and had to turn them down, there would be a hole in my heart even Dr. Oz wouldn't be able to fix.

Day after day, I sulked and grew bitter. I felt like the worst wife, mother, daughter, and friend by the minute. I wasn't who I was supposed to be and I became even more miserable while I watched my friends live out their dreams. Travel. Promotions. Adventures. I challenged myself every day to be the worst I could be and I was getting good at it! Just when I thought I couldn't go any lower, I'd dig myself into an even deeper hole. Soon I'd be hitting the Earth's core.

On November 20, 2009 I was rocked out of my misery. As I held my infant son and watched TV, Oprah announced that her show would end after twenty-five years. In eighteen months the red chairs would disappear. Panic and misery sent me into a tailspin.

That night I couldn't sleep. When the house was quiet, I tiptoed into the living room and cracked open the laptop. Navigating the cyber world, I made my way to Oprah.com. For a minute I hovered over the keyboard. Why didn't I do this years ago? What made me think I could do this now? Without knowing the answers, or perhaps knowing them all too well, I took a deep breath, filled out the audience request form and pressed the "send" button.

I could hardly believe what I'd done. I'd just poured out my heart, telling Oprah how lost I felt. That if I could just have this one thing my world would be all right. Tears rolled down my cheeks. I wiped them away and ran to soothe my hungry baby.

Today when I look back, I know this was the first time in my adult life that I made a decision that wasn't based on career, family or money. There was no logical rationale behind it. It was purely a selfish decision. Later, I would see that it wasn't selfishness as much as it was self-love.

For the next eighteen months I prayed to be sent to the red chair. I pleaded, wished and hoped. I had never let myself do that before. Every day I checked my e-mail, disappointed that I had not been chosen. Oprah's last show would tape on May 24, 2011 without me ever being able to so much as breathe on the red chenille chair.

At midnight on May 21st, I scrolled through my e-mail, already having accepted my defeat… and like the miracle I thought would never happen, the screen blinked back: OPRAH AUDIENCE TICKETS. RESPOND ASAP. I couldn't believe it — my essay had worked!

I clicked open the message and screamed. It wasn't just tickets to Oprah's last season, it was Oprah's last show — ever!

Within forty-eight hours, I had babysitting (bless you, Mom!), a flight to Chicago, and Evette as my date. My dream had finally come true. I was going to sit — no, dance — in that gorgeous red chair!

That day, Oprah delivered a valuable gift: a love letter. This is what she said: "Life whispers to all of us. If we don't listen, the whispers will get louder. If we insist on being stubborn, we'll get 'thumped upside the head' until we can no longer ignore it."

Ain't that the truth!

I came back from Chicago still not knowing what I wanted to be. But at least I knew that I wanted more and I didn't feel guilty about it. Oprah warned me about that herself.

Today, I know what whispers to me. I'm thirty-eight years old and I know who I am and what I want. I also know that I'm not there yet and that's okay. As I give my family the chance, I see how truly supportive they are.

I know all this because my prayers were answered. I had finally made it to the red chair.

~Ariffa Hosein

The Power of a Secret

*There is no exercise better for the heart than reaching
down and lifting people up.*
~John Holmes

I once had a secret that was so shameful it almost destroyed my health. I was always on guard, protecting the secret that would surely hurt my family if it saw the light of day. Ever alert, I changed the subject when a conversation got a little too close for comfort. I had ready-made answers in case I was caught off guard with a question. I tried to avoid socializing whenever possible.

It has been said that you're only as sick as your secrets. Mine led me into a bout of depression, gave me high blood pressure, and caused chest pains that sent me to the emergency room.

My secret was changing me. The positive person that I once was had become a hopeless shell of my former self.

I couldn't continue down this path. My family needed me to be healthy. I had to find a way to live with the painful secret before it destroyed me and my entire family.

My sister was one of the few people who knew what was going on and she was deeply concerned. She found a place that she thought would help so we went to check it out. Upon entering the room, we were greeted with friendly smiles and warm welcomes. I felt comfortable.

The session got underway. I listened as other people shared pieces of their lives. Some of their stories sounded very similar to mine. My heart began to feel safe amongst these strangers. Then, it was my turn to speak. For the first time, I said out loud, "My name is Rose and I am the mother of an addict."

My sobs came fast and furious until I could no longer speak. My throat felt like it was closing in, trying to hold on to words that were too painful to be spoken. I waved to indicate that we should move on to the next person. The members encouraged me to continue.

I finished my story using all the energy that I could muster. The kind, caring people surrounding me were so supportive. They understood how painful this journey was, how one day you are a regular mom to a beautiful child with hopes and dreams for the future, and the next you are the mom of a child struggling with addiction who may die before his time. They understood how your dreams become nightmares. Every person in that room had experienced this transition. I no longer felt alone. The weight of the world had been lifted off my shoulders for the first time in a very long time.

That was the beginning of my healing process. My secret lost its power to destroy me when I realized that I was not alone. I continued to go to support groups, and I read everything that I could find about addiction. As a result, I got stronger and healthier.

I was ready to take another big step. I wanted to go public with our family's "secret" as a way to raise awareness. My hope was that other families might be spared the heartache of addiction. There was one big thing standing in my way: I was gripped by a lifelong fear of public speaking. I was also concerned about what others would think of my beautiful family if they knew the truth.

I was determined not to let fear stand in the way of doing something that might save lives. I was going to start talking publicly even if it killed me. As far as what other people would think, I came to realize that no amount of stigma would ever hurt as much as watching my son slowly die from his addiction, and feeling powerless to save him. If I could make it through that, I could make it through anything!

Within weeks, I was invited to speak to a university class about our family's experience. The reality of what I was about to do hit me hard. I was terrified!

I began to have self-doubts and second thoughts but I worked through them. The silence around addiction was deafening and deadly. I needed to use my voice. I had so many things to say, and I was determined to say them.

When the big day arrived, I mentally prepared myself for the fact that I might pass out in front of the class or not be able to speak at all because of my intense fear. I was willing to take that chance.

The classroom was full. I took a seat while the professor introduced me. My heart was pounding. This was the point of no return. My secret was about to be shared with strangers who might or might not understand. I was opening myself up to judgment and stigma. It was about to get personal but I was ready. I said a little prayer to myself: "Dear God, please let the words that I want to say, and the words that they need to hear, be the words that come out of my mouth."

I walked to the front of the class, thanked the professor and stood at the podium. I looked into the eyes of the students. At that moment, I felt a calm come over me like I had never experienced before. It started at the top of my head and worked its way down to my toes. I no longer felt nervous. Instead, I felt empowered. I knew with every ounce of my being that this was what I was meant to be doing. It was my calling. That defining moment changed my life.

I have spoken publicly many times since then. I am a passionate advocate who works hard every day to give a voice to the voiceless. Now, instead of my secret having the power to destroy me, it has the power to help others. It is a powerful weapon that fights stigma, gives hope and saves lives each and every day.

~Rose Barbour

Dreams of Her

A moment in my arms, forever in my heart.
~Author Unknown

t was time to tell my son and everyone else. I had found her. "David, what if I told you that you have a half sister?"

I looked at my son with tears in my eyes. He looked at me with his eyes wide and said, "Really, a sister!" He was an only child you see.

I had given up a baby girl for adoption when I was eighteen, one of the hardest things I had ever done. The only people who knew about it were my parents, my siblings, a couple of close friends, my aunt and my grandmother. I kept this secret from others, even my ex-husband, for more than twenty-five years.

I had decided that when my son turned eighteen, I would tell him and start looking for his sister. I had dreamed about her many times over those years. All I had to go on was the one look I got of her through the window before I went to sign the papers to give her up for adoption. I always wondered what she looked like, what her life was like, and whether she had good adoptive parents.

One night I sat down at the computer and started doing some research about how I could find her. I came across a website for Texas adoptions. Birthmothers, birthfathers, and the adopted children could use the site to look for each other.

Before I entered my information I decided to do a quick search of the posts that were already there: "Female. The Edna Gladney Home in Ft. Worth, Texas. October 1973." My hands shook as I typed.

One result popped up. It had been entered two months earlier. I was the only woman who gave birth that day, so this had to be her. I got goose bumps. It was hard to believe that I had found her already!

I knew that if I saw her picture I would know for sure. I replied to her and asked for a photo. I also told her that her adoptive parents took her home in a yellow blanket that my mother had knitted. I hit the send button.

I had a gut feeling this was it, but I couldn't sit there waiting. I forced myself to turn off the computer and go to bed.

After a sleepless night, I saw my son off to school in the morning. He scurried around getting books together and grabbing a banana before he went out the door. I grabbed his coat and told him to hold up. I looked into his eyes and said, "David, I love you." He was taken aback but he said, "I love you too, Mom!" And out the door he went.

Finally, I went to the computer, and there it was: her picture. The minute I saw her smile I knew. She wrote that her adoptive parents had kept the blanket that her grandmother had knitted. Her name was Kate.

After I regained my composure I wrote back: "Kate, I know you are my birth daughter, I just know it. You have your father's smile." We both wanted to meet, but we had to go through some psychological counseling and fill out some paperwork before the home would confirm our match.

A couple of weeks later we got the good news. We were a match and we could meet. That's when I told David the news.

It felt like the weight of the world was lifted off my shoulders because there was no "secret" anymore. I told my ex-husband, and he told his family. I told the rest of my family and my co-workers. I later found out my grandmother had written Kate's birth in her family Bible.

Months later I flew to California to meet Kate and her adoptive parents. The tears flowed for me during those two days. Her adoptive parents were wonderful people and they gave her a wonderful life.

When I returned home I got a letter containing a paper that Kate had written in high school. Her adoptive mother wanted me to have it. It read:

It is quite difficult for me to write about an individual who means everything to me, yet I have never seen her or heard her voice. I suppose I could say that you see a likeness to her in me, but even that is enigmatic. This person I speak of, this hero is my biological mother. If there was one thing I could say to my hero it would be simply thank you for giving me such a wonderful life.

~Kate

Kate received an A+ on the paper and a comment: "What a wonderful story."

It was wonderful. My dreams of her, my impossible dreams, came true.

~Susan Kocian

The Good Deed

*No matter how scary the road ahead may seem, never
be afraid to chase your dreams.*
~Melaina Rayne

I always wanted to go to college, even though no one in my family had ever done it and there was no money for tuition. My mother had a ninth grade education, and I was the only one of my parents' five children who even graduated from high school. We were a lower middle class family, living on my father's income as a painter.

I had a perfect GPA and I had taken college level courses, but I didn't do as well on the standardized tests, so I didn't qualify for financial aid. My parents encouraged me to attend summer orientation at the state school that accepted me, assuring me that they would somehow make it work. This would mean enormous debt for all of us, but they wanted me to earn a college degree.

I went to orientation in July, but spent the entire three days with the overwhelming sensation that it was not where I was supposed to be. The school was huge and the experience impersonal. I was unable to register for any of the classes I needed and met no one with whom I could imagine becoming friends. I attempted to picture myself graduating from the institution, but could not envision it no matter how hard I tried. While I was upset, I had another and more powerful sensation that would not stop nagging at me.

It concerned the place my father worked, a private school in the town where I lived. It was the oldest private college in the state, and prohibitively expensive for us. My father had worked there on and off for almost my entire life, continuously contracted out to paint the many classrooms, gyms, and dorm rooms from year to year. I had never really considered going to school there because it was so expensive, but I now had the overwhelming feeling that I should try, and that somehow, even though it made no sense, it was my best hope for an education.

I went home from orientation feeling defeated and afraid to confront my parents about my new wishes. When I told my father that I didn't want to go to the state school, after all he had been through obtaining loans, he was speechless. He sat with his head in his hands, not believing what I was proposing now. My mother was surprised but supportive, and after a long while my father told me he would inquire about an application at the school. It was July after all, and most of my college bound peers were already getting ready to move to their chosen schools. It might be too late for me to attend that fall so I would need to find a job if I had to wait. I agreed and said I understood, and the next couple of days I waited for my father to bring word about whether or not I had a chance to get in for the fall semester, if at all.

What I did not know was that my father had not gone to the admissions office, but to the president of the college himself. My father had painted his house and was acquainted with him, as it is not a large school and it's the sort of place where everyone knows everyone. He went to ask the president not only if I stood a chance of being accepted this late in the year, but if he might honor all the years my father had worked on the college and treat him like an actual employee in this one instance.

This was a very meaningful request, since college employees were allowed to have their children and spouses' tuition waived, if they could first be accepted to the institution.

I was never aware of that fact, or of what my father was asking until after it was all over. I thought when my father asked for my résumé and test scores they were for the admissions office, not the president. But when my father came home later that week with not only the news that I had been accepted, but I was going to go to school at no charge, I couldn't believe it.

All these years later I still marvel at it. Before that time, I had met the president once or twice with my father, but I did not know him and he did not know me. And as I went to school there and saw him more and more, I never did ask him why he chose to give me such a gift. But I made sure that he never once had the chance to regret what he had done for me. I kept my grades up, contributed on campus with different student organizations, wrote for the school paper, and helped launch an institutional history project. In the summers, I joined my father in painting the same classrooms I sat in the other nine months of the year.

In the end, I finished my bachelor's degree a semester early, with the highest academic honors. And when I graduated, I walked across the stage to the president, who gave me a hug. It was the thirteenth and last commencement he oversaw at the college, as he left the institution the following month. But not before he went in person to give me a recommendation for my first job, which I did not know until after I had gotten it.

A master's degree, two jobs, and nine years later, I still have no idea why that man chose to bestow such tremendous kindness on my family and me. They say God puts it on our hearts to do good deeds for each other, and we should always listen and act on them. Perhaps it was like that for him. All I know is that if I hadn't listened to my gut on that other college campus, I would have missed out on the greatest blessing of my life.

~K.L. Werle

Silver and Gold

To dance is to be out of yourself. Larger, more
beautiful, more powerful.
~Agnes de Mille

When I discovered my passion for Irish Dance in my mid-forties I learned everything I could about it. This was despite the disparaging comments of some of my friends. They tried to talk me out of my dream, saying I was too old to master this art form.

I didn't listen to them. I took classes, practiced every day, paid for private lessons, went to workshops, and constantly listened to music for competitions and shows. Frankly, I never liked being in the competitions. But, they forced me to practice and improve my technical merit. Over the years, I accumulated a few silver and bronze medals.

And then, at age fifty, I won a gold medal for performing the hornpipe, a difficult solo step, at an Irish Step Dance competition in Estes Park, Colorado. This was the reward for all my hard work and the validation of my dream. I had done it despite the naysayers.

At the end of the competition, while I stood in the dancer tent admiring my medal, a pair of Irish dance shoes went flying past my head. The shoes were not intentionally aimed in my direction. But the words of an angry fellow competitor were: "You have no right to that medal, Padgett. You are way too old to be dancing, competing or even thinking about performing an art this demanding and athletic. Even if you were of an appropriate age to enter this level of competition, I should have won. I am so much better at technique, timing, and all around dancing than you will ever be."

I didn't know what to say. I felt like I was reliving all the negative words I had heard over the years, from all the people who said I couldn't do it. I stood there, hurt, trying to regain my emotional balance. Then I felt a hand rest gently on my shoulder. An unfamiliar voice asked, "Do you believe her?"

I turned to face the judge who moments ago had awarded me the gold.

"Yes ma'am. She has better technique and sense of musical timing. She is just all around better than me," I admitted.

"No, she isn't," the adjudicator told me. "Do you know the difference between the silver and gold? Do you know why you were awarded this medal today?" she asked.

I dropped my gaze from hers and shook my head.

She lifted my chin, looked into my teary eyes and said, "You reflected hours of practice and honing of your craft, just like many others. You managed to keep the beat and execute a difficult step, like many others. Your posture was straight, and you demonstrated ability to remember the intricacies required. You were up against some tough competition out there today, and you gave a flawless performance. From a judge's point of view, it can be difficult to select one dancer over another when awarding medals.

"But, if mechanics and technical merit are equal, the decision will fall to the one who dances with her heart. Some *do* the dance; others *are* the dance. Today, you were the dance. And that, my friend, is gold."

That was my last Irish Dance competition, not because I feared decapitation as the result of airborne footwear. It was because the calendar does not lie. My years of hard, competitive Irish dancing were over. I entered the contest knowing it would be my last.

I am not prone to melancholy over things out of my control — like the passage of time. And I honestly cannot say I spend a lot of time looking at the dance medals I accumulated over the years.

Nonetheless, the medals do come in handy once in a while. For example when someone tells me they cannot realize a dream because of age, perceived inabilities or opinions of critics, I extend this invitation, "Would you come to my house for tea, please? I want to show you something."

~Laura L. Padgett

Think Possible

Chapter 2

Starting Over

Success Is Failure Turned Inside Out

Success and failure. We think of them as opposites,
but they're really not. They're companions — the
hero and the sidekick.
~Laurence Shames

n December 2010, I won the Conference Championship as part of the Miami University football team. A week later, I walked across the stage with a bachelor's degree. I was on top of the world, as the odds had been against me for both. During the 2010 season, we made NCAA history with the biggest turnaround in college history, going from 1–11 to 10–4. I also made history in my family by becoming the first male to graduate from college. With a promising football career ahead of me, it seemed the sky was the limit.

The following summer I hired a trainer to ensure I would be prepared for professional play. It turned out to be the hardest I've ever worked to achieve something in my life. After training for months, I still had not been signed by an NFL team so I joined an Indoor Football League team, the Nebraska Danger in Grand Island, Nebraska. The first game I did well and things looked good... until the next day. They said I wasn't good enough. I went for a tryout with a team in Pittsburgh. I didn't make it. Soon after, I headed to Toronto and was told again that I didn't make it. I felt like a failure.

At this point I had a lot of pressure from people asking why I wasn't in the NFL. As an athlete, people associate you with sports and treat you accordingly. Even though you're more than just an athlete, you become one with your sport, like a marriage. Unfortunately, I was going through a divorce. Three years later it was time to accept that playing football was no longer my passion.

I was not sure what I wanted to do next. I continued working my part-time job as a mentor to children. While I loved my job and was great at connecting with the children, I felt like there was still untapped potential that I hadn't discovered. On a whim I decided to take the GRE and apply to grad school. The trend continued and I failed. Again.

I found myself at a local factory, working a dead-end job on the assembly line six days a week. This was a far cry from the promising NFL career I was hoping to embark on just a few months earlier. Despite all this, I held out hope that success was just around the corner. I made a promise to myself to practice what I preached — remaining positive and enthusiastic about my situation — because I knew this job was only for a season. Working in the factory allowed me to inspire people with my uplifting attitude and positive affirmations on a larger scale than I could've ever imagined. My social media posts that I wrote for my own motivation caught on like wildfire, and my network rewarded me with sparks of positivity and encouragement. It caught me off guard but made me realize what one already has can be a blessing to others.

It was during this time that an old friend, a firefighter, contacted me and asked if I would sit down with him to see if I was interested in the career. Soon after we met, he added some much needed perspective to a role many know nothing about.

To be a firefighter there are obvious skills one must possess, such as bravery, selflessness, humility, and perseverance. In addition, there is a major technical aspect that most are unaware of and takes approximately two years to complete: the interviewing process itself is quite a journey.

The first step involves passing a rigorous written examination — 150 questions covering firefighter knowledge, Emergency Medical Technician functions, spelling, and reading comprehension. Next, you must be selected to complete a thorough background check that takes four months. Everything is fair game, from an FBI background check to contacting elementary-school teachers, neighbors, old jobs, and friends to discuss your character. After this comes an oral interview in front of a board of firefighters, asking a series of situational questions. If you manage to successfully pass, your final test is to complete a series of demanding physical assessments.

That first step, the written exam, would be the hard part for me. I knew from college experience, as well as my attempt at the GRE, that I needed to study material longer to fully grasp the information. With my intense work schedule, I didn't have much time to study. I had to come up with a game plan.

There were only three things I would not give up: reading my Bible, going to the gym and going to church. By sacrificing sleep, I managed to squeeze in five hours of studying daily, surviving with only three to four hours of sleep. Knowing my history with test taking I knew I had to study harder than everyone else.

To make matters worse, word got out that the first class would only be twenty-five people. Over 1,300 people had signed up to take the test. It might have sounded impossible, but I had made up my mind that I was going to become a firefighter and nothing could stop me. I even made the difficult decision to cut off my dreadlocks ahead of time. They were nearly twenty inches long and I had spent years growing them. But this leap of faith was pressure I put on myself to test my confidence; I wasn't just hoping that I would become a firefighter — I was instead preparing for it as if I already was one.

Finally the day came to take the test. Arriving early, I studied a bit in the car. I was excited and nervous. They passed out the test and I was in my zone, quickly checking off the boxes with a confidence I didn't know I possessed. When finished, I walked out of the testing center feeling like the weight of the world was off my shoulders.

Several months went by before results were shared. Nearly 1,000 people passed, yet only twenty-five people would be chosen. I somehow managed to remain optimistic, convinced that things would work out in my favor. Finally, I got the call. I was selected for the first class! I broke down in tears, overwhelmed by the weight of my victory. It had taken two years of hard work, a positive outlook, and dedication to realize my dream.

~Peris DeVohn Edwards

Recession Blessings

*Trials teach us what we are; they dig up the soil, and
let us see what we are made of.*
~Charles H. Spurgeon

During the depth of the recession, my friend would call my media production studio two or three times a week to check in. One day he sounded different — desperate. "Have you heard? They just laid off twelve people at the station and I was one of them." Another friend walked into my office unannounced, normally a pleasant surprise, but this time his face told a different story. "I'm pretty sure I'm being set up for the end of my career at the paper."

These were my friends, my associates in television, radio and the newspaper business. The careers they loved were ending. They were creative communicators who had been in the business for decades, rising to the top — and that meant they were the highest paid. Therefore, they would be the first to go. The reporters who had been telling this tragic recession story had become part of the story.

"Do you have any work for me, Sue?" My heart sank. How could I help them? My business was taking a hit too. I had nothing for them. I was letting several of my own employees go!

What I'd found in my most desperate times as a freelancer and business owner was that the surest road to success was the one shared with others. I had learned that the best way to compete was to run faster than everyone else, not to knock them out of the race. In my hardest times, I found other business owners to connect with, and they always helped me talk through the tough decisions I had to make.

So, I began a "support group" of sorts, for my friends. I went online and found a low cost website where we could organize, communicate and coordinate our meetings. We called ourselves the Media Associates Group, because that's what we were and the initials were cool: MAG. That would make me the MAGnifier and they would be MAGnificent. We met in my building once a month, using our DVD players and monitors to show off our work. We would eventually be able to hire each other as the clients began to reappear. Sounded ideal.

I sent an e-mail to everyone who might benefit from this group. The response was immediate. "Yes, I will be there! Can I bring three others?" What happened next was magical.

The first meeting was like a high school reunion. Old friends who had been too busy to connect were now reconnecting. There were hugs, hellos and handshakes that lasted a good half hour. Then it was time to start. We sat in a circle and I asked them to explain their specialties and a bit about their current situation. The first round was painful, as each injured soul reflected on the end of his or her beloved career. They shared anger, hurt, disbelief, and fear.

The second time around, I encouraged them to share what they might be able to offer to each other. If someone needed to be trained in editing, for example, then an editor might offer to teach that skill. I offered our conference rooms for free, to those who might need to meet with a potential client in a professional setting. It was like lighting a fire. Everyone wanted to help. Elizabeth and her husband Fred owned a struggling photo studio: "We can do head shots for free for anyone in this group. You can use them to post online or for business cards." A graphic designer chimed in: "I'll build a website for our group and post your bios, head shots and demo reels. I won't charge — I just think it will bring in more business if we appear united."

It was happening. They put aside their own needs and reached out to each other. Their losses didn't take away their ability to give. Amazing.

There were even more surprises. I tossed out a challenge: "If we don't have any customers to pay the bills, let's create a video product that we could sell, or a TV series about something remarkable in our community—something that sponsors might get behind. We are creative folks. Let's just make it up!" The buzz began, "What about…" and "we could try…" The positive energy and ideas were contagious. Then a freelance videographer, Rusty, who had never produced anything for broadcast, spoke up. "I don't know if this is what you have in mind," he said hesitantly, "but I've been going to 2nd Saturday now for about six months, videotaping the happenings down there. Maybe we could use some of that video to sell."

2nd Saturday was a community event in Sacramento, and it continues to this day. The second Saturday of each month, many of the main streets are blocked off to traffic and all the art galleries open their doors for an "art walk." It was the perfect event to "cover," as we could report on how all those art galleries and restaurants were surviving the recession. I challenged the group to make it happen. Rusty and John jumped at the chance. The two had never met before. John was a seasoned TV news journalist, retired and now running his own small business out of his home. He would take the lead, instructing Rusty on how to shoot a story for television. John interviewed artists while Rusty shot beautiful video with his own gear. John wrote the story, and Rusty edited.

By our third meeting, John and Rusty had a couple of finished stories and they were fabulous. If we had stopped there, it would have simply been something that kept us busy during our mourning period. It could not stop there.

The next day, I contacted a local television station and asked to meet with their programming gurus. I wasted no time telling them that we had a show to propose, and then asked when (not if) we could meet. "Good timing Sue!" Those words were like honey on warm toast to me. "We have a program we want your company to consider producing for us and I've been meaning to call you! When can we meet?" I was about to win the recession lottery! If I accepted this project, I could actually hire some of my friends. A win/win! But, what about our MAG project? I figured I should meet about their project, and then slip in the idea of them buying our MAG production.

The day of the meeting was memorable. We did talk over the project they wanted me to produce — but I quickly pitched the 2nd Saturday show MAG had produced. The men looked at each other, smiled ear to ear, and said, "That's it!" They went on to say that they were lacking content for their upcoming art special, and had been looking for local stories to cover.

You could have picked me up off the floor. Our out-of-work support group had just sold our idea! Over the next week, I negotiated a contract for our production, agreeing to take less money up front in order to retain the rights to make the program into a series. We would consider this our "pilot" and have the freedom to present it to potential sponsors. They agreed.

Our fourth support-group meeting was full of high fives and huge smiles. We had done it! We created something from nothing! We were a bunch of individuals bouncing around on the stormy seas of financial insecurity, without a clue what our professional future would bring. By coming together, we found strength, hope and success. We didn't just hang onto the life raft — together we began to build a new one. A bigger one.

Had the recession not tossed us out of our secure places, we would have never come together to make this happen. And if that's not a blessing, I don't know what is.

~Suzanne Peppers

The Leather Skirt

Action is the foundational key to all success.
~Pablo Picasso

The day Kevin moved out he moved his money with him. I took a job cashiering in a grocery store to get food on the table.

I tried to avoid leaving the house in the morning at the same time as the lady across the street. She was a teacher who wore nice clothes and carried a briefcase. I wore a uniform — a white button-down shirt, aqua vest, bowtie, and polyester pants with a large elastic waistband. All I needed was a red rubber nose and a Bozo wig.

Each day I was allotted a fourteen-minute break. I'd head for the hot case, hoping to snag a warm snack, eating with my cellphone cradled between my shoulder and ear. But then unwelcome voicemails would divert my attention, all from creditors. I'd never get to have that snack.

One day, I was heading back to my register after yet another disquieting "break" when I saw my inspiration. It was that time of day when the "professionals" were vacating their offices and heading for their condos. It usually meant a stop for something to grill and a bottle of wine to complement their meal.

The first thing I saw was her feet. I don't remember exactly what her shoes looked like, but they were not purchased on a BOGO at a discount store: they were leathery perfection only seen in a Manolo Blahnik advertisement.

My eyes traveled upward. She did not limit her leather selection

to her feet. From her slender waist to just below the knee she was wrapped in a gorgeous shade of brown leather with no trace of reality-star overly tight tackiness. Perfectly paired with her masterpiece of a skirt was a short-sleeved, black turtle-necked sweater.

The minute she walked away her cellphone rang. I knew she wasn't hearing from her creditors. I imagined the new fashion lines from Paris had just arrived and Versace was calling to make sure everything was in order. I was hooked, fascinated, enthralled with someone who seemed so empowered while I was… how shall I say it? Not.

I did the unthinkable. I flipped my till light off and followed her. She pulled a fancy keychain from her matching leather bag and I heard a melodic chirp. I watched her walk over to a sleek, black BMW just like she owned it — because she did. Standing in the parking lot, wearing my clown suit, I watched her drive off.

Even though it wasn't the wisest thing to do, I started comparing our lives. There was no way that woman was in danger of her electricity being shut off. It was unthinkable that she had a combative, soon to be ex-husband making her life miserable. How did I know? Because what was on the outside was too powerful, too successful, too in charge. She would have hired the best attorney in town and crushed the person who tried to take her children, her life, her leather skirt, her BMW or her very essence.

Standing in the parking lot, still on the clock, wearing my bowtie, I made a decision. I wanted to be that leather skirt–wearing, BMW-driving woman when I grew up.

When I grew up? Yes, I needed to grow up.

I knew that if I wanted to get from here to there, I needed to grow. If I wanted to have more confidence, more options, more essence, I needed to become more. Some growth happens naturally. But sometimes we need to grow on purpose. I needed an intentional, daily plan to grow myself — to become more than a scared, clown-suit-wearing, low self-esteem victim. A leather skirt and a BMW became the symbols for me of what I needed: new skill sets, improved outlook, wise choices and a definite plan to succeed in life.

It was going to require daily action. No matter how crazy,

disappointing or unsettling life was, taking action to grow myself every single day would keep me moving forward.

So there would be less chance of failure, I kept it simple: I chose five things I could do every single day. I figured if I only chose two or three, it might not be a big enough commitment, but more than five would be overwhelming and cause me to abandon the process. I personally decided to:

1. Have a devotional time to build my faith.
2. Exercise for at least twenty minutes to feel confident about my physical appearance.
3. Read twenty minutes from a book written by someone successful so I could be motivated to better myself.
4. Set some goals for the year and review them every day so I wouldn't drift off target.
5. Use my drive time to listen to a positive, encouraging message on CD because I knew that my attitude would determine my altitude.

My five tasks gave me something to look forward to every day and empowered me in the sense that I was gaining knowledge, improving my health, becoming more proactive, and feeling more in command of my life.

I didn't get a leather skirt or a BMW right away, but almost immediately I noticed that my life became more stable, even though I still had to deal with unstable situations. My stability was starting on the inside and working its way out. As I became more stable on the inside, more grounded and secure, I became more able. I noticed I held my head higher and walked and talked with more confidence and authority.

Within two months, I was able to hang up my bowtie and accept a better paying position elsewhere. Six months later, I became a manager for an international organization and received a significant pay increase. In less than a year, I went from being homeless to qualifying for a quarter-million-dollar mortgage.

It really wasn't about owning a leather skirt — although I now have two — it was about wanting to improve my condition in life. In order to do that, I needed to improve. It all started with a decision that required daily action. And my diligence paid off.

~Debra Perleberg

I Can Do This

Bravery is being the only one who knows you're afraid.
~Franklin P. Jones

I was recently divorced and I needed to find work. I picked up a newspaper, flipped to the want ads and groaned. I hadn't been in the workforce for years. What was I qualified to do? I began to highlight the possibilities.

I crossed out way more ads than I highlighted before I found it: Waitress Wanted — Day Shift. I giggled and said out loud, "Why not?" I sat back, smiled and wondered whether I'd have a uniform.

I dressed quickly in a dark blue pencil skirt and white button-down blouse. I swept my long blond hair into a high ponytail. I slipped my black flats on my feet, paused at the mirror and pinched each cheek for a little color. "I can do this," I said to my image in the mirror.

The owner of the restaurant asked. "Have you had any experience?"

"Oh yes." I spouted a list of establishments I'd worked at years ago as a teenager.

"Great, I think we can use you. Can you start in a few days?"

"Yes, yes." I answered with almost too much enthusiasm.

On my first day, the owner placed me in a back room where it would be a little slower at lunch. This way I could learn the ropes. I busied myself. I filled salt and pepper shakers and took note of how the other waitresses set the tables. My little white lie about job experience made me a little uneasy.

I looked up from the prep station to see what looked like a herd of men coming toward my section. There were ten of them! I watched them take their seats and settle in before I calmed myself. "I can do this," I repeated several times to myself. I picked up menus. My hands shook and my legs wobbled as I headed toward the table.

"Hi ya'll, my name is Flo. I'm new and I'd really appreciate it if ya'all would order the fish special to make it real easy on me." I have no clue why I put on a silly accent and pretended to be a waitress I'd seen on a television comedy, but all the men laughed, and this put me at ease. Besides, they all ordered the fish.

The gentlemen had several rounds of drinks before the food was ready, which turned out to be a good thing.

I'd watched some of the other waitresses pile at least three plates on an arm. It didn't look so hard. When my order came up, I confidently placed three plates on one arm and headed through the swinging kitchen door.

Plate one made it to the customer, nice and easy. Plate two, the same. Plate three, however, teetered before it fell directly into the lap of gentleman number three. Yep, you can see it, can't you? Fish, fries and creamy coleslaw ran right down the front of the man's trousers.

"Oh no, I'm so sorry," I yelled. "Here, let me help you." I grabbed napkins from the table and started to frantically wipe the front of his trousers before I realized what I was doing. The entire table of men snickered, and then broke into raucous laughter. I know I turned red from the top of my forehead to the tip of my toes before I made it back to the kitchen.

Behind the kitchen door, the entire staff stomped their feet, held their stomachs and reeled with laughter. I leaned against the wall and broke into tears before I too fell into hiccupping laughter. I composed myself and once again said, "I can do this."

I walked calmly to the table, apologized and offered to pay the cleaning bill for the trousers. I also brought out the remainder of the order without incident. The gentlemen composed themselves, ordered a few more drinks and went about their conversation as if nothing happened. I retreated to the kitchen and continued to amuse the staff with comments about my ineptness at plate handling.

After I presented the bills, I continued to apologize, ask for forgiveness and smile. When the men left, every plate had a napkin with a smiley face drawn on it and a twenty-dollar tip. "Yep," I said to myself. "I can do this."

~Alice Klies

Riding High Side

I can't control the wind but I can adjust the sail.
~Ricky Skaggs

"Ready to tack," the captain orders, and my first mate releases the sheets on the starboard side. I furiously pull them tight on the port. We are headed for the shallows where the current is not as strong. 5 knots... not bad for a boat her size. I grab the handle of the winch and give the sheets one last heave. The sails billow in the wind. I tie off loosely and sit back and relax for a moment before we tack again.

It is 7 p.m. on this glorious but chilly spring night. In the distance I see a flock of white swans taking flight parallel with our craft. The sun is casting a hazy yellow glow as swallows dance in search of their evening meal. I ponder grabbing my phone, but decide some things are better captured in the mind's eye than on film.

The past year has been a difficult one and the winter especially hard. I was in a tumultuous marriage and my self-esteem had taken a beating.

Then, a friend invited me to The LaSalle Mariners Club. They were empowering women by teaching them how to sail. What I saw as an evening of escape soon came to be my lifeline. With every rigging of the hanks and raising of the jib my resolve became stronger. If I could hoist a main and pull a boat out of chains, then surely I could pull myself up and get myself out of this mess as well. I soon discovered that when the body is busy, you're able to think more clearly. I began to trust myself and plan.

Now, as I sit here three years later, no longer merely a piece of deck fluff, I can truly say sailing gave me the confidence to leave my marriage. Riding high side with the wind whipping my hair I realize I am at peace. Every once in a while a wave splashes up to lick my face. I lean into it. I am refreshed. I am empowered.

~Robin Martin Duttmann

How Gratitude Got Me Through

If a fellow isn't thankful for what he's got, he isn't likely
to be thankful for what he's going to get.
~Frank A. Clark

"My life will not end like this. My family needs me and I have to follow my dreams and start now." That's the promise I made myself one evening years ago. I was sitting in my work truck on a road construction site that was the culmination of my dead-end career. My dreams had faded to nothing, my marriage was stuck in idle, and my daughters only saw the remnants of the father they'd once known, when they saw me at all, which was seldom.

Riding on the power of that decision, I left my financially comfortable, soul-destroying construction career behind. I jumped into a success mentorship program, quickly discovering the power of personal development and opening myself to the idea that my life was in my hands. I believed I had embarked on a journey that was waiting just for me. Then the unexpected happened.

I was quickly building momentum and learning the principles of building a successful business when my wife of seven years began to change. She had gone so far into her new reality that it took all the courage she had to confess it all. "I'm seeing someone," she finally admitted.

All of the momentum I'd been building crumbled under the devastating blow as she hesitantly said, "There's more." A long pause, and then, "I'm pregnant."

In that moment my heart and soul were shattered. I grasped for a straw of hope. "It's mine, right?"

One word blew that straw away. "No."

I still wanted her as my wife. I held on to that thought and tried desperately to make it work and win her back, but it was hopeless. As much as I prayed for a miracle, I had to accept she wasn't in the relationship with me anymore. It was time to let her go and move out.

Almost overnight, I went from new success to new distress. That year I spiraled into a deep depression and found myself sitting at bars and drinking more than I ever had. The rage I was trying to suppress came out one night in a drunken bender. In a high-speed chase one hopes to see only in a movie, I eluded a deputy sheriff twice, finally losing the officer but causing an accident and totaling my Jeep. While thankfully no one was severely injured in the accident, I was a mess. Unsurprisingly, I was placed under arrest.

I'd worked with deputy sheriffs on construction sites and I had always respected the law. This behavior was out of character for me. I had to ask myself who I had become.

Sitting in that cell for four days straight not only sobered me up, but also woke me up to the reckless way I was living my life. I hit rock bottom sitting in that cell, locked up with people who were on trial for awful crimes.

In those four days of incarceration I went through a wide range of emotions, but what I found was clarity in my mission and the passion that would pick me up from the deep depression I was in. I prayed. I fasted. I found inspiration in others' stories. Most of all, the light was beaming brightly out from me again. I realized that I needed to forgive if I was going to move forward with my life.

Praying for everyone, especially for those who had created my nightmare, softened my heart and made things turn around faster than I'd imagined. Words, I learned, have power, and the ability of grateful prayer to change your life should never be underestimated.

I had fallen prey to situational alcoholism and depression. But now I held fast to my new vision. I would be grateful and wish everyone the best, including my enemies. I prayed for blessings for my ex-wife, her lover, and their unborn child.

Unfortunately, the day following the arrest, my name was plastered all over the news as a suspect in a high-speed chase. I was sentenced to six months for Driving While Intoxicated and Reckless Driving.

I saw the emotional effect my sentencing and conviction had on my family, and it was devastating to face six months behind bars away from my daughters when they most needed me. Although I thought this was the last thing I needed, looking back I realize it was, in fact, the best thing.

Those six months helped clear my mind from the nightmare and gave me the courage to accept professional therapy and get refocused. Most of all, it awakened my heart to a new relationship.

Before serving time, I had become friendly with a woman at work. Unbeknownst to me, she was also going through betrayal and divorce. The similarity in our situations was eerie, and it was obvious to us that our becoming friends was no coincidence. I began to write her daily, and the closer we became the more she was my ray of light in the storm I was living through.

She brightened my days with her letters and visits. She gave me hope, and it inspired me to keep going.

In the outside world, the life I once knew was being pummeled to dust. But in my incarcerated world I found contentment in writing, drawing, singing in the choir and inspiring others to chase dreams.

I learned something powerful — being incarcerated doesn't mean being unhappy. Happiness is a choice. You can choose to believe in something bigger and have faith that your journey will take you to better circumstances.

When my six-month sentence was over, traveling on that bus back to my reality was surreal. I was returning, but with a new level of awareness for life. Learning from others' stories gave me insight into how powerful the principles I learned from my success coaches and millionaire mentors really were.

I've learned that we all have the same twenty-four hours each day to sow seeds of abundance. And we can't receive greater gifts if we don't let go of the past ones.

It became obvious that I had been blind for many years to the power of visionary gratitude. I had taken so many things for granted for so long, including achieving my dreams. But by intentionally envisioning and being grateful in the now, it gives way to abundance in the future.

When I'm asked to speak to audiences about my story and how I persevered in spite of circumstances, I talk about the power of words and prayer, and about holding that vision of gratitude for what you have so that greater possibilities become real.

~Vidal Cisneros Jr.

The Winds of Change

Attitude is the difference between ordeal and adventure.
~Bob Bitchin

My partner and I both loved nature and sailing, so we decided to live aboard a sailboat and cruise. I could continue my consulting business by telecommuting from the boat with only occasional trips to see clients. He already handled most of his marketing work by phone. We were both healthy and in our forties. By working together and adopting a more frugal lifestyle, we could afford a boat big enough to live on within two years. Until then, the twenty-eight footer I'd bought would suffice for extended cruising.

He proposed marriage, but I was still gun-shy after my divorce and needed more time to be sure. He understood and said, "I'll keep proposing every year until you say yes."

Everything aligned for a bright future — until I discovered he led a double life. I'd had suspicions for a while. How many times could a person take business trips but never have a hotel receipt or a plane ticket? Several times he said he would be staying with a business associate at his home. When I insisted on a phone number, he gave me one, but nobody ever answered or returned the calls after I left messages. He received calls at odd hours on his line. Who calls about business at 11 p.m.?

Occasionally he used my computer. He was not very tech savvy, and one day when I was deleting old documents I found one that contained an e-mail from a Caribbean hotel that was unfamiliar to me. It explained that because his camera had been stolen from the room where he and his wife stayed, they both had to sign the form stating they agreed with the proposed reimbursement.

When he returned from another of his "business trips" a few days later, I confronted him. He had lied to me from the beginning. True, he had gotten a divorce. He just neglected to mention he'd married again after that divorce.

I stared at the creature who stood before me and hid my fear. The man I loved and thought I knew was suddenly a stranger.

Depressed by his betrayal, for months I did nothing but work, eat, and sleep. My whole life fell apart at the sudden loss of both my life partner and my planned future. Should I abandon my dream and sell the boat? None of my friends sailed. The few sailors on my dock would likely prefer to sail their own boats. I could not sail my boat alone. I never even liked taking the helm, preferring to deal with the sails, lines, and everything else. Being captain means you are responsible for your crew and I didn't think I had the knowledge to ensure their safety. Be at the helm when docking the boat? Forget it! I'd always refused that. Our plan to save money for a bigger boat and earn money as we cruised did not work for one person.

I looked up the phone number of the boat broker, but I could not dial it. Why give up my dream because of a failed relationship? I bought the boat because I wanted to sail, yet I never captained my own ship. "Time to end this pity party," I told myself. "You wanted to do this. You need to put up or shut up."

I knew from experience my broken heart would heal in time. I'd married in my early twenties and divorced in my late thirties. After a few tears, I'd lived happily alone for years. I could do it again.

My boat had been stored on land for the winter. In the spring, the boatyard launched boats at the other side of the marina. It would be my job to get the boat from there to my slip. Anticipating I would not do well, I scheduled the launch for a weekday when few, if any, people would be at the docks to witness my embarrassment. That also meant that no one would be near my slip to help secure lines. I was certain I couldn't dock the boat by myself, so on launch day I approached the yard manager, Dominic. "I've never docked the boat before. Could someone come with me?"

He hopped aboard. I took the helm, motored to my dock, and slowly turned into the slip. Amazingly, I pulled in straight and close to the short pier with room to spare in the front.

Dominic jumped onto the pier and we secured the lines. He looked at me and grinned. "That was perfect. Are you sure you've never done this before?"

I exhaled and smiled back. "When you want a big audience, you never get one."

Dominic waved and returned to his work.

My perfect landing at the dock boosted my confidence, but the next hurdle was to captain the boat on an actual sail. For that, my nerves required someone with more experience to join me on my first attempt. Thankfully, Rick and David, the two most knowledgeable sailors on the dock, agreed to sail with me sometime. I hoped they would each pick a different day so I'd get two days of solid practice, but no such luck. They decided to accompany me together.

When the day came, Rick said, "I think Janet should motor out of the slip."

David instantly chimed in, "I agree!"

"Absolutely," I said. I thought one of the gentlemen might have volunteered to back the boat out of the slip, but I would have rejected the offer. I needed to do this myself, and no better time than now with two experts aboard.

I motored out to the bay and told them which lines to use to raise the main and unfurl the jib. We had perfect weather and a wonderful time. I didn't need a bigger boat; I'd do just fine with the one I had. Not once did I ask anyone to take the helm, and I executed another perfect docking when we returned. Fortunately, I had wine aboard for just such an occasion.

That afternoon sail taught me the helmsman had the easiest job.

All this time, I had been doing the hard work, but that turned out to be a good thing. I knew how everything worked on the boat, plus how to deal with minor problems that occurred while sailing. From that day on, I captained with one or more friends on board.

Later that season, I sailed with a friend who knew very little about the sport. As we sailed from the bay into the river on our way back to the marina, she looked up at me and asked, "Don't we have to turn?"

"No, I can just adjust the helm."

"You really know what you're doing," she said.

Her words, music to my ears, blended perfectly with the wind in my hair.

~Janet Hartman

19

Affirmations Changed My Life

An affirmation opens the door. It's a beginning point
on the path to change.
~Louise L. Hay

n 1998, I was miserable. I had a three-year-old son whom I adored, but his father was a different story altogether. I was in a miserable marriage and in poor health. I lived in a small town and worked a job I hated. We were so broke all the time that we were always one paycheck or financial disaster away from being homeless. It was not a good time.

Things had grown so bad that my husband and I slept in separate bedrooms. Every night, I retreated to my room and buried my head in a book or my journal. One day, after reading an article on the Internet about affirmations, I realized I was desperate enough to give them a try.

I'd always thought affirmations were silly. I associated them with the old Al Franken *Saturday Night Live* character, Stuart Smalley, who would gaze at himself in the mirror, saying aloud, "I'm good enough, I'm smart enough, and doggone it people like me." While that was a funny running gag on *SNL*, I didn't think I could bring myself to do it, because it just felt embarrassing.

Still, after reading the article about affirmations earlier that day and reflecting on my current misery, I realized I needed to do something—anything—to change my life. I threw caution to the wind and started making affirmations.

Unlike Stuart Smalley, I didn't say them out loud while gazing at myself in the mirror. Instead, I pulled out a spiral-bound notebook. I closed my eyes and envisioned the life I wanted for myself. I saw my son and me living with a man whom I truly loved in a supportive and honest relationship. I pictured us living in a comfortable home. I saw myself in a well-paying job that I loved that still allowed me plenty of time with my son. I pictured myself whole, happy, and filled with vibrant health. I imagined having a happy family and lots of friends, as well as engaging in activities that filled me with joy and purpose.

Once I had a picture in my mind of exactly how I wanted my life to look, I wrote ten statements that affirmed each of the things I visualized. Instead of writing them as statements of want, I wrote the affirmations as if I already had the things I envisioned. For example, I wrote, "I am grateful I have a job that intellectually, creatively, and financially fulfills me while allowing me to spend plenty of time with my son."

After I settled on ten affirmations, I wrote them by hand in my notebook. Every night, I wrote each affirmation ten times. Then, I closed my eyes and visualized the life I wanted. I ended by expressing thanks to the universe for giving me such a wonderful life.

I did this for months, filling two notebooks full of the same ten affirmations, written over and over every night as I sat alone in my room.

Slowly, life took over. Eventually, I only wrote my affirmations once a week, then once a month. Then, I forgot about them altogether. My life went on, and it changed drastically.

My husband and I separated and divorced, but we worked out an arrangement between the two of us to support what our son needed from both of his parents. I moved to a new town and started working a job in a field I loved: writing. The job paid extremely well, and I was allowed to telecommute several days a week so I had plenty of time to hang out with my son. I was thrilled.

At my new job, I met a wonderful man. After a few years, the two of us married. We both made good money, and I was no longer a paycheck away from financial ruin. My husband was also an amazing stepdad to

n, and he had a son who gave my child the sibling he'd always
ed. As I grew happier, my health improved significantly, as well.

In 2003, we moved into a lovely new home on a hillside with a beautiful view of the valley. Along with working from home and spending time with my son, I also had the time to engage in hobbies and volunteer activities that enriched my life. Through my activities, I made many new friendships. Life was good on our hill, and I was very happy.

One day, shortly after moving into our home, I was digging through a box when I came across two battered spiral notebooks. I opened them with interest, wondering what I had written. In their pages I found my ten affirmations, repeated over and over again.

As I read the affirmations I had written five years earlier, I was shocked. Every affirmation I'd so carefully repeated and visualized described precisely the way my life had turned out. Through affirmation and visualization, I had created exactly the life I wanted for myself.

With such a powerful example of how well affirmations and visu-alizations work, I now realize that Stuart Smalley was on to something, after all. Using these tools can set the wheels in motion to bring about lasting change in your life.

Today, I use affirmation and visualization as a regular tool, and it is one I am grateful to have. Occasionally I forget about the tools when life gets in the way. However, I always return to visualization and affirmation. Whenever I do, I see the visualized outcomes manifest-ing quickly as my mindset changes and I am spurred to action. I am eternally grateful.

~Karen Frazier

20

Birds of a Feather

When life gives you a hundred reasons to cry, show life
that you have a thousand reasons to smile.
~Author Unknown

When my best friend died exactly three months after my divorce was finalized, an eraser swept across my life. I had a job I loved, but when the weekends came I had no one to run and play with. No one to laugh with as we pigged out on ice cream. No one to tell me to "get off the couch and do something." No one to hold me accountable for anything.

One evening several days after my friend's funeral, I found myself in front of the TV finishing another pint of mint-chocolate-chip ice cream. Soon, stomach cramps made me painfully aware that things needed to change. I needed to break out of my shell and leave the comfort of my nest.

I dried my tears and considered the options. I could sit at home and eat junk food every night or I could step out my front door, meet people and embark on a new journey without knowing the final destination.

With a yellow pad in front of me, I wrote out the hobbies I enjoyed. Gardening, which I did alone. Hiking, which I hadn't done in years. Antique shopping, which I couldn't afford. Writing, a hobby that required hours of alone time. All of these options had the potential to keep me in a solitary cocoon. I needed to grow by being with others who had similar interests.

First, I researched local clubs and organizations focused on my interests. I'd always fed birds in my back yard and enjoyed bees and butterflies flitting about my perennials so I chose an Audubon meeting as my first get-out, step-out event. My game plan? Arrive late, use the back entrance, and fly the coop if it wasn't for me.

Everything changed when I arrived at my first meeting. The back entrance? Locked. At the front entrance, through a glass window, I noticed a group deep in conversation. I entered and tried to slink past.

However, one of the ladies saw me and gave me a large grin. "Hi. Welcome."

Before I could choose a seat, I was surrounded by friendly people sharing their names and asking mine. Another person asked, "Are you a first-timer?" My wide eyes and sweaty palms must have been clues. When a gentleman stepped to the microphone, we dispersed. I noticed a projector pointed toward the front screen. For a better view, I sat closer than planned, spoiling my plan for a quick get-away.

I chose a row with two people and sat with a few seats between us. As the lights dimmed, a woman sat down beside me and whispered, "Hello. I don't think we've met." She smiled, gave me her name and said, "We'll talk after." And we did. She also introduced me to others who mingled after the program. They each encouraged me to come back and suggested I join the next field trip.

Even though it was late when I got home, I visited the organization's website for field trip details. I needed to put the date and time on my calendar so my fears wouldn't prevent me from going. I printed out a map and put it on the entry table. Every time I picked up or laid down my car keys, I would give myself a few words of encouragement: "You'll have a good time when you go." "It'll give you a chance to explore a new place." "Perfect weather for a day outside."

On the designated day, I left early in case I got lost on the way. When I arrived, there were already several birders with binoculars. They were engaged in conversation, but as soon as I approached they introduced themselves. By the end of the day I'd traded phone numbers with others who wanted to carpool to yet another field trip. I'd spent the day outdoors, learned new birding skills and gained new friends with a common interest.

During the field trip, the sighting of a Yellow Warbler became my symbol of hope. This bright yellow bird sang as it hopped from one branch to another. When joined by other birds, it became part of a flock. Exactly what I wanted for my life — a positive attitude and being part of a group.

I attended many meetings and went on many field trips during the following months. It didn't take long to be engulfed with fun activities and new faces. I soon found myself sitting on the board. I've made lifelong friends who travel in and out of the country to chase rare birds and attend nature-focused conferences.

After this first adventure, it became easier to try other groups. I attended a local writers' conference and became active in a writers' group near my home. Our weekly gatherings inspire and stretch me in new directions. Just when I'm worn out from staring at words on my computer screen, my friends' smiling faces refresh me and get me out of my writer's shell. Their critiques challenge me to go beyond my self-imposed limits.

I also visited several churches to find a group of active women and singles. Once I made a choice, I didn't just show up to perch on a pew. I got involved. Doing so granted me the blessing of a flock of friends. It's also an opportunity to bring other single gals under my wing, extending friendship and a place to nest.

My days have settled into a rhythm of work and activities with people I hadn't expected, but ones I can't imagine being without. Each week, I eagerly wait for time with fellow writers, nature lovers and activities with my "peeps" from church. Who knew my life could be so full after two such devastating losses? Certainly not me. But, all my friends and activities have become, as the song says, the "wind beneath my wings."

~Gail Molsbee Morris

21

Making Time for Possibilities

Every new day begins with possibilities.
~Ronald Reagan

P eople needed me so I needed to tick off every item on my holiday checklist. No self-respecting Martha Stewart devotee would get caught dead without a checklist. Mine read like a NASA flight plan.

Do. Do. Do. I was so busy doing for others. With bread dough rising for our church bake-sale and cookie batter calling my name from the fridge, I had to keep moving no matter how exhausted I was. And that's how I landed in a heap at the bottom of the staircase when I was rushing to answer the phone.

The next thing I knew I was pulling myself along the floor inch by inch until I reached that phone. This time the mission was to dial 911.

My husband Joe arrived home from night school just in time to see the paramedics load me into the ambulance. By sunrise the next morning four stainless steel screws held my left leg together and a plaster cast stretched from my knee to my toes. Shattering bones is not for sissies.

No worries about the holidays though. I already had Christmas in the bag. Our tree glistened with soft twinkling lights and shiny glass ornaments while brightly wrapped gifts festooned its base. In the kitchen dozens of home baked cookies awaited distribution to friends and family. Procrastination is for lackluster elves and homemaker rookies. We wouldn't be missing Christmas, despite my broken leg.

What got me concerned though was when I heard the doctor say to Joe, "She'll be laid up for several months." Apparently he missed the memo announcing my status as linchpin of the Universe. When news of this catastrophe rippled through the realm, bedlam would follow. The world getting on without me? Impossible.

I sailed through the first day of my recuperation on a morphine-induced flying carpet ride. Resting comfortably in my hospital bed I could almost hear every bake sale, craft show, church committee, and volunteer project within a ten-mile radius come to a screeching halt. My inability to say "no" had made me a volunteer-recruiter's dream come true.

I always felt like a celebrity at work, church, the local neighborhood association, the nearby grade school, and the county resale shop to benefit the needy. That's the status you get when you're a volunteer junkie.

Now that I was laid up, that was all over. In the care of my parents the days turned into weeks and my mood swings ranged from grumpy to intolerable. How Mom and Dad put up with my insolence for so long I'll never know, but I clearly remember the day when they'd had enough. After one of my particularly surly remarks Mom came into my room, looked me right in the eye and said, with a healthy dose of candor, "Daddy and I are getting a little bored with 'sour-puss' being the recurring flavor of the day around here. You'd better figure out what's ailing you and fix it." Her eyes fixed on me. She meant business! I clenched my jaw and glared right back at her.

"What's wrong with me?" I shrieked, piercing a hole in the silence. I knew darn well what was wrong and so did she. I could no longer hide from the fact that the world marched on without me and never missed a step. No project, charity event or group volunteer effort collapsed without my tireless efforts. And that hurt me, a lot. Oh, how the tears flowed. I don't even know how I put it into words but somehow my mother got the idea and she sat down on the bed with a box of tissues in hand.

"Annie, you fell because you were so exhausted. You spread yourself too thin. You always have and you're not the only person who suffers from it. It's very nice to feel indispensable. You know what is even nicer? A full night's sleep. Try it some time. If you don't, you'll be no good to anyone. It is possible to find balance, but not without taking a good hard look at what motivates your choices."

Mom delivered a dose of truth that was pretty difficult for me to accept, but deep down I knew she was right. I'd convinced myself over the years that no charitable project would survive to completion without me on the team. What a self-centered notion that was, and one that left me exhausted most of the time.

Through many more months of recuperation I spent considerable time contemplating the possibilities ahead me. I realized that I needed to choose my projects wisely. Along the way I not only stopped feeling sorry for myself, I rediscovered many simple pleasures that had fallen through the cracks. That little chat I had with Mom set me on the right path.

As I neared the end of my recuperation I signed up for a writing course, something I'd always wanted to do. Three days before my first class the phone rang. It was our church secretary. She was thrilled that I would soon be back on my feet. She asked if I would oversee a teen car wash event scheduled for the same day as my writing class.

"I'd love to, but I'm taking a class and I'm not available that day. Thank you so much for thinking of me. Goodbye." And I hung up the phone. I'm sure I sounded nervous, but still, I did it. I had said no. I made a wise choice. I had the power.

I still love volunteering, and work it into my schedule frequently, but I don't allow it to reign supreme in my life. Now I carve out time for me, just to explore the possibilities. Today I am a published author, an avid crocheter, and I play a mean game of *Scrabble*. I read for the sheer pleasure of it and spend many happy hours singing and recording Irish and American folk songs with Joe. I have a balanced life and look forward to every day knowing I will enjoy it rather than endure it. The possibilities are endless.

~Annmarie B. Tait

Regroup, Reboot, Reroot

You may have a fresh start any moment you choose,
for this thing we call "failure" is not the falling down,
but the staying down.
~Mary Pickford

When I was eight years old, my science teacher asked each of us to select our favorite tree. She wanted to make understanding photosynthesis more personal for us. If her third grade class could establish a connection with the subject at hand, in this case a tree, we'd have a vested interest in the learning process. I selected the fig tree.

Looking back, it is amazing that what may have been viewed as a random decision by a child could have life-long implications. Unbeknownst to me at the time, the humble fig tree has one of the deepest root systems in the botanical world. Unlike the mighty redwoods in the California forests whose root system is described as "shallow," a fig tree can sprout deep roots that even damage cement foundations.

Growing up, I developed my own roots — as deep-seated and strong as the fig tree. I had a small circle of devoted friends, a close-knit group of co-workers, and a fulfilling career of twenty-six years. When that career abruptly ended after the company declared bankruptcy, I was devastated.

More adventurous souls than I would have viewed this "tragedy" as an opportunity — a chance to spread one's wings, explore other options, test the waters for a new career. But I was distraught, anxious and even angry. In my mind, I had given the best years of my life to a job that no longer existed, putting in endless hours and working hard. If everyone else had shown that same dedication, I reasoned, I would still be employed. I'd still be a vice president, still occupy that corner office, and still have all the trappings that went with the title I had worked so hard to attain.

Exacerbating that dilemma was my age — a woman in her mid-fifties. While by no means "old," fifty is not the "new" thirty in the world of marketing and public relations. In my early twenties, armed with newly acquired bachelor's and master's degrees, along with an impressive list of work-study jobs and summer internships, I felt ready to take on the world — and in one way I had. My generation had left the confines of the kitchen and the secretarial pool, and forged our way into the working world, competing with our male counterparts, demanding equal pay for equal work, and smashing glass ceilings in the process.

But that world had changed radically in the years that I had spent climbing the corporate ladder. Human resources had migrated from a physical place in the company's headquarters to a virtual office, a hyperlink on the company's website. Longevity, once viewed positively as "company loyalty," was now viewed as "ludicrous." Why would anyone spend so many years with the same company? And the new world of social media presented its own set of challenges — what was a Twitter handle? Who was following whom on LinkedIn? And what was the best way to use search engine optimization to showcase a résumé?

As I struggled with the loss of my job, I thought a lot about the Swiss psychologist Elisabeth Kübler-Ross. Renowned for her work on death and dying, she wrote about the five stages of grief — denial, anger, bargaining, depression and acceptance. Though I was not confronting my own mortality in a physical sense, I was facing the death of someone I used to be. I was no longer the corporate success, the vice president, the career woman. In fact, I didn't even have a job. For the first time in forty years, I was unemployed. And like a person struggling with an agonizing diagnosis, I was in a state of disbelief and denial.

After a few weeks, the painful reality of my situation worsened. I had lost my job in the summer, and those first few weeks of disillusionment were softened by the mild weather. But when autumn rolled around, I became angry. How did I ever get in this position? And more importantly, how would I find my way out of it?

With an energy fueled by anger, I began responding to every job opening on every website — positions for which I was grossly overqualified, positions that were nearly a hundred miles away. I would take anything. I had to get back in the game, I reasoned, regardless of the title or distance. And while some of those inquiries resulted in a handful of interviews, I did not receive a single offer — which is when the depression over my job loss truly hit home.

There's an old expression that sometimes the only way out of a bad situation is through it. The challenge is that when you're in the middle of it, it becomes almost impossible to imagine the other side and how to get there. For months I struggled, but looking back, what saved me was sheer activity. Despite not working, I continued to get up early, shower, eat, dress, and walk to a local coffee shop. There, I pored over the morning newspapers and then "rewarded myself" with the daily crossword puzzle, something I didn't have time for when I was working. From there, I walked to the library and spent hours looking for career opportunities on the Internet, researching companies and networking with my increasing list of contacts on LinkedIn.

During this time, it also occurred to me that if and when I landed another position, I would not have the luxury of a secretary. For so many years I had been blessed with a support staff — individuals who typed my reports, prepared my PowerPoint presentations, and formulated my Excel spreadsheets. Swallowing my pride, I registered for a series of classes on Microsoft Office, and to my surprise, became quite efficient with PowerPoint and Excel.

While I was celebrating these small successes, I had my first promising interview. It was at a retirement community, and the job in question was a new one — director of community outreach. The position required marketing, writing, public relations, and familiarity with the nearby area. And there was a major silver lining — the retirement community was located less than three miles from my home. Two days later, I received an offer, and the following month, I was the newest member of the management team.

It has been more than three years since I "reinvented" myself as a community outreach director. I no longer wear designer suits, carry a corporate credit card, or occupy a corner office. In fact, most days my car serves as my "office," as I am often visiting a senior resident at a nearby hospital or representing the retirement community on a local board. And while I vowed never to become so involved in a job again, I find myself reverting back to my fig tree behaviors — for very cautiously I have once again started to put down deep roots.

~Barbara Davey

Chapter 3

Think Possible

Overcoming Adversity

Kidney Tomorrow

If you don't like something change it; if you can't
change it, change the way you think about it.
~Mary Engelbreit

When I met the woman who eventually became my wife, we were both young and struggling to get our footing in the world. For me, the struggle was compounded by the fact that I had a kidney transplant that was failing. I was heading for dialysis again in the near future.

Making a relationship work between two healthy people in this world is difficult enough — but we made it work. We grew closer and closer as I returned to the chair in the hemodialysis center, three nights a week, four hours a treatment. She was in nursing school, and spent long hours studying between the menial jobs that she did to pay for school. She would often come to visit me at dialysis, where we would sit and talk. It wasn't the usual course of romance for two twenty-somethings, but it was amazing how close we became. So, it was the easiest thing to do when I asked her to marry me a year and a half later.

My dialysis center had made me aware of a new home hemodialysis program they were offering — you'd get a small "portable" machine and supplies sent to your home. You'd have to train a partner to help attach you to the machine and monitor your treatments; you'd be able to dialyze in the comfort of your own home and have more control over your schedule. With some careful planning, you could even travel with it. My soon-to-be wife immediately demanded that I sign up and that she train to be my partner. She was working on a floor in a hospital then, doing twelve-hour overnight shifts. For the next two weeks, she finished her shift and then went with me to dialysis to be trained on the intricacies of the dialysis machine. Because of her dedication to home dialysis and to us as a couple, when we got married a few months later, we were able to pack the machine in the car with us, and have a honeymoon — our first vacation ever.

So, the years rolled on, and we continued much in the same way — she would work her shift and then put me on dialysis. We met with the local kidney transplant center and I was put on the list. Every day, we'd do dialysis — and we'd always say, half jokingly, "Tomorrow is the day we get the call!" which ultimately, over time, became shortened to our battle cry, "Kidney Tomorrow!" We used to say it to each other all the time to buoy our spirits on difficult days. Over time, the years wore on us — many days were filled with tears, exhaustion and despair, but somehow, whenever we said "Kidney tomorrow!" to each other, we felt better.

One summer night, we went out on a rare date. We played mini-golf and had a water fight to cool off from the hot July temperatures. I remember sitting on a picnic table with her, outside the golf course, watching the sun set. I talked about how exhausted I was, and how I wondered how much more I could endure. She just smiled and said to me, "It's okay. Kidney tomorrow!"

The next day, we woke up and I drove her to work. I dropped her off and mentioned that I was going to the store that morning. She asked me to pick up some milk. So, I shuffled off to the store and began to walk toward the milk. My cellphone rang in my pocket; it was rare to get a call so early in the morning, and when I answered it, the voice at the other end exclaimed, "Steven! This is the transplant center. We may have a kidney for you. Please come up to the hospital now."

When you're on dialysis and waiting for a kidney, you dream about this moment. You plan for it — we had a plan in place, and a bag packed at home for it. But there I stood, in the middle of the grocery store, surrounded by people, and time slowed down. Reality can seem to bend when the fulcrum of your life tips unexpectedly. I put the milk back in the cooler. "If I was going to be in the hospital, it might go bad," I reasoned. So, because we needed the milk, I did the next best thing.

I purchased a box of powdered milk, and called my wife. "Honey, the hospital called. We have to go there now; they may have a kidney for me."

"What? Oh my… uh, hold on…" she said.

I could hear her shout to her co-workers on the floor. "I have to go! They've got a kidney for Steven!"

I heard the cheers of all the workers and patients on her floor over the phone.

"I'll see you in a few minutes," I replied, "I, uh, got powdered milk…"

"You're absolutely silly, Steven — put the milk back!" she cried.

Soon, I raced to pick her up — she got in the car wearing the biggest smile I had ever seen. As I pulled out of the drive and we headed toward the kidney transplant center, she grabbed my hands and looked me in the eyes.

"Kidney today?" she asked.

"Kidney today," I said. "Kidney today."

Less than twenty-four hours later, I woke up very groggy after an extremely successful surgery. I had a functional, healthy kidney. Our days of dialysis were over.

It's been almost four years now, but we still talk about how a silly positive mantra, "Kidney tomorrow!" helped us during such a trying time. Being together has been the greatest experience in my life, but staying positive together has made all the difference — and it makes this new life we've been given all the more sweet. So, even now, when the tough times of "normal" life creep in on us, I turn to her, smile and say, "Kidney tomorrow."

And everything is all right.

~Steven Alexander

The Tale of Tabby

You cannot do a kindness too soon, for you never know
how soon it will be too late.
~Ralph Waldo Emerson

t was a cold and rainy October day in 2003, when the animal shelter where I worked received an elderly, emaciated, blind, virtually hairless Cocker Spaniel. We did not hold out much hope that the dog we named Tabby would find a home, but we were committed to helping her anyway. Because Tabby was a stray, she had to be held for a period of time to ensure that her owner wasn't looking for her. Based on her condition we were fairly certainly that no one would be coming forward to claim this poor little wretch of a dog.

Tabby received treatment from the attending vet and was then bathed, fed and settled into the quiet of the administration building, where we felt she would be less frightened and better able to heal. I should explain that the admin building was in an old house and therefore retained a sort of homey feeling. Tabby quickly endeared herself to our staff, who noticed that she appeared to be deaf as well as blind. She slept very soundly, and at about fourteen years of age, she liked her naps. She also quickly learned her way around the building and its various offices. With time and care she gained weight and grew in a luxurious coat of soft cream-coloured fur.

Despite or maybe because of her various challenges, Tabby had a great attitude. She high stepped along walls, feeling her way and never missing a beat. She boldly navigated obstacles, recovering from any missteps quickly. The one concern we had for her successfully being placed into a home was that she was easily startled, particularly when asleep, which caused her to nip. Tabby would require a special home in many ways, including one that did not include children who might be accidentally injured.

The days turned to weeks and then to months and Tabby settled into a comfortable routine. She seemed to like everyone she met, but she claimed a couple of our staffers as her own special friends. Her ability to know when one of these folks arrived on the shelter property was nothing short of remarkable. We attributed it to her keen sense of smell as we had no other explanation. Tabby would bark and bark until her person came to say hello. She insisted on being acknowledged and only when she had her fill was her person allowed to carry on. Tabby would then happily go back to napping.

When winter began to turn to spring and not a single person had asked about adopting Tabby, we assumed she would live out her days with us. She was happy and our staff loved her. Her life at the shelter was good, even though we normally hoped for a home for every animal.

The promise of spring began to turn into the long days of summer when a mom named Loretta came by the shelter with her three children, including her son, Andrew, a young boy who suffered from seizures. It was this boy who had noticed Tabby on the shelter website. What drew him to her was the note on her profile explaining that she had special needs. As a special needs child, he identified with Tabby and insisted they pay her a visit.

With three active young boys, including a toddler, this well-meaning family hardly seemed like the ideal fit for Tabby. They were shown other more suitable dogs to consider for adoption, ones that did not startle easily and sometimes nip. The child who somehow seemed fated to be Tabby's boy would simply not hear of it. He would not leave without his dog and as far as he was concerned, Tabby was that dog.

After having a long and very frank conversation with Loretta about our concerns that Tabby might nip a child, we reluctantly suggested that the family try fostering Tabby before making a permanent commitment, fully expecting them to call us the next day asking to bring her back. Call us they did, but only to tell us they loved her and wanted to adopt her. Tabby had, indeed, nipped everyone in the family, but no harm was done and they took it all in stride. They agreed to continue to foster her for the next week. At the end of that week, mom and son were at the shelter when we opened to sign all of the adoption paperwork. Tabby was officially their dog, or perhaps more importantly, Andrew was Tabby's boy.

This story could end here and be one of a thousand happy shelter memories, but Tabby's tale was not yet finished. Through tears, Loretta told us about the bond that had developed between her special needs son and his special needs dog. Where once Andrew suffered from four or more seizures a day, he had not had a single one since Tabby came home with them. He was no longer afraid to go to bed at night, as he had no fear of the terrifying seizures that would wake him from sleep. So concerned was he for Tabby's needs that he did not think about his seizures at all. It was clear that this once lost, broken little dog had not only found a happy home, a family and a child who loved her, she had found a purpose.

We heard from Tabby's family fairly frequently. Her boy went almost two weeks without having a single seizure. His mother attributed this to Tabby's presence. Although fewer in number and further between, the seizures did eventually return. Then something truly magical happened. Tabby began to alert Andrew before each seizure. This allowed him to prepare by getting into a safe place and position.

So Tabby, our little wretch of a dog, a dog with so many challenges and few options, a dog that most other shelters would have euthanized, found her perfect home with a boy who needed her as much as she needed him. Tabby, our blind, deaf, fourteen-year-old Cocker Spaniel, had not only found her perfect home, but her perfect job, where she enriched, enlivened, encouraged and inspired a young boy. Together these two indefatigable spirits marched bravely on.

Unfortunately, Tabby's age meant that her time with her boy was shorter than anyone would have liked. They supported and cared for one another for two years until Tabby closed her eyes for the final time. Andrew and his family mourned her passing, but also cherished their time together. The bravery she inspired and the selfless nurturing shared between them are memories that live on, as does her spirit, forever etched in the memories of those who were touched by this remarkable dog.

~Tammy Zaluzney

From Oppressed to Success

One's dignity may be assaulted, vandalized and cruelly mocked, but it can never be taken away unless it is surrendered.
~Michael J. Fox

n August 25, 1992, I stepped off the school bus — number 144 — and headed to Ms. May's classroom. As I walked to class, I felt an unexpected jolt; my pink Barbie book bag had been yanked from behind. A student who stood much taller than me (and a person who would become one of my meanest bullies) had grabbed my book bag and dumped my things on the ground. My pens, paper, pencils, notebook, crayons, and coloring books went tumbling down, and I frantically tried to grab them before they hit the ground.

I heard the bully laugh and say, "Do something about it! I wish you would!" By this time, a crowd of students gathered around me, and they began laughing, pointing, teasing, and taunting me. I was determined to not let them see me cry. I prayed that the teasing would stop and that someone would come to my rescue. Heartbreakingly, no one did. With fear and a heavy heart, I slowly bent down and picked up my things and put them back in my book bag. This was my first day of kindergarten, the first day of thirteen years of bullying.

From kindergarten through twelfth grade, I was bullied unmercifully for my size, stature, complexion, achievement, and love of learning. I was called "Geek," "Nerd," "Sell out," "Oreo," "GEICO Direct," "Teacher's Pet," "Goody Two Shoes," and more. The name that hurt the most was "Oreo," because kids said I was black on the outside, but white on the inside because I spoke properly, made good grades, and pronounced the "ing" on my words. I was physically bullied too. Students pushed me into lockers, threw food at me, tried to break my arm, tripped me, and told me that I would not amount to anything in life.

The bullies also took my lunch money, refused to pass the ball to me in gym class, and then threw the ball at me when the teacher was not looking. I hated lunchtime because I never fit in: White students accepted me, but black students made fun of me. The black students made fun of me because I did not wear name brand clothes and because I was the only black in honors classes. It always perplexed me as to why black students bullied me. We know the cruelty and torment our ancestors endured, but instead of uplifting or encouraging me, my own race tore me down. This hurt me so badly, both emotionally and physically.

After an award ceremony in fifth grade, students walked by the awards I had on my desk and knocked them on the floor. "You only won those awards because you are a teacher's pet!" the students shouted at me. Yet again, just as I had done on my first day of kindergarten, I fought back the tears because their words were excruciatingly painful. It was at this moment that I decided to prove them wrong.

I have always been self-conscious about my eyes because bullies made fun of them and said I looked like a frog. They told me I could probably see the whole world because my eyes were so huge. One student relentlessly called me GEICO Direct. To make my eyes appear smaller, I squinted when I talked to people, or I would avoid making eye contact altogether. I began to question God and asked Him, "Why did you make my eyes so big? Was it so people can make fun of me? Why didn't you make me normal?" I became so depressed that I put a picture of my sister under my pillow and fervently prayed to God that when I woke up, I would have normal size eyes like her. Each morning when I woke up my eyes were still big and I had to face another day of torment.

I was so low that there were times when I wondered if I should even live because I had very few friends, I was always being picked on, and I hated going to school. One time a bully picked me up and dangled me off the edge of a second story building, pretending that she was going to drop me. Because I was so small and afraid to speak up, bullies enjoyed making my life miserable. I am thankful for my parents and brother who told me to keep the faith. They set an example for me, sharing their own stories about how they overcame challenges through perseverance. Hearing their stories gave me the motivation and determination to keep living!

My mom and dad grew extremely concerned about the torment I experienced at school, and they talked to my teachers, principals, and even the bullies. However, after my parents talked to the administrators, things backfired and the students bullied me even more; because of this, I stopped telling my parents about what happened at school. Yet, I continued to tell myself that I would succeed, and I was determined to prove the bullies wrong. I often gave myself a pep talk, and from these pep talks, I coined my own saying: "I used other people's desire of wanting to see me fail as more motivation to see myself excel." I wanted to succeed, and I did!

In 2009, I graduated with a B.A. in Communication and minor in Psychology from North Carolina State University in Raleigh. I then worked for the University of North Carolina General Administration system and North Carolina State University before heading out west to graduate school. In 2014, I graduated with a Master of Education in Postsecondary Administration and Student Affairs from the University of Southern California (USC), and now I work at USC as the Manager of the Black Alumni Association. In addition, I am a red carpet host for Rich Girl Network and I interview celebrities at galas, award shows, and charity functions. How ironic that those who bullied me in school and said I would not amount to anything are now telling me, "I always knew you would be successful." Ha! I laugh and keep going.

My advice to people is simple: Never give up and never let anyone tell you what you cannot do. If I had listened to the bullies, I would not be where I am today. Because I ignored their cruel comments, worked hard, persevered, and kept the faith, I am making my dreams come true.

~Tensie J. Taylor

26

The Disney World Dream

All our dreams can come true, if we have the
courage to pursue them.
~Walt Disney

As a twenty-six-year-old single mother I became an expert at juggling bills, getting good deals and cooking balanced meals on a meager budget. Ryan had no idea that we lived just above the poverty line and I was happy to keep it that way. I was also very good at finding inexpensive or free entertainment.

However, in January of 1986 Ryan threw me a curve ball when he decided we were going to go to Disney World. He was five years old and enamoured with the Disney World commercials that always seemed to be playing on TV. I wasn't sure how to respond at first. The financially stressed part of me wanted to scream that we could barely afford to live, let alone go to Disney World! But, I didn't do that. Instead I grabbed my penny jar and got out a pad of paper and a pen.

I sat down on our living room floor and asked Ryan to help me figure out how much such a trip would cost and how many pennies we would have to save to get there. By the time I added up the costs of airfare, hotel, food and Disney World spending money we were well over $2,000. Then I dumped out our pennies and we began to count them. We had $3.48. Honestly, getting to Disney World was not part of my reality but I decided to turn the prospect of going there into a learning opportunity that I expected Ryan would tire of fairly quickly.

"I'll make you a deal," I said to him, "I will not buy a few things each week that I would normally buy and I will put the money that I don't spend in this jar. But, you have to do the same thing. If you ask me to buy you a treat that I would normally buy for you then you have to decide whether you want the treat or you want the money to go into our savings jar. That way we will both be contributing. What do you think?"

"It's a deal," he said. "When can we go?"

Never, I thought to myself, but out loud I said it would probably be only a few years. I felt guilty at not being truthful but the prospect of squashing his dream was even less palatable to me. The next day I stuck to my half of the bargain. I didn't buy myself a coffee when I normally would have and I passed on buying a pack of gum. After picking Ryan up from daycare we stopped at the grocery store. At the checkout counter he looked at the candy display and asked if I would buy him a chocolate bar, which is something I would buy for him once a week.

"Do you want the candy or the money?" I asked him.

"The money," he replied with a satisfied grin.

That evening I put $2.25 into our jar.

As the days continued the oddest thing started to happen. While I'd always thought I'd been good with money I noticed how often I spent money on small treats like a coffee or a magazine as a little reward for myself. I began to realize those small splurges added up. And, much to my surprise, Ryan didn't give up either. Friday nights after dinner we would dump out the change jar, count our coins and roll them in coin wrappers.

At the end of our first month we took over $30 in coins to the bank, where I opened a savings account. While going to Disney World was still not a reality for me I was pleased to have opened our savings account and I began taking pride in not spending money on things that I didn't need. Ryan also engaged Nana in his quest to get to Disney World and when he came home from visiting her would immediately put the spare change she'd given him into our jar.

Ryan turned six years old in October of that year and by the end of November we had almost $650 in our savings account and getting to Disney World had become real for me. We'd even gone to the travel agency and picked up brochures on vacations in Florida.

I rarely mentioned our travel goals to anyone, but one day in early December I was talking with a client and the fact that Ryan wanted to go to Disney World came up. She said she had a condo in Madeira Beach that was available the first week in January and we could have it for only $400 for the week. It was a two-bedroom unit with two double beds in each room. I was embarrassed to admit to her that this incredible offer was out of my range so I told her I would get back to her.

During the drive home I realized that if I could talk my mother and sister into going with us then it would only cost me $200 for one week of accommodation. I stopped in at the travel agency to inquire about airfare and the travel agent promised to get me the best deal she could find. That evening she called with the news that not many people wanted to fly to Florida at 7 a.m. on New Year's Day so there was a massive discount on the seats on that particular plane. I almost cried when she told me I could get round trip flights from Toronto to Tampa for $98 including tax!

As soon as Ryan was asleep I phoned my sister, Cathy, to ask her if she wanted to go to Florida with us and when she heard that her accommodation and airfare would only cost $200 she immediately said yes. This cost was also within my mother's budget and she was thrilled to be invited. On my way to work the next day I stopped by the travel agency, paid for our airfare, and then visited my client to accept her offer.

When I picked Ryan up from daycare and told him that he would be going to Disney World in just a few weeks he was over the moon with joy. And so, at 7 a.m. on January 1, 1987 the four of us were on our way to Florida. We loved the condo and everything Madeira Beach had to offer us. But the best part of our vacation was the day we took our bus trip to Disney World. Ryan went on the rides he wanted to go on, met some of his favourite Disney characters and enjoyed a live musical performance.

As I watched him sleeping that evening I couldn't help but feel an amazing sense of accomplishment. It seemed hard to believe that only the year before taking Ryan to Disney World had been inconceivable to me, yet we had done it. And, what had started out as a learning opportunity for Ryan had ultimately become an education for me in the power of owning a dream.

~Laura Snell

27

Getting from Here to There

Holding on is believing that there's only a past; letting go is knowing that there's a future.

~Daphne Rose Kingma

The Mimosa tree was in full bloom and provided the perfect canopy against a powder blue sky that Sunday afternoon. It was my time for peace and quiet. My only time. Life on a farm was difficult and exhausting. Living with an angry, alcoholic father brought additional challenges and heartache. These afternoons were a nice respite from my daily misery as I found escape in the pages of someone else's adventure.

My peace was interrupted when my mother stormed out of the house yelling at me. As she rushed toward me and began striking me with the all-too-familiar round curtain rod, I scrambled to assess what could have possibly brought on her wrath. Then I saw it. My diary! Mother had found my diary.

My secrets were in that journal. My most private thoughts. My pleas for encouragement. My appeals for help. No family, friends, or teachers seemed to care enough to investigate the source of my sadness, much less offer solace. In that diary were accounts of the torment endured when my bedwetting became habitual. In her frustration, Mother attempted to correct my behavior in the only way she knew, through punishment. I wrote about how each morning she would bend me over the bed, rub my nose in the urine-stained sheets, spank me with the curtain rod, and send me to school without a bath. The hot South Georgia school days intensified my stench. I was scolded in the hallway and relegated to the back corner of the classroom so as not to offend my teacher and my heckling classmates.

My mother was angry. Most mothers would have been concerned, not angry, after reading the accounts of molestation I documented in the journal. It had been going on since age five when a doctor's examination revealed the sordid family secret. The white-haired hometown doctor's words echoed still: "Lola, someone is hurting your little girl, and it has to stop." It didn't. If my own mother wouldn't help me, then who would? Consequently, I shared my woes with my diary. Now, my diary had exposed my mother to another ugly truth, the fact that my dad was having another one of his affairs — this time with a church friend.

The last six months had been the only time our household had known peace. My dad had accepted The Lord, turned his life around, left his honky-tonk lifestyle and brought his talented barroom cronies to church with him where they formed a band. A church lady brought her alto harmony to the group and, shortly thereafter, discord struck an ugly note again within our home.

Mother's tiny, frail frame was defenseless against the twice-her-size husband who had brought horrific physical harm to her for as long as I could remember. As she always did, Mother released her frustration on me. After she beat me, she ripped the pages from my diary and tossed its remains at my feet.

I pulled my knees under my chin, leaned against the Mimosa tree, and with tears streaming down my cheeks, I peered through the limbs, leaves, and blooms at the heavens above and had a tête-à-tête with the Lord. "God, if you really loved me, why would You let me be born into this family? I don't belong here!"

My way out finally came just before my eighteenth birthday, when I met my future husband. He was a youth minister who had pledged to serve the Lord after he was saved from a congenital heart defect.

We have lived happily ever after. Well, almost. For the first seventeen years of our marriage, my husband was unaware of my past.

I had managed to mask it. Until my husband was asked to minister to a beautiful young girl who claimed she was being abused. "Does she look like anyone who has been abused?" my husband asked. A thousand questions raced through my mind, all leading to the major one — would he still love me when he found out? An eternity passed in those few seconds. Webby broke the silence. "Does she, Joyce? Does she look like someone who has been abused?" It was time for the truth. I simply asked, "Do I?"

I held my breath, not knowing if I could draw another. Webby wrapped his arms around me and partnered with me as I began shedding the past and stepping out of my emotional prison. The next time my dad made a 2 a.m. phone call threatening to burn my house down or to bring harm to my family and me, he dealt with my husband. It never happened again.

Continuing to serve alongside my husband in ministry, I began speaking as an advocate against child abuse. I began writing again, but not in a journal. I had never written in my diary again after that Sunday afternoon. Instead I became a writer of books, starting with a pair of books about marriage.

The books helped me become a relationship expert on a local Kentucky television station. Soon thereafter, *Today's Woman* magazine asked me to join it as a columnist. The articles have been so well received that I now write for *Today's Family* as well. The *Just Ask Joyce* show, where real life and family values connect, can be heard every Monday through Friday on the Louisville Salem Network stations.

I am still getting from here to there. Having moved out of my past here to my present there, I press on because even though I am now here, there is another there on my GPS. We should never belong to a here. Everyone can dream, regardless of background, financial means, or educational level. A dream is a "there" waiting for someone to step out of a "here." For I have learned that "all things are possible for one who believes" (Mark 9:23). And even when you doubt yourself, the God of Impossibles believes in all of your possibles.

~Joyce Oglesby

28

Sure-Footed Faith

I remember my mother's prayers and they have always
followed me. They have clung to me all my life.
~Abraham Lincoln

My mother gripped my feet and ankles firmly but with tenderness. "This will work," she said to herself as she looked at me. I was lying on a thick blanket folded into a makeshift bed that was sitting on the dining room table. I cooed and stared at my mother, unaware of the prayer she said while she moved my feet around. "Please, God, make this work."

My feet were pointed inward when I was born. My condition was a mixture of being severely pigeon-toed and a minor case of being club-footed. My legs were twisted a bit like corkscrews, in that the tips of the big toe of each foot touched naturally and the knees bumped together when bent, making it impossible for me to walk if left uncorrected. I wasn't in pain. I was unaware of the crippling effect that my legs could have on me in my future. Instead, I lay on the bed my mother created on the dining room table and watched my mother turn my little legs from the inward position in which my toes touched to the outward position in which they pointed forward. I smiled each time.

"This isn't going to work," my father had bellowed at the doctor who began fitting my little legs with braces a week before in his office. I was squealing uncontrollably, as if the metal of the braces burned me with every touch. "No, this is not going to work. Get them off him."

"He needs them to realign his legs," the doctor said, holding the tiny braces up for my father to see. They looked like torture devices from the Inquisition. "We talked about this."

"Jimmy," my mother said. She had scooped me up in her arms. She held me close to her bosom, and her raven hair fell across me like a veil, protecting me from the suffering of the world. "He won't be able to walk."

"There's got to be another way. If you think I'm going to let him put that on my son," he pointed at the braces the doctor was holding, "well, it's not going to happen. I'm not letting that happen to my son."

"We'll have to operate then," the doctor said. He dropped the braces onto the table in the room; they clanked heavily, silencing my father. "We'll need to operate on him when he's older if we don't use the braces."

"He's not going to wear those," my father roared before he stormed out of the room.

"Is there anything else we can do?" my mother asked. Tears ran down her cheeks. She was not going to challenge my father. "Please."

The doctor said nothing for a minute before he looked up at my mother. "There's an exercise," he said. He opened a drawer and pulled out a prescription pad. He began to write on it. "There's an exercise you can do with his legs that has been known to work."

He eased me from my mother's arms and touched my chin briefly. There was a bluish line on it intersecting another like-colored one, although shorter. Like an X, he thought to himself, even as he checked the mark to ensure that it was made up of veins still visible through my slightly transparent skin.

"Like this," he said as he knelt on the carpeted floor and placed me on the ground gently. My mother knelt next to him. She looked as if she were in prayer. The doctor held my feet loosely, deciding what to do, and then slowly turned my feet so that the toes that faced inwards faced forward. My knees rolled with my toes and my feet, which were turned on their side, adjusted accordingly. I cooed again. "You try."

My mother slid over, exchanging places with the doctor. She took my feet in her hands and did what the doctor did.

"If you do this every day for half an hour," he said, trying to calm my mother, "there's a small chance that the surgery will be easier."

"Easier?"

"Just do it," he said. "It'll help you."

"It'll help him," she said. "This will work."

"Come back in three months."

After the appointment, my mother took me home and placed me on a blanket in the living room. She bent her head slightly and folded her hands and prayed for her son's legs. "This will work," she whispered to Him. "I know You will make it work."

She took my feet into her hands and began to exercise them while reciting nursery rhymes and singing children's songs and religious hymns. She talked about my brother and my father. She talked about her faith in God.

Ten minutes turned into twenty, and twenty turned into an hour. Soon, she and I sat together for the better part of every day. And as the minutes turned into hours, the days turned into weeks and those weeks turned into months.

"This will help you," she said to me again and again. "I have faith in Him."

"Where's your son?" the doctor said to my mother three months later as he examined my legs.

"This is my son."

He smiled awkwardly. He looked at my legs and didn't recognize them.

"This is not your son. Your son's legs were twisted like the roots of a tree," he said and checked his chart again. He calmed himself. "This child's legs do not look like your son's legs."

"He's my son," my mother said quietly. She picked me up. "He's my son."

The doctor examined my legs as I cooed at him. They were straight, with the toes pointed toward the heavens and the knees only turned in slightly. Then he looked at my face before touching my chin softly.

"It looks like a cross now," he said out loud, but to himself. He allowed his finger to trace the intersecting lines on my chin. He had remembered the mark from before. "He is your son."

"He is," my mother said, smiling through her tears. "And he is healed."

"What did you do?"

"I did what you told me to and more."

"It shouldn't have worked," he said. He looked at my mother apologetically. "There's no such exercise. I made it up. It shouldn't have worked."

"It wasn't the exercise that cured him, doctor."

And in my file in a doctor's office in Pennsylvania is a note pinned to the documents pertaining to my crippled legs. It reads simply Cured by Divine Intervention.

~James Foltz

29

I Believed Despite the Odds

*An attitude of positive expectation is the mark of the
superior personality.*
~Brian Tracy

was born with cerebral palsy in Johannesburg, South Africa. I
had my first seizure at age four. Later, I was diagnosed with
localized epilepsy. We had no 911 so my mother would drive
me to the hospital when I had one long seizure or back-to-back
seizures. Sometimes, I'd even have a seizure on the way home from
school.

I went to a school for disabled children, but we moved to the
United States when I was ten. I had to adjust when I was integrated into
a mainstream school and just went out for one special education class.

Having a physical disability, a learning disability, and a seizure
disorder made me feel like such an outcast. Everyone knew who the
"special ed" kids were and mocked us on the playground. Why do
kids have to be so mean?

When I was a teenager, despite going to mainstream classes, I was
still being told what I couldn't do. My neurologist said that I had brain
damage and I wouldn't be able to do analytical things. I wanted to be
a counselor more than anything in the world, but he said I wouldn't
be able to handle it.

That doctor crushed my dreams. When I told mother what he

said, she said that she empathized, but the doctor was the expert.

When I graduated from high school in 1994 I enrolled in a local community college. Two people there changed the trajectory of my life. One was my college counselor, who thought I was an amazing, articulate student with a knack for establishing interpersonal networks. She encouraged me to enroll in the Human Services program at Western Washington University in Bellingham, Washington. The other person was my boyfriend, who helped me with my math homework. He figured out a way to see the subject matter through my eyes and he also showed great faith in my abilities. He himself was visually impaired, but he never quit on his dreams. His positive attitude was a great influence for me.

Sometime around 1997, I felt this passion and fire grow in me — the likes of which I never experienced before. I knew exactly what I wanted and I was determined that no one was going to stop me — not even my concerned parents. I wanted to get married to my wonderful boyfriend and attend Western Washington University together. I aimed to apply to the Human Services program and he was interested in computer sciences. We had already planned how we were going to apply for financial aid and receive campus housing.

My parents had a hard time grasping that I could go to university and get married. I think they were generally concerned about my wellbeing, naiveté, and general lack of experience. They did not want to see me get hurt. But, I was willing to get hurt, if necessary. To me, that was part of growing and gaining experience. More than anything, I wanted to be educated and experience the same opportunities as everyone else. I wanted to see what I could do in a world that told me I was limited. I refused to give up on myself.

Not only did I receive my bachelor's degree in Human Services, I went a step further and got a master's degree in Psychology! While in school, I became a member of two honor societies and won an essay scholarship that covered tuition. I soaked up every piece of knowledge I could. I was thirsty to learn and to connect with other students.

It was amazing. It was also one of the hardest experiences of my life. My challenges had less to do with the subject matter and my ability to learn; they had more to do with learning the art of interpersonal communication in a world with so many perspectives. I had been overprotected my entire life and was ill prepared for other people's judgments, thoughts, life experiences, and worldviews. Nevertheless, I was resilient. My relationship with my husband survived. And, I got more of an education then I could have ever imagined. It was an education in life.

Ironically, after finally becoming the counselor I always wanted to be, I realized that I wanted to pursue a new direction. This new direction had something to do with writing and inspiring others to see their inner power, as well as their freedom to choose their own life path. I came to this realization after a few major life transitions.

I am fortunate to have family and friends who support me and stand by me through all the successes and failures. They remind me that I am worth it. They remind me that I've made it this far, despite the odds.

Here's what I tell myself every day:

Challenges make me resilient.

I have the will and inner strength to overcome my challenges.

It's all a matter of perspective; if I can't do something one way, I try another way.

I will adapt.

I will never quit or give up on myself.

~Mandy Traut

No to Nearly Impossible

*Never give up on what you really want to do. The
person with big dreams is more powerful than
one with all the facts.*

~Author Unknown

Exiting Dr. Gyimah's African American Lit class, my emotions sprang into action. Who did she think she was? She couldn't tell me what I could do. Why was everyone against me?

The walk through the parking lot was an excruciating blur. There were colors, but nothing distinguishable to my eyes. The only thing I saw was my resolve to do what everyone kept saying I couldn't do... finish school on time.

Two weeks earlier, I'd had a sweet baby girl via C-section. I was sewn up tightly and sent along to sort out my new life as a teen mom finishing her sophomore year in college. I flip flopped between desperation and determination. I didn't know which way I was going until Dr. Gyimah weighed in: "It's hard enough to pass my class as a regular student with no other responsibilities. It will be nearly impossible with a newborn baby, Deborah."

My grandmother had cautioned me too. In an effort to encourage an abortion during the early weeks of my pregnancy, she had warned that I'd have to give up track and field, which meant I'd likely lose my scholarship and be forced to quit school. She spun a web of dreams deferred and implored me to think about my future.

"What should I do, Antoine?" I wept as he drove down Beechwood Street in our small college town. "I don't think I can do this."

"It's going to be okay," my daughter's father said soothingly. "You have to do it. Just take it one day at a time."

On that frigid March day of 2003, I allowed my anguish to run its course as we made the short trip home. I was intent on leaving it in the car; carrying my desperation beyond the passenger door of the car would be detrimental to what I was slowly deciding would be my new goals. I was going to run again, and I wasn't going to just pass Dr. Gyimah's class, I was going to ace it. From that moment on, I began to coach myself into positive thoughts.

Each day, I woke up and took my daughter to the indoor track with me where I went from barely able to walk to a slow jog. It was humiliating at times to feel the eyes of my teammates watching me with pity. I averted my eyes and continued to show up.

With fifteen credits to complete, if I wasn't on the track, I was attempting to balance studying and catering to the needs of my new-born. I thanked God for her calm temperament; I'd seen plenty of babies who were far less easygoing. This was a sign to me that I had to trudge onward.

As flowers opened and warmth descended on the town of Princess Anne, Maryland my legs grew stronger, my stride became more confident, and the warrior within me emerged. Early May brought with it finals and essays, but I'd worked hard, so I was fearless. Sitting in front of the computer in my living room, I skimmed through my final grades. There were fifteen credits worth of A's, but my heart leapt at the sight of the A beside African American Lit. I knew it!

The momentum from attaining perfect grades took me through a summer of hard training. If I could do it in the classroom, I could do it on the track and maintain my scholarship. The following track season, during my junior year in college, I suffered a bad breakup, but I refused to allow any pain to derail what I said I would do.

As the gossip spread about the split, I stayed focused. Before me, there were always two choices: give up or fight. Each day I had to choose one, and the more frequently I chose to fight, the more consistent I became at commanding my success. My freshman year I peaked at 2:18 in the 800 meter run, my specialty event. By the spring of my junior year, I peaked at 2:11. I was stronger and faster than I had been before becoming a mother. Every whisper was silenced, and I again ended my year with two semesters of straight A's.

My greatest victory was holding my daughter in my arms after crossing that stage with my *summa cum laude* degree in hand, all because I made the choice to never allow quitting to be an option. I woke up each morning prepared to fight and refused to allow "nearly impossible" to be part of my language.

~Deborah J.

Autism Is My Superpower

*It does not matter what sixty-six percent of people
do in any particular situation. All that matters
is what you do.*
~John Elder Robison, Look Me in the Eye

My parents were concerned because my speech was not as advanced as other children at age two and a half and I did strange things like lining up all my toys in rows throughout the house, spinning around in circles, and throwing tantrums. In addition, my motors skills such as running and hand strength were delayed. I also had a lot of trouble with balance.

My neurologist recognized the signs immediately and informed my parents that I was autistic. My parents asked what my long-term outlook might be and they were told that I would most likely never be independent. They were told that because of my lack of motor skills I probably would never be able to ride a bike, motorcycle, or drive an automobile. This news made my parents very sad as they had lost my older brother in childbirth two years earlier.

My parents immediately enrolled me in speech and occupational therapy classes. I don't remember much about it, but they said I went to classes five days a week for four years. Early on my parents believed that if they could get me enough training that somehow I would outgrow or no longer be autistic. As I went to classes later I noticed that almost all of the parents believed the same thing. It wasn't just about helping their children fit into society. It was also about trying to hide the autism from the world. A lot of the kids sometimes felt like Rudolph in the movie *Rudolph the Red-Nosed Reindeer* when his dad tried to hide his red nose.

While my autism caused me to develop slower than other children in some areas it also gave me some abilities that others didn't have. I learned my alphabet at age one and I could read at a fourth grade level by eighteen months. In preschool the teacher always read a story before naptime to the class, but was so amazed at how well I could read that I took over and was the official storyteller for my preschool. It was easy for me to read the words on the page fluently, but I had difficulty having a simple conversation.

My dad had been a star athlete in high school and college, but because of my delayed motor skills I was not able to play organized sports early on. I really wanted to follow in his footsteps because he enjoyed football so much, but it just wasn't possible. Instead I joined the Cub Scouts. It was so much fun, and at each meeting I learned a new life skill, from cooking to tying knots to hiking. It was also the first time that I spent a lot of time with neurotypical children. This was important because I would copy how the other scouts acted and that's how I learned to interact and take part in organized events. All of the physical activity improved my motor skills too.

I earned the Arrow of Light Award and the Cub Scout Super Achiever Award because I had earned every pin that the Cub Scouts offered.

Since I had such a wonderful time in Cub Scouts I bridged over to Boy Scouts. It was not an easy transition as Boy Scouts are "boy run." This means that I was no longer taking classes from patient adults, but being given orders from older scouts who were in high school. It was difficult because I could not process what they wanted me to do as quickly as regular developing children. I was sometimes overlooked for leadership positions and not given a chance. I did come home very upset sometimes, but I always remember my father saying, "If it's easy everyone would do it. It's the hard that makes it great." He always knew what to say to motivate me. I doubled my efforts and slowly I was able to do the jobs that were needed and in turn I was given positions of responsibility.

I believe that scouting is very good for autistic children because they learn hands-on life skills through merit badges. An Eagle Scout must have twelve Eagle required badges and twenty-one total merit badges to even be considered. The Eagle requirements are very difficult. Everything from First Aid, Citizenship, Accounting, Family Planning, and Physical Fitness are learned along the Eagle Trail. I currently have all of the Eagle required badges and a total of forty-five merit badges. I enjoy learning new things from the experts in the field who teach the merit badges. My favorite was the Aviation merit badge. We went to an actual flight school and learned all about navigation, instruments, weather conditions, and the different planes. We then got to ride in a small plane and I even got to fly it for a little bit. It was amazing!

When I was thinking about an Eagle Scout project there were so many options to consider. The churches all needed help with their facilities, and all of the fraternal organizations like the Elk, Moose, and Veterans clubs had things I could have helped with, but none of the options seemed quite right.

Then a little over a year ago I came down with a terrible fever and my mother took me to the emergency room. The EMT who was there took my information and when they were told I was autistic the doctor asked him to stay in case they needed to hold me down while I got shots. I guess the doctor had experience with other children on the spectrum. I calmly allowed them to give me the shots and the EMT and doctor were both shocked when I didn't put up a fight.

The EMT stayed with me and asked a lot of questions about being autistic. Then he followed us out into the parking lot and explained why he was asking all the questions. It seemed that his nephew had just been diagnosed with autism and he and his sister were very upset. With a tear in his eye he told us that I was such a well-mannered young man and in control of my surroundings, which gave him hope for his nephew's future. He said that I inspired him and he was so happy that he met me.

As I thought about what he had said it came to me that maybe I could help other parents. I could make them understand that autism is not something to be ashamed of and that if their child is on the mid to higher end of the spectrum anything is possible. I want parents to embrace their children for who they are and not carry the guilt that they did something wrong. According to the CDC, one in forty-two boys in the USA is somewhere on the autism spectrum. If I could inspire new parents who are so devastated by the news then maybe I could make the world a better place.

Currently, I am a high school sophomore and enjoy playing the piano and the trumpet in our marching band and jazz band. I'm also in ROTC and was honored by being inducted into the Kitty Hawk Honor Society for members with good grades. I take advanced classes and I am on track to graduate with honors. I currently have a 3.75 GPA. I threw shot put and discus for my school's track team and also ran the 100-meter dash. I will be attending a university upon graduation. I am hoping to get accepted into the Wharton Business School at Penn, or another Ivy League school, but if not then possibly Baldwin Wallace University in Berea, Ohio. After graduation I would like to own my own business, possibly in computers.

How would I define my autism? I was never considered an "Aspie" because of my diagnosis. I use the word "autistic" because it is a word most people understand, but in the end it is just a word. To be honest my answer may sound strange, but I am not defined by my autism. I am Michael Whary. I cannot be defined by any set "definition." What I have learned is that no matter who you are or what disabilities you have to overcome in this life if you want something badly enough anything is possible! God gave everyone a special gift, a "superpower" if you will. Autism is mine. It has taught me to overcome my physical, mental, and social difficulties.

Every year we celebrate my birthday with a cake and candles as most people do. When I blow out the candles and make a wish it's always the same, "I wish that all of the suffering in the world would end and in so doing there would be peace on Earth."

I thank the powers that be for giving me this life. I thank my parents for their guidance, patience, love, and understanding. And I wish nothing but good things for others on the autism spectrum.

~Michael R. Whary

Editor's note: For his Eagle Scout project, Michael made a video for parents of kids newly diagnosed on the autism spectrum, to show them what they can expect. You can see the video at https://www.youtube.com/watch?v=86MXGIDG7UM. We highly recommend it!

Anything Is Possible

When you have a disability, knowing that you are not
defined by it is the sweetest feeling.
~Anne Wafula Strike, In My Dreams I Dance

The sun was shining down on me as I sat motionless on the steps of the pool, watching everyone else swim back and forth. This reminded me of all the times as a child I sat watching my classmates run around during recess. It was then that I realized that most of my life had been spent watching others enjoy themselves as I sat back and did nothing.

After coming to this realization, I noticed a little girl staring at me as she swam back and forth. She had a look of confusion on her face as she tried to understand how it was I got into the pool in the first place. I smiled at her, hoping to break the ice and have her ask me why I wasn't swimming. Unfortunately, my attempt failed and she just kept on staring.

The awkwardness of the situation escalated before I decided to lose myself in some of my favorite show tunes. However, my happiness bubble was quickly burst when a little boy swam up to me and said, "I feel sorry for you."

I looked at him and asked, "Why?" He just turned around and swam away.

After the encounter, I decided I had enough for one day and wanted to get out of the pool. I lifted myself up the stairs and reached for my mom to help put me in my wheelchair. I told her what had happened and how uncomfortable it made me. Then, in a moment of complete clarity, another thought came to me. If I wanted to change how the world viewed me, I would have to take action. That's when I decided to write a children's book. I felt this was a good idea because it was children who stared at me the most. I would write a story that taught them about disabilities in a fun way. This is when I came up with the concept of KatGirl, a super hero in a wheelchair who helps children that are being bullied.

Anxious to start writing, I quickly wheeled inside my apartment and locked myself in my room to begin creating the story. As I wrote each word, I could envision my future as a world-renowned author and public speaker. This feeling grew so intensely that every fifteen minutes I brought my mother into my room and read to her what I had written. My excitement spread like wildfire as we both fantasized about interviews with CNN and being on The New York Times bestseller list. In the end, regardless of what happened, I knew one thing for sure — I was done watching the world pass me by.

I continued writing for the next twelve hours, with very few bathroom and food breaks. I was so focused that by the time I was ready to go to sleep I had written eighteen pages. This was just the beginning though, and over the next year and a half the story went through many changes before it was ready to be unveiled.

The book was published in the spring of 2011. I was so excited when I received the call that the printed copies were ready. I couldn't believe the day had finally arrived that I would see the outcome of all my hard work.

When I picked up the yellow book with The Adventures of KatGirl written on the cover and saw the drawing of a brown-haired girl like me sitting in a wheelchair tears began to well up in my eyes. There it was: "Written by Katherine Magnoli." I hugged the book the same way a mother would her newborn baby. I opened the book slowly, making sure not to wrinkle any of the shiny pages. As I read each sentence I couldn't help but cry as I saw my words come to life in a book.

Shortly after getting the books, I visited several bookstores and libraries, enduring a lot of rejection. I did not rest though, and eventually my perseverance came in handy when I was contacted by a local bookstore looking to put my book on their shelves. I was thrilled by this achievement but knew there was so much more to be done. Eventually it came to me: I would offer to visit schools and read my book to the students. I immediately started to contact every school in my surrounding area. I had very little luck getting calls back until one day all that changed.

I was on my way home from college when my mom called to tell me she had just received a phone call from a principal inviting me to speak to the students at her school. I went home and began preparing for the presentation that I would be giving the following morning. I barely slept that night due to so much excitement and apprehension.

The next day I confidently wheeled into a classroom filled with students who stared at me just like the little girl in the pool. However, this time, instead of looking away, I decided to ask the question: "How do you feel when you see me?" The kids paused and then bravely responded: "I feel sorry for you." I listened intently to their answer and simply replied, "Okay."

I opened my book and started reading. In no time I noticed the children's stares turned to smiles. When I finished reading I asked the question again: "How do you feel when you see me?" Without hesitation they replied, "You are so cool! Does your chair fly too?" I just smiled and said; "No, not yet, but maybe some day." I knew in my heart that this was true, because the past two years had proven to me that with determination anything is possible.

~Katherine Magnoli

The Most Important Day of My Life

*You are never given a wish, without also being given
the power to make it come true.*
~Richard Bach

"He has suffered brain damage," the doctor gravely told my mother after I was born. "We're not sure about the extent, but he will never walk or speak. He's probably severely retarded, and I suggest you find a suitable institution in which to place him."

That's what people did with their developmentally disabled children in 1960. They called them "retarded" and they put them in institutions. Mom's response was a stubborn determination to prove him wrong.

Due to a prenatal injury, I was born with a subdural hematoma on the top right side of my head. It was the size of an orange, and the blood put pressure on my brain. Doctors assumed the injury was severe enough to significantly limit my muscular and cognitive functions. They had not, however, met a mother so fiercely devoted to her children.

My mischievous four-year-old brother had played a role in this saga. He had asked why the baby hadn't arrived as scheduled. Mom had shrugged and told him I just wasn't ready.

"What would make him ready, Mommy?" he asked.

"I don't know," she replied. "Perhaps if I slipped and fell..."

You can guess what happened next. Billy spread magazines all over the tile floor. Then he yelled "Mommy, Mommy, come quick!"

Mom flew through the door, slipped on the magazines, and fell. I was born the next day.

The next year should have been one of firsts, but mine came slower than average. I lacked any muscle tone. The lump gradually melted away, and portraits show a healthy child. What you can't see are Mom's hands supporting me from behind because I couldn't sit up. Although my motor skills were lacking, my cognitive abilities convinced her I was normal.

Mom began to exercise my flaccid limbs. She cross-patterned left arm to right leg, reversed, and repeated after each diaper change. Challenging me to push and pull against her pressure, she coaxed my muscles to work. Progress was slow, but she persevered.

Several trips to "crippled children" hospitals didn't convince specialists of any progress. At eighteen months, I refused to speak to doctors. This convinced them I was also mentally disabled. During one visit, *after* the doctor left the room, I asked, "Go home now?"

Accelerating the "workouts" earned dividends. At age two I could sit up and scoot around on my behind, yet I didn't crawl. A torturous device was added: the "standing box." Locked into an upright position, I screamed for freedom. Mom had to reassure the neighbors I wasn't being abused. Gradually, my leg muscles strengthened. My brain learned balance. After each session, she would hold me close, reassuring me I would someday walk. She was gentle but firm in her resolve.

For six months this device was my daily nightmare, but it worked. One day, as I was mimicking TV cartoon characters, I jumped up and started running around the room. Laughing and jumping around, I called out to Mom. She watched silently from the kitchen doorway, nodding through a veil of tears. Finally, her little Patrick had defied the "experts."

Although I don't remember this specific moment, I'm told this bright March day became the most important of my life.

Mom took me back to the hospital, where I walked for the stunned specialists. Her dedication had trumped their expertise. They remained convinced I was mentally deficient because I still refused to speak to them. Mom's disdain had evidently rubbed off on me; it would be a while before I spoke to a doctor.

Although the doctors stubbornly disagreed, my parents enrolled me in preschool. Already able to read and write, I excelled. Therapy improved my slurred speech. I grew into a happy and healthy little boy.

When I reached third grade, I did not get along with my teacher. I decided she was a worm-faced monster. She was mean and insulting. I lost interest in school.

"He's retarded, Mrs. Coomer," Mrs. Battle-Axe said. "He doesn't belong in my class."

My mother responded fiercely, in front of the school principal and psychologist. "No, he's not," she exclaimed. "You're the one who's retarded. Patrick just doesn't like you, and I don't either. He's plenty smart enough to succeed, but he needs someone who inspires him. You are right about one thing: he doesn't belong in your class."

I was transferred into a class taught by a young lady who was sweet and patient. My grades soared.

As I grew into adolescence, my legs grew stronger. I played basketball, but my upper body remained weak. I ran twenty miles daily on my high school cross-country team, which won two state championships. An honor roll student, I wrote for the school newspaper and participated in several clubs.

During my first year of college, I was editor of our award-winning student newspaper. Mom urged me to keep writing when I left journalism. She encouraged boldness, refused to accept excuses, and cheered every success.

Ornery yet fun, Mom was intelligent and opinionated. Her love of history and literature inspired me to read the classics. She respected diversity and resented bigotry. As our political beliefs diverged, our debates were spirited but respectful. Her grasp of history demanded I argue with facts, not rhetoric. We became close friends, even during some rough stretches. Although she could make me angry, I knew her love for me was steadfast. Many who were diagnosed as I was were indeed forgotten. Because of her, I've challenged my own children to never say, "I can't."

Mom passed away nine years ago, but not before I provided my parents with plenty of grandchildren, including my first child, Anna, who even gave them a great-grandson.

Knowing Mom would be angry if I melted with grief at her passing, I coached my son's basketball team that evening. Later, on my nightly walk, each step was a memorial to her devotion. Tears of gratitude mixed with the cold Oregon rain, and I lost track of my lap count. It seemed fitting to walk for hours. It was the best memorial I could give her.

At her service, I recited Robert Frost's poem, "The Road Less Traveled."

Thanks, Mom… the road you chose has made all the difference.

~Patrick B. Coomer

Chapter 4

Think Possible

Proving that Persistence Pays

Princess's Posse

An effort made for the happiness of others
lifts us above ourselves.
~Lydia M. Child

went to veterinary school later in life. Due to the fact that I had to hold a job during the day, when it came time to log numerous hours in an internship, my choices were limited. Finally, at the last possible moment, I was taken on at an urgent care/ emergency veterinary hospital located deep within the inner city. The facility was open 24 hours, 7 days a week. Nights were long and heart wrenching. Most of our clients did not have the means to pay for the care their pets required. They often came to us far too late, when nothing could be done to save their pets. Clients would spread out meager sums on the counter and beg for whatever services that precious amount would buy. Most nights I dragged myself home at 3 a.m., exhausted and heartsick.

One night started about the same as the others but soon became very special. An elderly woman arrived carrying her small Poodle wrapped in a bloody blanket. She said they had been out for their evening walk when a large dog had attacked her Princess. A man came and pulled the large dog away. She had grabbed Princess and come straight to us.

The Chief of Staff and I took the small bloody blanket to the exam room.

We were expecting the worst. No movement or sound came from

the bundle.

As we peeled the bloody layers away, a small white Poodle emerged. She was alert and looking at us. There was a lot of blood, but as we examined her we grew more excited. "There are a lot of lacerations, but nothing major has been damaged! I think we can sew up this little gal!"

He formulated his plan and what the estimate would be for our client. My mission was now to speak to Princess's mom.

I brought her into the office. "The good news is," I said, "that it looks far worse than it is." I then told her the bad news — a several hundred-dollar estimate for Princess's care.

She asked, "How long would I have to pay that bill?" I immediately began my rote speech that we had no payment terms, that payment must be made in full at the time of service, etc.

"That's not what I meant," she said. "How long tonight?"

I felt a glimmer of hope.

"How long do you need?' I asked. She wanted to know if she could stay in the office and use our telephone to make some calls. She handed me two crumpled twenty-dollar bills and gave my hand a squeeze. "Is that enough to start? Give me a little time to get some people down here."

I relayed the information to the Chief of Staff. He had given Princess some pain medicine and cleaned her up in order to get a better look. His decision was to prep Princess and let her owner have some time to work on a few things.

Shortly afterwards, chaos ensued and we became very busy. Our receptionist walked into the exam room, waving a twenty-dollar bill over her head, and said, "Some lady just gave me this and said it was for Princess. What am I supposed to do with it?" Before we could answer we heard our bell ringing nonstop at the front desk. A woman and three children were there. I went out with the receptionist. The woman handed us $30, and each child opened his hand and dumped a fistful of change on the counter. "We brung that for Grandma and Princess," the little boy said.

Next came a young woman who handed me four credit cards. She said that each one had about $20 left on it. Her direction: "Fill them up for Princess and Grandma." The funny part is that after they made their contributions they stayed. Our little lobby filled. Where it was usually deathly quiet or the only sound you heard was crying, it was now filled with joyful greetings and phone calls to others to get up here quick to help Grandma. Our receptionist would holler out the current total and cheers would erupt. Our lobby now contained at least twenty people rooting for Princess. The man whose dog attacked Princess arrived and laid a one-hundred-dollar bill on the counter. He wanted to personally apologize to Grandma, so I went to get her from the office. I told her that all of her children and grandchildren were arriving and were in the lobby contributing funds for Princess. She laughed and told me that she had no children or grandchildren of her own. She said, "Everybody in the neighborhood has always called me Grandma — I've always tried to take care of all of them the best I could over the years."

Our Chief of Staff went into the lobby and thanked everyone and said that since our lobby wouldn't hold anyone else, he figured we had enough for the bill! Princess recovered beautifully and she and Grandma bring us treats all the time. My heart swells every time I see them and think of the entire neighborhood that came out to take care of the grandma who had always tried to take care of them.

~Peggy Omarzu

Grace Revisited

God respects me when I work; but God loves
me when I sing.
~Rabindranath Tagore

am a church girl. I was born and raised in the church, eager to
participate in all things "churchy." For me, that meant music.
My grandmother says I could sing better than I could talk. A
close second was my love for words, so together, words and
music kept me sane during my darkest hours. Life was not easy for
me; I was molested as a child, raped in college and I have an ongoing
battle with anxiety and depression.

Due to my bouts with depression and anxiety, any stress was
distress and I spent a good portion of my twenties heavily medicated
and in treatment. The toll this took on my body was great, so great
that my discs herniated. After a year of physical therapy, injections
and even heart catheterizations, it was determined that I would need
a cervical fusion.

I was experiencing so much physical pain, and at times partial
paralysis, that I agreed to have the surgery. On the morning of the
procedure, the surgeon, rolling me in to be sliced, said cheerfully,
"Oh, you might not be able to speak properly again after this. So take
it easy after the surgery so that your voice has a chance of returning
to somewhat of a 'normal' capacity."

I was horrified. I had been singing since the age of five and still
had plans to record and pursue an acting and singing career. Chills ran

down my spine, the same spine he was about to operate on. I needed the surgery, but I also needed to sing. In that moment I might as well have been told I was going to die. Then I felt a gentle nudge in my spirit reminding me that my attitude had been less than stellar. I was filled with conviction.

In the months leading up to the surgery, I had been neglecting my leadership duties in church due to pride and hurt feelings. A family member who was younger and noticeably less talented was chosen over me to lead the worship team and I was simply not interested in sharing my gift of singing anymore. I sang, but without any emotion or spirit. I didn't believe in the words. Hatred and jealousy had replaced love and joy in my heart.

Now that my ability to sing was being threatened, I fervently bartered with God. I promised that no matter what the outcome was, from that point on I would honor him with my gifts.

Those weeks following the surgery were the worst I ever had to endure. I felt like I had been dropped from an airplane without a parachute. Unstoppable pain radiated throughout my body day and night and I could not speak at all. When I tried, the words were raspy and deep, not to mention I had limited range of motion and could barely hold my own head up.

I was determined to overcome. I prayed and believed God's promises concerning his plans for my life regarding music. I slowly started to speak, pushed myself to sing, went online and found vocal exercises to practice while in recovery and then tested my new instrument at an open mic poetry reading. No one knew I was struggling to maintain tone or pitch or that my range had greatly diminished, but I kept singing. I never stopped singing. I sang every chance I got.

I used this experience as a testimony of God's grace and mercy, but also as a modern day reminder of the parable of the men with the talents. God gives us all gifts and talents, but it's what we choose to do with them that can create an atmosphere for worship. Pre surgery I took for granted those talents. Now, five years later, I am eternally grateful for every opportunity I have to share the gift he gave me with other people, and they have taken notice.

Since the surgery, I have recorded two studio albums, starred in three plays, recorded over ten compilation projects and I am currently working on projects with individuals who all have experience in the recording industry.

I had forgotten how precious God's grace was, and I am glad he gave me another chance to revisit my first love: music.

~Shantell Antoinette

Flag Girl

If you are not willing to risk the unusual, you will have
to settle for the ordinary.
~Jim Rohn

I had been trying for months to get a summer job, any summer job, as my second to last year of journalism studies drew to a close. I had applied at newspapers big and small, close to home and across the country, to no avail. Although I knew my parents would ensure that I could continue my studies in the fall, I wanted to prove that I was an independent young woman and could make my own way in the world. But to do that, I would need to make money and to make money I would need to have a job.

It was shortly after I completed school for the year that I decided to apply for a highway construction job. "Flag girls" were a rather new phenomenon but most construction companies had begun hiring young women to direct and control traffic. Everyone said the money was good. The job couldn't be that hard, I told myself. I had driven by lots of "flag girls" and had always admired their dark tans. If I stood outside in the sun day after day, not only would I make more than enough money to return to school but the resulting tan would look phenomenal against the pale yellow bridesmaid dress I would be wearing at my sister's wedding later that summer.

I decided a written application wouldn't do the trick. My rather thin résumé hadn't resulted in a position anywhere else. So, I drove to the job site and very boldly asked a rather rough-looking man carrying a shovel if I could speak to the foreman. With a grunt, he motioned toward a very pleasant-looking man wearing a white hard hat and standing in a ditch talking to a group of men.

Showing more bravado than I actually had, I walked over and requested a word with him. The timing was perfect. That very day he had decided he needed one more "flag girl." He offered me the job. I would need a hard hat, which the company would provide, but I was responsible for getting my own work boots with steel toes. I was to report for work at 7 a.m. Monday and would be working five days a week, from 7 a.m. to 7 p.m.

It was with a mixture of anticipation and downright fear that I put on my newly purchased boots with the steel toes and showed up at the construction site Monday. The sun hadn't been up for long. I was more than aware that I knew nothing about highway construction, just as I knew nothing about the duties of a "flag girl."

There was no training. The foreman gave me a bright orange reflective vest to wear and the Stop/Slow paddle to hold, a red Stop on one side and a yellow Slow on the other. He positioned me at a point where the highway had been reduced to one lane, graders and diggers and all kinds of equipment I couldn't name working on the closed lane. He said I should watch the seasoned flag girl at the opposite end of a strip of one-lane highway. When she flipped her sign to Slow, I was to flip mine to Stop, each of us giving the traffic a fair amount of time to travel along the strip of road. It was as simple as that.

Simple it was not.

The very first time I flipped my sign to stop the traffic, a transport truck slid to a stop with the dust flying, the driver laying on the horn and shaking his fist. I had no idea that a transport truck driver didn't just step on the brake to stop, the way the driver of a car or a pickup truck did. He had a few choice words for me and I certainly never forgot that to stop a transport truck isn't instantaneous, that the driver has to gear down. I didn't make that mistake again.

The first time I looked at my watch that first day, thinking it must be almost lunchtime, I was shocked to see it was only 8:30. I had only been on the job ninety minutes. I was tired of standing, and although the stopping and slowing of traffic had gone smoothly since the first transport truck fiasco, I was getting a little bored by the whole process. By noon the morning breeze had died down to be replaced by a merciless sun. Even with just a T-shirt under the reflective vest I was hot and my arms were already sunburned. Had I had a mirror, I would have seen that my nose was a brilliant red. By the end of the day my legs were aching, my hair was crunchy with dust and I had a blister on my heel the size of a nickel from one of my new steel-toed work boots.

One look at me when I got home that night, dusty and dirty and red, and my family and friends asked if I was going to give up on the idea of a summer job as a "flag girl." Although my mind shrieked "yes" my answer was a resounding "no." As much as I wanted to quit, I had a point to prove.

I stuck it out all summer.

I learned to wear layers of clothes so that I could shed them as we moved from the cool early mornings to the relentless heat of the afternoon. I learned that a red and peeling nose was my cross to bear because no amount of sunblock would stop it from happening. I learned that thick wool socks inside the work boots stopped the blisters, although they kept the sun from tanning my ankles. I also learned that wearing a reflective vest does not result in a nice even tan. I looked absolutely ridiculous in the bridesmaid's dress at my sister's wedding, with my stark white ankles and my brown and white striped shoulders and arms. It's a good thing she loves me and didn't blame me for sticking out like some sort of brown streaked abomination in her wedding photos. But I was also pleased with myself for having seized the opportunity to make good money for the summer, even though the lovely tan part hadn't worked out as I hoped.

The next spring, as I was finishing my journalism studies, I once again began the process of sending out applications to every newspaper big and small. My résumé proudly included being a "flag girl" the previous summer.

I got an interview at a small town newspaper, was hired as a junior reporter, and spent my entire professional life there. A few months in I was the senior reporter; a couple of years later they offered the editor's position. I retired many years later as the editor and general manager of several publications.

One night early in my career the publisher who had hired me made a confession. He had received dozens of applications for the junior reporter position, he said. He decided to interview me, he confessed, because he wondered what a "flag girl who studied journalism" would look like. He had asked me about flagging during the interview and I told him candidly about seizing the opportunity when I couldn't find a newspaper job, about sticking it out through sunburn and blisters and everyone thinking I would give up. He said that he knew right then I was the reporter he wanted at his newspaper, a person with tenacity who wasn't afraid to go outside her comfort zone to get what she wanted.

One of my first assignments at the newspaper, a copy of which I framed and hung on my office wall, was to write about the trials and tribulations of being a "flag girl" on highway construction. I started with the headline: "I heard the money was good."

~Lynne Turner

37

Andrew's Emmy

To accomplish great things, we must not only act, but
also dream; not only plan, but also believe.
~Anatole France

A late call on September 8, 2007 could mean only one thing. But by the time I put down the afghan I was crocheting and scrambled to find the phone, I missed it. I was on pins and needles until the phone rang again.

"How'd you do?" I asked when I heard my son's voice.

"We won!"

I caught my breath. It was one of those moments in life you never forget. Andrew and five others from his company, Atmosphere Visual Effects, had won Primetime Emmy Awards that evening for outstanding visual effects for a television series.

Less than a dozen years before, Andrew was jobless. Tonight he clutched an Emmy on Los Angeles's famous Shrine Auditorium's stage. It was the pinnacle of an incredible journey — and one big answer to a mother's prayer.

Growing up, my firstborn had two passions: art and fishing. He always had incredible patience and persistence for both. It was like he was born with a fishing rod in one hand and an artist's brush in the other. He spent hours dangling lines in nearby lakes or the ocean — or sketching dragons and monsters.

School wasn't Andrew's thing, but he excelled in art. At age fourteen, he took private painting lessons. His first oil, an ocean sunset, hangs in my office.

Andrew's dad and I separated the same year he graduated from high school. It was devastating for him and his two younger siblings, but he was determined to get on with his life. He took art courses at a local college and got a job pumping gas. But when his best buddy enticed him with a job offer in the big city, he was gone.

Andrew thrived in Victoria, British Columbia. He sold cars at a dealership and within two years was promoted to a service advisor position. He liked his private office, his relationship with customers, the challenge — and the good fishing in the Pacific.

But something was missing.

I've always prayed my children would fulfill God's vision for their lives. "Do what you love to do — and get paid for it," I often told them. "God has a purpose and plan for your life. That's why he's made you the way you are."

Andrew was twenty-five when he called to say he had quit his job. "Mom, I'm having a quarter-of-a-life crisis," he confided. "Working at a car dealership is not what I want to do for the rest of my life."

I felt my chest tighten. I was remarried and living near Vancouver, so my son and I were separated by the Strait of Georgia. I wanted to hug him and tell him he would be okay. But all I could offer were my prayers.

God's answer came faster than I expected. One day, while scanning a flyer, I spotted the word "animation." The Vancouver Film School was offering a one-evening information session on how to make a career in either classic or computer animation. It cost $35.

When Andrew was a teenager, he talked about drawing comic strips. He enjoyed creating cartoon characters, cute little things with personalities (a nice change from monsters!). I reminded him that the great cartoonist Charles Schulz followed his dream — and was successful.

About that time, my husband, Allen, happened on an animation studio while working in Vancouver. He came home excited. Wouldn't it be neat if Andrew could get a job as an animator?

I called Andrew, gave him the information, and offered to pay the fee. He couldn't wait to catch the ferry to Vancouver!

When he returned from the school, his eyes sparkled like they did whenever he caught a big fish. "Mom, this is something I've always wanted to do," he exclaimed. "I'd like to take the computer animation course!"

But then reality hit. The full-time course was pricey. He was jobless and we didn't have the money to give him.

I then thought back to my own dream of attending a particular college when I was eighteen years old. It was a miraculous journey of faith for me.

"Andy, there will always be money for what God wants you to do," I told him. "We can't pay for these courses, but we can give you room and board. I'll pray with you that God will work out the rest."

My son returned to Victoria with a dream, and I prayed.

Andrew first applied for a student loan to the Vancouver Film School. He was granted the largest one the school had given up until then. He then sold his car and worked a month for his brother-in-law. He still didn't have enough money for the full-time course, so he chose the part-time one. He moved in with us and took public transit to school.

Andrew quickly learned that computer animation was far more complicated than drawing cartoons! It was hard work. In order to succeed, one must be adept in both computer skills and art. Sometimes he came home discouraged, but I encouraged him to keep trying.

He finished the course several months later with high marks. To his delight, his instructors chose the top three students to stay on and tutor the incoming students. They could take the full-time course in lieu of pay!

While taking the course, Andrew composed an animation of the eye of a tornado. His instructor was so impressed he showed it to a film producer. It was just the shot the company needed for a particular scene. Andrew had his first break!

At that time, Vancouver was fast becoming known as Hollywood North. The American-dominated film industry had discovered the picturesque Canadian city was ideal for making movies, for both its location and its lower costs. Animation and visual effects were becoming big business, and artists were in demand.

Andrew had no problem landing jobs with visual effects companies. He rented an apartment with a friend and was on his way.

Seven years later, the company he was working for folded. Once more, Andrew was jobless. But not for long. He and two co-workers started their own company. With a contract for a TV series and about six thousand dollars they worked out of a spare bedroom in Andrew's apartment. They named their company Atmosphere Visual Effects.

When they got contracts for more series, they leased office space and bought more computers. When more work came in, they rented a 4,500-square-foot studio. As business increased, they added computers and employees.

Over four years, the company got work for the Vancouver-shot sci-fi TV series *Battlestar Galactica* and a number of other series. They also did all the visual effects for Disney's *Air Buddies*. The company was nominated for a Primetime Emmy Award three times before the big win came.

Andrew was the digital effects supervisor when he won his 2007 Emmy for an episode of *Battlestar Galactica*. It was the first win for Vancouver in the visual effects category for a television series.

My son, Andrew Karr, then bought himself a twenty-six-foot Bayliner fishing boat. I think God added that for good measure.

~Cathy Mogus

38

Overcoming Obesity

The power to achieve the extraordinary is within each
and every one of us. Believe that you can, work harder
than everyone else, and never, ever give up!
~Heidi Powell

I remember the moment I realized I was an emotional eater. I was angry with my husband about one thing or another, and I found myself in the kitchen stuffing my face with chocolate chip cookies. It was like I was having an out-of-body experience. I saw myself... and it wasn't pretty.

I realized at that moment that I was destroying myself because I was angry with someone else. Whenever I was happy, sad, or angry I would eat. I ate myself to more than 300 pounds.

That day I saw what I was doing to myself, but it felt so overwhelming, so impossible to change. I did not change that day. In fact, I continued the cycle for three more years.

Then, a couple of things happened. The first was when I was eight months pregnant with my third child. At my prenatal checkup my doctor said, "You cannot gain any more weight!" I was 328 pounds. She gave me some suggestions. "Cut back on white carbohydrates and sugar." That is what I did... after shedding some tears and wondering how I was going to do it. In the last few weeks of my pregnancy I lost twelve pounds.

But then after having the baby, and all that comes with recovering from a C-section, I started eating again. My husband was taking care of meals and I just ate what he made.

The second thing that happened finally got me to change.

My new baby boy was three months old and some of the older ladies at church were admiring him. "He's gonna be a big boy like his mama!" one lady said.

"I wasn't always big," I said.

"Oh really?" she said, and she sounded so surprised.

At that moment, I had my "aha" moment. You see, my mom is obese, and her mom before her was obese, and I don't know for sure, but I could imagine that her mom before her was obese, and so on. It infuriated me that someone just assumed that I was always fat, and that this boy was going to take after me and be fat, too. Nope. Not going to happen. I would not do that to my children! I decided at that moment that I was going to break the cycle of obesity in my family.

That Monday I began a journey. I cut out carbohydrates and sugar. It wasn't easy. I'm an Italian girl. We eat pasta and bread at every meal, pizza every Friday! But, I had to do this. I made up my mind. I told myself that I had eaten enough of those things in my thirty-five years of living that if I never ate them again I still had eaten a lifetime's worth of them!

I wanted to put things in perspective. I told myself that even if I only lost one pound a week, I would be down fifty-two pounds in a year! But, if I gave up, I would be once again saying "I should've" and "I wish I had…" at the end of the year.

You can't start a journey like this and say, "I'm going to lose 150 pounds." You will fail. Who can lose 150 pounds? That is too over-whelming! My goals were to be a better "me" each day. I told myself, "I am going to put healthy food into my body *today*. I am going to move more than I sit *today*." I started by asking my husband if I could mow the grass instead of him. Baby steps.

There is a big picture. We tend to see only what's right in front of us. I didn't set out two decades ago and say, "Hmm, I think I'd like to be over 300 pounds one day. I am going to eat without restraint and become totally inactive." It took me years to put on that weight, and even if it took a few years to take it off, that was okay. I was still improving, still bettering myself. Still becoming a healthier version of myself.

I wanted to be a better example for my three kids. I wanted to be someone they could emulate, someone they would be proud to call "Mommy." Now, kids don't really know the difference when they are young. And I know my mom has always been the most beautiful woman to me; her weight never mattered. But for me, and for the sake of my family, I needed to press on.

I set small, reasonable, attainable goals for myself and celebrated every one of them! But not with food! Every time I refused cake or cookies or chips, I felt stronger! I could do this! It was possible! I could envision my future self, and that was the image that I pictured in my mind as I was exercising.

It has been two and a half years since I started my journey and I have lost 150 pounds! I did it one decision at a time. Not one day, not one week... solely one decision at a time. I learned to say "no thank you" one decision at a time.

This is my body; I control what goes in it! I am thrilled to say that at age thirty-seven I feel healthier than I did at seventeen! I can say things to my kids like "race you to the car!" I take them for walks and bike rides, and I can go down the slide with them at the playground! My life isn't limited anymore. My daughter, who is five, said to me the other day, "Mommy, I didn't know you could run that fast!" Baby, I didn't either! I am still discovering my strength and all my body can do!

In the words of A. A. Milne, "You are braver than you believe, stronger than you seem, and smarter than you think."

~Gina Tate

A Treasure-Filled Life

Failure will never overtake me if my determination to
succeed is strong enough.
~Og Mandino

t was a hot August day, nineteen days after my fourth birthday, when my life changed dramatically. One day I was a lively, active little girl who rode a bike, dragged her little brother along on adventures, and loved riding horses. The next day I was falling every few steps and getting up only to stumble and fall again. For eleven months I was unable to breathe on my own, needing an iron lung to pump air in and out of my lungs. Whereas I had been active and independent, I became ninety percent dysfunctional, without the use of my limbs. Bathing, dressing, eating, and using the bathroom were no longer things I could do for myself. I am a survivor of the polio epidemic.

The following nine years were filled with surgeries on my hands, my legs, and my spine. I soon learned that much of life was about adapting. Each surgery required changes. I would write with my hands a certain way, and after the surgery I would need to find a new way. Once, during a prolonged stay in bed, my mother stuck a pencil in my mouth and encouraged me to write my algebra equations. I made it work.

As a teenager, I started thinking about what life could offer. Living independently, a career, marriage, children, travel? These became my dreams. I was a shy, quiet introvert and kept all of these images of victory close to my heart. I learned I needed to project an open, friendly, positive attitude toward others so they would get past my appearance as a young woman with a twisted torso, in leg braces, in a wheelchair. As time passed, I worked with myself to truly become that open, friendly, positive person.

I was active in high school, carrying a full academic load. As treasurer of the French club, I coordinated bake sales and dances. I went to basketball and football games and hung out with friends. My classmates pushed me to and from classes and events. Those blessed kids gave me legs, even on our senior trip to Knott's Berry Farm and Disneyland. My first power wheelchair didn't arrive until I was in my early twenties and oh, how I loved the freedom!

I attended two years of college, my brother being my ride the first year and friends working out rides for me the second. Wheelchair accessibility was not as available in those days. I acquired lots of friends — girls who were willing to hold my books and many good-looking guys who carried me up and down stairs.

One of my college friends received a job offer in Maryland and needed a live-in babysitter for her six- and eight-year-old children for the summer. I accepted the job, the kids and I had fun, and I stayed on. I have lived in Maryland ever since.

I qualified for a computer programming class for persons with severe disabilities, which included the opportunity to live in with full care provided. Without finger mobility and dexterity, I had to learn a way to type, so the school taught me to use a stick in my mouth. I have never won a typing contest, but I still type 14.5 words per minute!

In 1980, I was encouraged to enter the Miss Wheelchair Maryland beauty pageant. The pageant focused on women in wheelchairs who were accomplishing goals in their lives. I entered and won. Later, I went on to the Miss Wheelchair USA pageant.

The pageant afforded me many opportunities. I met government officials, made personal appearances at various disability-awareness events, and was invited to represent the pageant at the Pimlico Race

Course. I had liked riding horses as a child, so visiting Pimlico and being up close and personal with two-thousand-pound racehorses was a dream come true. The pageant prizes included a set of Samsonite luggage that I still have, some money, and a clothes-shopping spree. It was wonderful for someone like me who would be out looking for a job soon.

Like many young people, I furnished my first apartment by shopping at Goodwill and flea markets. My teachers gave me a set of wineglasses and groceries. It was Christmas time, and two classmates gave me their hand-me-down tree and ornaments. I still have one of those ornaments thirty-five years later.

My mother moved in with me while I searched for a job. Daily I would pore over the newspaper ads, and with a loaner typewriter my mother would type my application letters as I dictated them. A computer keyboard easily responded to my typing with a mouthstick, but this borrowed typewriter did not. To my delight, the Social Security Administration hired me. When asked if I had transportation, I replied affirmatively, even though I had no idea how I was going to travel back and forth to the job. I scrambled to pull rides together, soliciting the help of a cab driver who lived in my building. That sufficed as I waited for special transportation through the local bus service. Thus began my fourteen and a half years of service at the Social Security Administration.

Retired now, I have what I need to take care of my ninety-year-old mother and myself. I travel, enjoy Ravens football games, attend plays and concerts, and do anything else I set my mind to.

As a child, I wasn't supposed to live past my teens. Those innovative, painful surgeries I endured early in my life, and medical advances as I've aged, have enabled my lifespan to be extended. As I approach seventy, I am looking forward to many more years of quality living. My latest goal is to go on a cruise, and I can hardly wait for the ocean view, a stack of books, and, of course, more new friends.

It does not matter that I am in a wheelchair and need people to help me with life's details. What matters is that I have never given up on my dreams. I have held onto them and believed they would come to pass, taking advantage of every opportunity that presented itself. No — I haven't married, but I have had many a gorgeous hunk carry me over the threshold. I haven't given birth to children, but I have enjoyed the antics, pouts and love of my friends' children. I attained an education, have enjoyed a career, and live independently. For goodness' sake, I won a beauty pageant! I have ridden across the countryside on Christmas Eve and delivered baked goods and presents to my friends as if I were Santa Claus. I have gotten up every morning of my treasure-filled life and lived each day to the utmost.

If you never give up, you can achieve anything you set your mind to!

~Sydna Elrod

Hooking My Way to Fame

*My disability has opened my eyes to see
my true abilities.*
~Robert M. Hensel

To most people, this looks like military code: With mc, ch 4, joining with sl st to form a ring. Rnd 1: Ch 3, work 2 dc in ring; *ch 3, work 3 dc in ring, rep from * twice, ch 3, join with sl st at top of beg ch 3 and turn. Rnd 2: Ch 3, work 2 dc in ch 3 sp, ch 3…

To me, it's a recipe for happiness. My heart soars in anticipation of colors, textures and patterns. Countless pieces of needlework have provided fanciful and practical wear for me and mine for half a century. I've kept the snuggly woolly and synthetic lovers decked out in most all of their requests, even doll clothes.

Our daughter's cheerleading squad put in their order for mittens to match their outfits. After ogling deep purple for days, I found myself knitting mitts in my sleep. I worked with flashy colors and faddish styles for my nine growing granddaughters, and was always ready to make the latest popular throw for someone's new piece of furniture.

Notion departments and specialty yarn shops within hundreds of miles turned my patient husband into a car napper. Minutes turned into hours while I fingered downy skeins of delicates and bulkies to please individual tastes. Varieties of needles and threads spawned perfection, a trick taught to me by a grandma who intuitively sensed gauge and feel. As a child, she took me to an occasional Saturday matinee, along with her latest project. While enjoying the movie, her tiny hands flew back and forth crocheting intricate pieces in the darkened theater.

But needlecraft was the last thought on my mind the day the unthinkable happened, a brutal accident in which I lost my dominant right hand. Hooking a simple daisy chain was far down the list of things I would need to manage. I had to invent new ways to put on a bra, butter bread without it shredding, stir the brownie mix without sending the bowl across the kitchen floor, feed myself politely, and fold clothes with my teeth.

Then I discovered a place across our state that specializes in orthotics and prosthetics. What was left of my right arm labored hard those first grueling weeks to achieve skill which every prosthesis offered. I finally returned home with a dainty hook, a tough farm and ranch hook most men ran from, and a very fancy myoelectric hand. I called it my go-to meetin' arm.

Weeks passed and my precious old lefty was being worked to the hilt. My hand and wrist had swollen so badly that I eventually couldn't turn on the garden faucet or set the sprinkler, simple things I had taken for granted. The following day my doctor announced I was well into rheumatoid arthritis, not what I wanted to hear.

Years slid by and one of the grandchildren instinctively asked if I could knit a bluish ski hat to match her new outfit. I laughed and quipped that I could probably get a half dozen out before the weekend. I don't know who felt worse as she bent down to give me a tearful hug.

Suddenly, the thought of holding a crochet hook in my hook sent my mind reeling. The following day I rummaged through my yarns, got out the box of prosthetic accessories, and spent the afternoon practicing. With the crochet hook locked firmly onto my prosthesis, I took yarn in hand and began... Ch 3, work 2 dc in ch 3 sp, ch 3... oops, try again, and again.

My husband arrived home to find the floor littered with crochet hooks, yarns, and a sea of practice squares. Provided the rheumatoid arthritis didn't put a hitch in my plans, I felt confident enough to begin a simple project — like maybe a young girl's blue ski hat? Renewed, and all wound up like a ball of yarn, I went to town picking and choosing new weights, colors and patterns. Instead of turning myself into a reclusive wimp, the good Lord had fostered His plan within my soul. God helps those who help themselves, and I was living again.

Mindless ski hats driving me loony, I turned out stunning sweaters in all shades and styles for each granddaughter before another year was out. My Christmas present that year was a granddaughter portrait taken in their treasured pullovers and cardigans, all of which I had made. Who could imagine my new *pièce de résistance* would end up a cherished legacy barely before my antiquity?

Is it any wonder all my sweethearts call me "Granny Hook?"

~Kathe Campbell

Emerald Dreams

> *The world is a book, and those who do not*
> *travel read only a page.*
> *~Saint Augustine*

"**A**nd this is me kissing the Blarney Stone," says my seventeen-year-old daughter. She turns the pages of her new photo album, recounting her recent ten-day journey abroad, and my mind wanders back... way back to when she was only five.

"Someday I'm going to Ireland," she had said, holding her *Childcraft* book in her lap. Her blue eyes sparkled as she looked at the beautiful pictures. One could almost smell the fresh, clean air and hear the contented bleating of grazing sheep.

"When I get big," Carrie repeated, "I'm going to Ireland."

"Well, maybe you can!" I said, having faith in her ambitions. Already she was an industrious, dependable child. Her chores (helping feed the baby calves and caring for several domesticated rabbits) were performed promptly and skillfully. I knew she had the potential to make her dreams come true. I realized, however, that she would need a good job to pay for the luxury of traveling. We were only a step above poor dirt farmers. In fact, we were poor dairy farmers, and all profit had to go back into the dairy operation to keep it going. While we would provide for her education and needs, she would have to pay for her wants, and I believed she would work to make her dreams come true.

Five years later, when Carrie was ten, a tornado roared through the hills of Tennessee, destroying our dairy barn, our outbuildings and all our fencing. We were forced to sell the milking herd immediately. One day a dairy farm, the next day rubble.

This disaster completely changed our lives. My husband, Charlie, was disabled by the tornado. He tried to rebuild the dairy but was physically and emotionally unable to resume the 24/7 workload. After trying and failing at several methods of earning income, he decided to become a baker. Admittedly, this was a giant leap from his dairyman persona, but he had always been "a chef in the kitchen," so this seemed a logical option and was better suited to his disability. We purchased a small bakery, fully equipped, and relocated it onto our farmland. Meanwhile, I began working as a secretary.

Tennessee Mountain Air Kitchen began selling sourdough and yeast breads, nut-breads, cakes, pastries, pies, etc. The business did very well. Regrettably, Charlie did not. His disability was so severe that after several months of trying he simply could not continue. The doors to Tennessee Mountain Air Kitchen closed.

While our family was admittedly going through difficult times — emotionally and financially — the dreams and spirit of our children were not shattered. They were doing well in school, and I smiled the day I read Carrie's essay entitled, "Things I would like to do." Topping the list were these words: "I want to go to Ireland someday." Again I whispered, "Maybe you can someday."

A few years later, Carrie entered high school and during her sophomore year enrolled in a German language class. This class occasionally organized an optional chaperoned trip abroad, usually to Germany. Given our situation, I did not think it was a viable option for Carrie, until she came home from school one day, hardly able to contain her excitement, and said, "Mama, you'll never guess where the class is going."

"Where?" I asked.

"To Ireland," she smiled broadly, "…and then on to England, for ten days!"

"You're kidding!" I said. "Ireland! Where you've always wanted to go!"

"But it would probably cost a fortune to go," she said.

I thought she was probably right — it would seem a fortune to us. My salary paid the bills, but nothing was left; and Charlie was still unable to work.

"Well," I said hesitantly, "you never know. Ask the teacher what it will cost. It won't hurt to ask."

Carrie came home the next day and announced that the trip would cost $2,100.

"This covers everything except spending money," she said. "The trip is planned for year after next, and the $2,100 can be paid in installments." Then she added, "But that's too much… isn't it?" Her voice was hopeful yet doubting.

"Well," I said slowly, "for ten days abroad — all expenses paid — that doesn't sound too bad. Daddy and I can't help much; still, you have two years to earn the money. Maybe doing odd jobs, saving your money, you could pay it off in time."

"You think so?" Carrie's face lit up like a Christmas tree to think she might go to Ireland.

"Well," I reasoned, "you can save your birthday money. Maybe we can have yard sales. Or you could use the bakery and sell baked goods."

Sell baked goods? We stared at each other. The idea had just popped out of my mouth, but it was a good one. Lots of people had bought baked goods earlier, so why wouldn't they buy them now? And the bakery was sitting idle. Plus, Carrie was an excellent cook! This would work!

So the plan was laid. Carrie began working, making a variety of baked goods. Soon, however, fried dried-apple pies became the customer favorite and her signature product. Selling them for one dollar each meant she would have to fry a lot of pies to pay for the trip to Ireland… but it could be done.

Dried-apple pies (or "turnovers") are an age-old, standard dessert in Tennessee, and Carrie made them the old-fashioned way! She used dried (never fresh or canned) apples, cooked, seasoned and spiced to perfection. All ingredients were natural — real shortening, real butter — and the crust was handmade and hand-rolled. Finally, in a cast-iron skillet, the pies were fried to a beautiful, golden brown! The finished product was a delectable treat, winning praise from even the little old ladies in these hills who have been making dried-apple pies for decades.

Orders began rolling in, and the Ireland fund grew. Coffee shops, restaurants, and convenience stores stocked Carrie's pies. Individuals placed orders for ten, twenty, sometimes fifty pies. Local factories purchased them as coffee-break treats. Business was booming. Carrie began to dream of shamrocks and leprechauns!

A local newspaper featured a story about Carrie's endeavor to travel to Ireland by selling dried apple pies. This, too, spurred business, and well within the allotted time the trip abroad was paid in full. Carrie was ready to pack her bags for the Emerald Isle.

Now I'm looking at her album as she proudly points out the sites she visited: castles of Ireland, historic bridges and cathedrals, cobblestone streets of Dublin, rolling green pastures and peaceful grazing sheep... so much like those in her *Childcraft* book. She talks of England: Big Ben, Stratford-upon-Avon, Stonehenge, and more. She chatters endlessly, relating details of the trip of a lifetime.

I listen and smile with delight. Surely, my daughter has been blessed and will forever remember this dream come true... a dream that began in the heart of a five-year-old girl and was ultimately made possible by the lowly, delicious, fried dried-apple pie!

~Linda Garrett Hicks

Whatever It Takes

He conquers who endures.

~Persius

How long does it take to fulfill a lifelong dream? For me it was eleven hours fifty-seven minutes and twenty-nine seconds.

It started when I was a little kid, back when I was a fan of *Charlie's Angels* and TV dinners were a treat. One day I was in our family room, spending a lazy afternoon watching television. They were showing the wheelchair division of the Boston Marathon. People in wheelchairs were pushing their bodies to the limit. That image stayed with me.

Physical therapy was a huge part of my life back then, and I had never considered what came after perfecting my ability to walk with my feet flat instead of on my tiptoes. Outside of the confines of basic function, that might have been the first time I wondered what I was physically capable of doing. Without telling anyone, I always kept my desire to complete a marathon in the back of my mind.

Five years later I joined a sports team for people with cerebral palsy. For the first time I was around people with disabilities who were older than I was and had disabilities similar to mine. Mentors and coaches pushed me beyond the limits of what I thought I could do. Nobody focused on my limitations, and during grueling workouts several people randomly called out "whatever it takes!" It became my mantra.

My passion was track. Training for hours became part of my routine. Over time, and with the help of the head football coach at my high school, I could bench press more than my body weight, went to various competitions, made the Paralympic team and challenged the world record in the 400-meter dash. Still, I wanted more. I wanted to know if I could literally go the distance.

After practice one day I was talking to Kerry, one of my coaches. Just like others on that team, she was more focused on what I could do than what I couldn't. Because I was preparing to go to college, she asked me if I had thought about what I wanted to do. My mind wasn't on academics when I blurted out that I wanted to compete in a marathon. I had rarely said that out loud before and for a split second I thought she might laugh. I was wrong.

Within weeks she found the Woodlands Marathon. The relative flatness of the course and the fact that it was in a community that was half an hour away from where we lived made it perfect. But because of my limited upper body strength, I knew completing this race would take me a very long time. I wondered if people would be willing to accommodate that.

Kerry made an appointment with Doug, who was organizing the race. He instantly put me at ease. Not only was he willing to have me participate, but he designed an alternate course to keep me off the main roads until daylight. He also made sure that the last part of the course was the same as everyone else's so that I could finish with the other runners. The plan was to start at midnight and finish at noon.

When Doug asked me why I wanted to "run" this particular race, the answer was easy. "So many people look at me and make assumptions about what I can't do," I said. "I want to prove to myself that they are wrong, that it is only my expectations of myself that are important."

The first few miles of the race were easy. Kerry and her boyfriend had volunteered to walk with me the entire way for security and encouragement, and my parents followed in the car with supplies and food.

About ten miles in, my excitement started to give way to fatigue and I didn't know if I would finish. I had finally reached the wall I had heard others talk about and I wasn't sure I could climb over it. More friends showed up at about 4:30 a.m. when I was finishing mile 14. They encouraged me to just keep doing what I did for hours every day of my life — PUSH!

At mile 20, I thought I would finish. I had done several 10Ks in the past, so I thought I could go that distance again. At mile 25 I questioned whether it was possible for me to push another stroke. I was exhausted. Physically my strength was gone. Emotionally it seemed like every good feeling I ever had seeped away with my energy. Blisters covered my hands, my arms were aching and I was having severe spasms.

At that point my dad drove the car about 500 feet in front of me. He stopped and got out and said, "Just come to me, Lorraine." When I was about ten feet away from him he got back in the car and did the same thing over and over, until I entered the stadium and completed two-tenths of the last mile around the track.

"Whatever it takes," echoed in my head, reminding me of all the grueling workouts I had finished in the past and the self-doubts I had overcome on the journey.

Doug saw me coming close to the finish. Looking at my face, he knew I needed some encouragement. He stood before the crowd and told my story. Then he said, "Lorraine has been here since midnight folks, and she looks pretty tired right now. Let's all show her we think she can accomplish her goal."

The roar of encouragement from hundreds of people gave me the lift I needed to cross the finish line. I set out to complete the Woodlands Marathon in less than twelve hours. I succeeded with barely two and a half minutes to spare. As people took my picture and shook my hand, I thought back to that Boston Marathon I watched on television so many years before. As an awkward kid, I didn't know what was possible. But a dream was born, and I never lost sight of it. In the minutes after the race, I hoped I had come full circle. Maybe my completing this race could motivate other people to question what was possible and realize their dreams, just as the athletes in the Boston Marathon had for me.

A seed of confidence sprouted in me that day. For the rest of my life, I know I can do anything.

With the support of the right people and a belief in myself I now understand that anything is possible. Lifelong dreams can be accomplished in less than half a day.

As long as you are willing to do whatever it takes.

~Lorraine Cannistra

One Last Dance

*Someday I may find my Prince Charming, but my
daddy will always be my King.*

~Author Unknown

For most fourteen-year-old girls living in a border town, the world revolves around *quinceañeras*. Yet there was no mention of such an event in my household. There was no talk about *damas* and *chambelanes* or about the color schemes or the dresses. There was no planning about where to hold the coming-of-age celebration or what music to select. There was no discussion about the guest list or the main course.

I helped my friends plan their parties and went to what seemed like dozens of *quinceañeras*. I must've had five to six fittings for all the ruffled dresses I wore as a *dama* that year. Whenever anyone asked if I was having a "quince" or "*¿Que van a ser tus colores?*" my go-to response was always, "I'm saving up for a car." I even had myself convinced until that night when I cried while the band played "*Tiempo de Waltz*" at my friend's *quinceañera*.

I went home early from the party, and although I tried to conceal my runny nose and red eyes, my mother could tell something was wrong. I did not want to lie, but what I feared most about telling her the truth was that I didn't want her to think I was selfish. You see, it's pretty petty and self-serving to be pining over a silly party when your dad is dying.

I finally confessed. I shared with my mom that I wanted nothing more than to have my own father-daughter dance. My dad had been diagnosed with Stage 5 cancer and given five months to live. By this time, he was in a wheelchair and had trouble remembering his children's names.

My mother pawned the little bit of jewelry she owned, and borrowed money from friends and family in order to raise enough money for my *quinceañeras*. In two weeks time we had printed homemade invitations and cleaned up and decorated my back yard by wrapping peach ribbons around the mesquite trees. We covered the borrowed tables with white plastic tablecloths, and set up a makeshift dance floor by draping Christmas lights around the basketball hoop. My *madrina* baked a three-layer cake covered in white frosting with peach flowers. My friends gathered with me in our satin, peach dresses and high heels on December 7th, six months before my actual fifteenth birthday, so I could have my very own father-daughter dance with my dad.

As the music started my mom pushed my dad's wheelchair up the ramp toward the center of the basketball court where I stood waiting. My dad motioned for her to stop and slowly raised himself from the chair and took my hand for the first and last waltz we would share.

~Erika Chody

44

Aloha

*Your destiny is to fulfill those things upon which you
focus most intently. So choose to keep your focus on
that which is truly magnificent, beautiful,
uplifting and joyful.*
~Ralph Marston

"I wish I could move there!" I've lost count of how many times I've heard those six words in the past few months. From the moment I put in my two-week notice at my old job in Tennessee that has been the single most common reaction when people hear about my move to Hawaii.

I could not have done it without the love and support of my *ohana* — who were also my housemates in Tennessee — one of whom has been my best friend for twelve years. There are others who contributed big-time to this happening, of course, but my dream of moving permanently to the state of Hawaii could still never have become a reality, even with their assistance, if I hadn't first changed my way of thinking.

From the time I was four, I heard stories about the island of Oahu from my great-grandfather, who lived there for quite some time with one of his daughters, and from my beloved grandparents, who visited and talked often with Great-Grandpa.

My first memories of this came from camping with my family and other friends of theirs. We sat around playing card games at a picnic table (Granny used to tell me that at age three I was a card shark who beat the pants off everyone at rummy) and were regaled with stories about this chain of islands out in the middle of the North Pacific Ocean. It seemed so very far away, and so impossible to get to.

It was that feeling of impossibility that stayed with me for nearly forty years. And I wasn't alone. Ever since hearing my "big announcement," there were two reasons co-workers, friends and acquaintances all gave me, over and over again, as to why they could not do what I was doing. One: It costs so much to move that far. Two: Hawaii is so expensive.

Those had been my reasons for "I can't" too.

Looking back, I realize that I started thinking seriously about where I really wanted to live in 2011, when the Canadian government decided not to renew my temporary foreign worker visa after I'd worked there for more than three years. I had to return to the U.S. right away, leaving not only my job, but the family I had created there as well. It wasn't easy, and luckily my *ohana* in Memphis opened their arms and hearts to welcome me.

Even then, I thought, "I should go to Hawaii." But again, as soon as the thought popped into my head, I immediately said to myself, "I can't."

For the nearly four years I was in Memphis, working a very good job with wonderful co-workers, and forming even stronger bonds with my *ohana*, I knew that wasn't my final destination. Yet I had no idea where I should be going, nor how I was going to get to wherever that was. Where did I want it to be? Hawaii. But… "I can't."

Then came a moment during that time when I took stock of my life and asked myself the all-important question: "Why can't I?" Which led to more serious thought. "If I want to go to Hawaii, what will I need to get there and to sustain myself once I'm there so I can stay?"

To answer that, I returned to the two major reasons that I and everyone I'd ever talked to always gave for not being able to move: It costs too much to move all the way out to the middle of the ocean from Mainland USA, and Hawaii is too expensive.

But the difference now was that I was finally mature enough to think of Hawaii as a place, not as a paradise where everybody wanted to vacation but nobody really lived. The second obstacle, the high cost of living, would be taken care of by getting a job that paid what I'd need to live comfortably in the state's economic environment. But how to tackle the first obstacle? That's when it came to me: relocation. If I could find an employer who wanted my skillset badly enough, they might pay for me to move all the way from Tennessee to Hawaii.

My Inner Nag said, "Nope, won't happen, not in today's economy. Nobody's going to pay thousands of dollars to move you to Paradise and then give you a really good job on top of it. Come on, get real."

I still didn't believe, but the annoying inner voice that wouldn't shut up, the one that wanted me to move, countered the Nag with: "For heaven's sake, what would it cost you to send out a few résumés? A little bit of time, maybe, but nothing else. Besides, nothing will happen anyway, right? Right. So, why not?"

Why not, indeed.

For the next two years, I submitted résumés to various companies located mostly in Honolulu. And I was right: nothing happened. But I now know it was because while I was going through the motions, my mind — and my heart — still weren't in it. I still didn't believe.

That's when the turning point came for me, and it came from my *ohana*.

My two best friends and I began talking seriously about leaving Memphis and finding somewhere we all wanted to make our permanent home. Where did we want to go? Somewhere tropical. We looked at various options, mostly non-U.S. ones at that point, since we were being budget conscious — but did we really want to leave this country? What would we do? We'd have to be completely self-sufficient, able to do our work remotely via Internet if we went someplace like Belize, for example.

Although I was already a published novelist, and we all had other irons in the fire, we were nowhere near self-sufficient.

We dithered. Hemmed and hawed. Finally, I thought, hey, I haven't submitted any résumés to Hawaii in a while. I talked to Best Friend #1 and Best Friend #2. Huh. Hawaii? Hmmm. Well, okay. Why not? Let's focus on Hawaii.

I submitted five résumés the next day to five different prospective employers. A month later I got a call. A week after that, I had an interview. A week later, a second interview. Two weeks later, a job offer.

With relocation.

Two weeks later, I flew from Memphis to Honolulu.

That's how fast it happened. Why? Because not only did all three of us decide to pull in the same direction to make our dream come true, but I, personally, stopped saying "I can't," and said, "I'm going to."

The power of positive thinking truly is power. And all you have to start with is your dream and two words: I can.

~Christine Davis

45

Welcome Home

Henceforth I ask not good-fortune, I myself
am good-fortune.
~Walt Whitman

"**H**ow long have you been trying?" asked the fertility doctor, peering over his glasses.

Answering simultaneously, my husband said "one year" and I said "five years."

I looked at him. "Where've you been? Maybe we've got more than a fertility problem."

While I've always had an "I think I can" attitude, struggling to get pregnant month after month, year after year, was building a case for "I think I can't." This doctor had a plan.

"There are some his and her things we can do," he said, "but because you're thirty-eight years old, we should get started right away." I was labeled an "elderly primigravida."

"Is that Latin for old and headed toward a really primo grave?" I asked. He handed my husband a cup and told me to see the nurse to schedule a laparoscopic procedure. I marveled at how unsexy talking about sex is.

We ran through a variety of tests and performed laparoscopy to roto-rooter my "elderly primigravida" fallopian tubes. The doctor decided casual sex wasn't cutting it for us. We needed a well-synchronized, scientifically assisted meeting of the his and her components to make a baby. Spin the sperm, find the best swimmers, net them, inject them and send them in search of a hopefully salmonella-free egg. I was having a hard time shaking that "elderly" label.

Two weeks passed. I bought a home pregnancy test and went to bed knowing my life could be completely changed in the morning. I awoke and quietly padded to the bathroom where I unwrapped the test stick from the foil wrapper. Three minutes passed at glacial speed. When it was time, I took a deep breath, squinted my eyes closed, then opened them. Two vertical lines. Yes, it was unmistakable. I was pregnant. I ran to wake my husband. Elated, we immediately called his mother. There was no holding onto this secret. She knew how desperately we wanted a baby and she was our only parent out of four still living. After screams and tears of joy, I quickly dressed and set off to the hospital where I worked.

My pregnancy began easily and my only symptoms were I was hungry and tired. I never missed a meal, a day of work, or my pre-natal yoga class. I loved visiting my OB/GYN to hear the comforting hoof-like thumping of my baby's heartbeat, but because of my age, my doctor ordered an amniocentesis and ultrasound. I wasn't nervous, just eager to see and learn more about my baby.

The ultrasound proceeded in the normal way. I heard a lot of tapping on a keyboard establishing markers and measurements. Then another person was called in. There was a lot of muttering and I strained to hear what they were saying.

"What's wrong?" I asked. They stammered and hesitated, carefully choosing their words.

"We have concerns about the baby's kidneys and spine." They recalculated my trimester. More tapping on the keyboard. Then they performed the amnio portion of the test, inserting a long needle into my belly to suction fluid to test for genetic deformities. I felt queasy. The baby was moving a lot, but they mentioned other concerns about his size. A boy, I'm having a boy. I took that in momentarily, but I couldn't shake the troubled look on their faces.

"Take it easy for the rest of the day. We'll call you with results."

The next day I felt good enough to walk around. It was December and I wanted to get a jumpstart on holiday shopping, so I went to the mall. I was moving slower than usual and began cramping. I went to the restroom and saw spotting. I lay down and called my doctor.

"Rest till the cramps stop. Then go home and stay resting. This is not uncommon after an amnio."

Panic welled up. I drove home and spent the next day in bed. The spotting thankfully subsided. On Monday, I went to work and answered the call from my doctor.

"I have some difficult news; are you sitting down?" I stopped breathing. I was ill before he even spoke the words.

"Your baby has a rare genetic defect. It has Trisomy 19. These babies don't usually come to term and if they do they don't live long, perhaps days or months. They have multiple life-threatening problems, including heart, lung, brain, and spinal defects. I am so sorry."

When I finally breathed it was a gasp, a mournful heaving sob. How could I lose this baby that I'd grown to love so fiercely? How could this be fair? I drove home in a blur of tears and despair. A few days later we visited the doctor, who confirmed our loss. He prepared me for the procedure to remove my baby and sent me home, explaining everything would be finalized the next day. Late that evening I began cramping heavily and called the doctor. A female physician whom I'd never met was on call.

"It's possible you'll deliver into the toilet," she said casually.

I wailed at the cruelty of her words, clutching my belly and determined to make it to the hospital.

After the hospital procedure, I returned home and headed straight for my bed. Normally a buoyant early morning riser, the light of day now hurt my eyes. Though I forced myself into simple activities, even going out for breakfast and to my husband's holiday office party, I retreated as quickly as I could to my bed and isolation.

My husband encouraged me to move on, but try as I might, my body knew it had given birth. I reluctantly returned to work with constant reminders of my loss. My breasts leaked milk unexpectedly at meetings and random moments. The only thing born was grief.

As the months passed, I knew if I wanted new life to come inside me I had to clear the psychic space of darkness and uncertainty. I had to let go of what I didn't have to get what I wanted. What soul would want to hang around for nine months in that environment?

I remembered my yoga teacher sharing a story about a woman who had had four miscarriages before giving birth to a healthy girl. She'd worked with a practitioner whose real name was Faith Hope. The irony wasn't lost on me. "Faith" guided me through a series of visualizations enabling me to stop perceiving my body as a failure. My jokes about my elderly state, though funny, were masks. I really feared I wasn't good enough. I connected with my baby, Max, and allowed him to go peacefully.

My words and thoughts were powerful. I now chose words supporting my wholeness and my ability to conceive. My lightness returned and my thinking shifted to the "welcome home" I was creating. I focused on life and embraced the doctor's assistance without the story that I was broken. Six months later I was staring at two vertical lines.

"Welcome home, Zoe," I said, gently stroking my belly. Certain she was a girl, I called her Zoe, the Greek word for life. "Enjoy your stay."

Zoe was born six months before my fortieth birthday.

~Tsgoyna Tanzman

Think Possible

Chapter 5

Facing Your Fears

46

The Pivotal Moment

As a girl, you're supposed to love Sleeping Beauty.
I mean, who wants to love Sleeping Beauty when
you can be Aladdin?

~Ellen Page

t's at this moment, as I'm lying on the roller derby track with a pain in my shoulder that feels like a knife, that I begin to question just what in the world I was thinking when I said I could do this. It's like time has stopped as I lie here staring at the ceiling of the old warehouse in North Battleford, in the middle of my first proper game of roller derby. The seconds feel like hours following the body check that grounded me, and in a haze I wonder if I've made some gloriously bad mistake. Like a picture sparking to life on a blank TV screen, I remember the act of insanity that got me into this mess in the first place.

As with most pivotal moments, in retrospect, the whole story behind it doesn't look that earth shattering. But it started something like this: A good friend posted on Facebook she was having a "Who do you want to be?" party for her nineteenth birthday. The idea was to dress up in a costume related to something you always wanted to do, or someone you always wanted to be. Naturally, having seen the movie *Whip It* nearly six hundred times and having spent hours imagining myself as Ellen Page speeding down the track in roller skates like her character Babe Ruthless did, I made myself a roller derby player costume.

And then my friend cancelled the party.

I will be honest in saying that I was actually sort of relieved, as I didn't own a pair of proper roller skates, had only a hockey helmet I probably got when I was six, and possessed no real knowledge (outside of what I'd learned from *Whip It*) on how to actually play roller derby. But the idea was planted. And then a few days later, like some sort of cosmic joke, a booth was set up in our local mall. A booth advertising a recruitment night for the local roller derby league.

Who knew people actually played roller derby in Saskatchewan? At least that's what I was asking myself as I stared at the posters. Saskatoon Roller Derby League was scouting people who were old enough to play — eighteen and up. Again, a cosmic joke, because guess who was finally old enough to join? So at that point I was pretty shocked, and reduced to shaking my head at the sheer coincidence of it all.

Oh, and remember when I mentioned the tipping point, that act of insanity that led to this whole disaster? This was it: Ignoring the fact that I had never really played a team sport before, hadn't roller skated since I got that pair for Christmas when I was four, and had dislocated a knee skiing a year and a half earlier, I marched right up to the booth and said, "Where do I sign up?"

I realize that sounds pretty ordinary, but to the widely proclaimed Queen of Boring from the kingdom of Never Does Anything, taking a leap of this sort truly was an act of insanity. And it started a journey wilder than any I had ever been on.

Fast-forward down the line, and I found out I was pretty good on skates. And fast. I felt like a true and proper Babe Ruthless, whistling down the track and scoring points with the other girls in Regina during a mixed rookie scrimmage. I was feeling pretty great about myself after that, and I can definitely say my head got a little big. Despite this cranial swelling, however, it was with a mix of terror and excitement that I found out the first real game was coming up in North Battleford, where our league would be facing off against Battleford's finest players. I wouldn't be playing with rookies anymore. It was my time to play with the big girls, the ones who had both skill and experience, and I was delighted.

I was even on my team's Jammer line, which meant I would get to race against the other team's jammer, dodge blockers, and hopefully score points without getting killed.

Getting killed. Right. That part.

So I'm lying on the track after getting hit by a blocker whose nickname should be Wrecking Ball, and everything from the past year is racing through my head. The magic from that moment of insanity has disappeared; my shoulder feels like it's going to come off, and as the game continues around me, I suspect something's torn. Vaguely, I also recognize one, important thought amongst these things.

I have a choice.

Choice number one: Give up. Keep lying on the track and let the referee blow the whistle to put an end to the two minute "jam" and maybe the other team's jammer won't score too many points because the jam ended early. Consequence — I get to live with the fact that I stayed down when I might have gotten up if I tried.

Choice number two: Forget the pain in my shoulder, get up, and finish the jam. Consequence — possibly fail to get enough points. But, show them all I'm made of tougher stuff. That they can't keep me down.

Biggest barrier? Shoulder hurting. Burning. Spontaneously combusting. Yeah.

So the choice sits on my chest like an iron weight, and for whatever reason, I start to see that party invitation on my friend's Facebook page, my mouse hovering over the button that will tell her whether I'm going or not. Lying there, I see the event heading, burning in my mind like fire.

"Who do you want to be?"

I take a deep breath. Then I take choice number two.

~D.J. Morhart

47

Three Simple Words

You will never fully believe in yourself if you keep
comparing yourself to everyone else. Instead, compare
yourself to who you were yesterday.
~Author Unknown

"Maybe I would be better off if I became an angel tonight," I thought to myself. "I could go to Heaven and watch the show from up there. Then I wouldn't have to be on the stage, and no one would ever call me gimpy or depressed or a burden ever again."

Thinking about hurting myself was the most terrifying thing in the world. I didn't want to die; I just didn't want to feel anymore. But as soon as I thought about the people I loved, I was ashamed for even thinking of doing such a thing. Cerebral palsy didn't have to take over my life. I was lucky mine was extremely mild and something I learned to deal with. My mom and dad raised me with the attitude that I could do anything I set my mind to, regardless of the fact that I spent time in physical therapy. So how did I go from simply walking a little differently to feeling like I could never be good enough because of my limp?

Three months earlier, life could not have been any better. I had been cast in the role I wanted in our upcoming musical. Performing provided me with the greatest rush. I can only describe it as a wonderful mix of feeling like I was simultaneously dreaming and flying. After being a member of the ensemble during previous productions, I was excited that this time around I would have more stage time, including choreography. This was a big accomplishment for any high school performer, but having your talent rewarded while trying to balance a physical challenge, too? That was like the cherry on top.

Our director Anthony was right out of college and one of the hardest working people I knew. His love for theater was always apparent, and it was rare that he was working on less than three shows at once. But as busy as he was, he always found the time to give me a hug or reassurance when CP was giving me a rough day. The trust that the two of us shared was unique to any person I had ever worked with. We made a deal from the start. I promised that I would work as hard as my body would let me, and he promised that he would tell me if something looked awkward on stage because of my weak leg. We shook on it, and from then on he never questioned when I asked for a break because my muscles were sore, or if choreography needed to be altered a bit so I could feel comfortable and confident in what I was doing.

But as many times as Anthony tried to help me feel secure, I eventually became my own worst enemy, convinced that if I didn't push myself as hard as possible, someone would say that cerebral palsy made me weak and unworthy of being a performer. My insecurities began affecting everything I was doing. I became more and more depressed and felt isolated from the rest of the cast. My usually respectable grades began to drop, which caused even more frustration during what many agree to be the most stressful year of high school — junior year. I left rehearsal each night angry at myself that I had gone from feeling great about earning the part to feeling like I couldn't handle it. Ironically, the motto of our show was "Anything's Possible!" But at the time, it felt like those words couldn't possibly apply to a girl who was stuck in such an overwhelming rut.

Something deep down inside told me I needed to get it together. Not only was our show opening that weekend but previews were happening the next day. The entire school would be coming to watch us perform select scenes from the show. This time around, I was featured in one of the dance numbers, which made me feel incredibly vulnerable. So, after our final dress rehearsal, I found myself standing backstage with Anthony… again. Standing up against the wall in full make-up, I crossed my right leg over my left in an attempt to hide the fact that it was shaking uncontrollably.

"I'm so afraid about tomorrow," I started. "I know I have to get up there and dance but I'm so nervous. What if someone calls me Gimpy again? I don't know if I can handle it. It's killing me!" Everything came flooding out of my mouth so fast that I'm not sure if it made any sense. It was only pure exhaustion that kept me from bursting into tears.

"But Annie," he answered without missing a beat, "why do you care what everyone out there thinks?" His question was so matter-of fact that it startled me, but it made me think. Why did I care so much?

"Listen," he went on, "go out there and forget about what every single person in the audience is thinking. You perform because it is what you love to do. So just go out there and make yourself happy."

Those words rang in my ears for the rest of the night. "Make yourself happy."

His advice was so simple, yet so powerful. Anthony didn't know about my failing grades, crumbling friendships or the rock bottom I'd hit the night before, but somehow his advice helped me find the power to look at my situation differently. Limp or no limp, I still loved the feeling I had when I was performing. I was glad someone had faith that I could find it again.

The next morning, as I walked into the theater, Anthony looked at me with a smile and said, "Remember what I told you!" While I waited in the wings, I whispered "be happy" to myself and let my mind go blank. The music started. I didn't think, just performed, and I was once again blessed with the joy I thought I had lost. I consider that afternoon to be one of my happiest moments. Not because of some huge epiphany or raving audience, but because my heart felt ten pounds lighter as I walked off the stage.

I'm not sure either of us realized it at the time, but my director's words to me as a high school girl changed me and will always stay close to my heart. I have not only remembered them… I've lived by them. My CP will never go away, but I know that it's a blessing in disguise, made even more valuable because of my experiences in theater. Every day I am grateful for the journey that helped me become a better, more positive person. One that began because of three simple words: make yourself happy.

~Annie Nason

48

The Only Way to Fail Is by Not Trying

*Don't worry about failures, worry about the chances
you miss when you don't even try.*
~Jack Canfield

While driving my car one day, a vision appeared before me. She was one of the most beautiful women I had ever seen. I was waiting to make a right turn, and as she came closer, I recognized her. It had been a while since I had seen her, but she was somebody you wouldn't forget. She played third base in the co-ed softball league I participated in the previous year from my job. I was on second base and could have scored on a base hit, but I stopped at third just so I could be near her.

Even though we worked for the same company, it was a big company with several buildings so I never saw her at work. I never even bothered to look for her at the time because I was shy and I didn't think she would go out with me. I wasn't exactly a smooth talker. Now I was getting a second chance.

I called out her name as she was walking by, but at first she ignored me. As I said, she was a really pretty girl and was probably approached by guys all the time. But as she got closer, she recognized me. I asked her where she was going, and she said she was meeting her mother at

Jewel Foods. I got up the courage to ask if she would like a ride, as it was about a six-block walk. Shockingly, she said yes.

I couldn't take my eyes off her while I was driving. I came close to hitting a car in front of me. I couldn't believe she was actually in my car. Since it was such a short ride, we reached the destination in no time.

That's the exact minute my life changed, even though it didn't happen overnight, but rather over time.

As she was getting out of the car, there were several things I could have said to her, such as, "It was great seeing you again. Do you think I could give you a call some time?" It's a nice innocent question that requires an answer.

She could have said, "Not if you were the last guy on the planet." Or maybe, "No, I prefer women." Or, she could have said, "That would be great! Here's my number."

I never found out the answer because I never asked the question, and I never saw her again.

I don't think I realized it at the time, but I started to think about it. Why didn't I ask if I could call her? What was the worst thing that could happen to me if I asked that question? It wouldn't have killed me. A plague of locusts wouldn't have descended upon me. The only bad thing that could have happened is that I wouldn't have received the answer I was hoping for. While it would have disappointed me, how bad would that have been?

It weighed on my mind. Then it hit me — a solution.

I wrote down the entire incident and typed it up on a 3x5 card that I put in my wallet. Every time I was afraid or fearful of making a decision, I pulled it out and read the words that changed my life: "The only way I can fail is if I don't try."

Instead of living life in fear and negativity, I now had the freedom to determine what my future would be. It opened up an entire new world for me and that was empowering.

This quiet, shy guy changed occupations and became a car sales-man. Yes, the guy too scared to ask a girl out started asking customers to spend a lot of their hard-earned money on a car. I became very successful at it, even winning Salesman of the Year in my second year on the job. Many awards followed. My new career allowed me to live a comfortable lifestyle.

More importantly, my newfound courage allowed me to follow my heart and pursue my first love — sports. I wanted to combine sports with my love of writing, something I hadn't done since my late teens.

I sought out publications and places to write for. If I saw an opportunity in front of me, I pursued it. I didn't always hear the word "yes," but as I learned from sales, the word "no" won't kill you. My profession taught me that every time I heard a "no," I was one step closer to the "yes" I was seeking. If you can visualize a seeming failure as a positive, it empowers you to move forward and keep on trying. The word no became my friend.

I have written for several sports websites along with local sports publications that I pursued. *Vine Line*, the magazine of the Chicago Cubs, asked me to write some articles.

While I love to write, I also love to talk sports. That was a passion I wanted to explore. I put out feelers to various Chicago radio stations about opportunities to get on the air. One answered, and I have hosted the *Sunday Sports Shootout* on WLUW for the past eleven years. I gained media access to both the Chicago Cubs and White Sox, along with the Chicago Bulls, because of my affiliation with the radio station. I also had the opportunity to be a guest on the *Chicago Tribune Live* show on Comcast SportsNet TV in Chicago.

My connections allowed me a fantasy so many sports fans around the country can only dream about. I have interviewed players, coaches, managers, general managers, Hall of Famers and more in my second job. I have had the opportunity to have a career along with living my fantasy of being involved with sports, and it's all because of the young lady I met whose name I don't even remember.

I do remember the first interview I conducted with one of the heroes from my childhood, Ron Santo of the Chicago Cubs, before the game. He was a color analyst for the team at the time on WGN. I remember thinking to myself, "I can't believe I'm sitting here in the radio booth at Wrigley Field talking to Ron Santo."

It taught me a lesson that I can have anything I want as long as I try. Nothing is out of the realm of possibility if you put your mind to it. You can live your dream as long as you are not afraid to pursue it. The only way you can fail is by not trying in the first place.

~Darrell Horwitz

The Name Tag

*Before I can tell my life what I want to do with it, I
must listen to my life telling me who I am.*
~Parker J. Palmer

"What are you doing, honey?" Mom asked, her face a mixture of amusement and concern.

"Nothing, Mom," I said, quickly hiding the notebook in my hands.

"Why are sitting on the floor in your closet? And why did you drag your pillow and blanket in there with you?"

"To be more comfy," I said.

"Comfy while you're doing what? Why not just sit on your bed?"

"I can't," I whispered. "I don't want anyone to know what I'm doing."

Mom sat down next to me, her concern evident. "What's going on?"

I hung my head. The jig was up. It was time to come clean. Soon, the whole world would know my secret.

I took a deep breath and confessed, "Mom, I've been writing."

I was eight years old.

In fifth grade, I won a prize at the Young Author's Fair at school. My story was terrible, and slightly plagiarized, I think. At the end of the story, the villain melted because of the rain and as his body became a glob of ooze on the ground, he groaned, "I melted because I'm so sweet." I stole this. My mother used to say that to my siblings and me when we fussed about carrying in groceries while it was raining. "You're not going to melt," she'd say. "Only sugar cubes are that sweet."

Plagiarizing a story from your own mother isn't sweet at all.

Clearly, my roots as a writer are iffy at best. My childhood included lots of closet hiding, spiral-bound notebooks, and, apparently, theft of my mother's intellectual property.

I'm not sure where I got the idea that writing was something to be done in secret, but that notion followed me into adulthood. As a high school senior, I won college scholarships because of essays I'd written. But never for a second did I consider journalism as a major. Writing for a career? That was way too risky.

Not financially. I didn't worry about that back then. It was risky… emotionally.

I majored in education and taught elementary school for a decade. I loved it, and I'd like to think I was good at it, but it didn't feed my soul. Not like writing did.

I wrote late at night when my husband and children were sleeping. I even sent some of my stories to editors and a few of them got published.

But I never told anyone.

It wasn't that I was ashamed. I just didn't want to answer any questions. I pictured telling someone I was a writer, and the questions that would follow:

How many books have you written? Answer: zero.

How many times have you been published and in which magazines? Answer: six times but not in any magazines you've actually heard of.

How much money do you make? Answer: enough to take my kids to lunch — at a fast food joint, if I have coupons.

I loved writing, and I didn't want anyone to steal the joy I felt at doing it. So I kept it a secret.

Until I wanted to attend my first writers' conference. I was nervous to tell my husband about it, but he encouraged me to go. So I did.

At the conference, they gave me a lanyard to wear. The tag inside read, "My name is Diane and I am a writer."

My breath caught. What was I doing there? I wasn't a writer. Not a real writer, anyway.

I put the lanyard around my neck, feeling like a liar.

That afternoon, I met with the editor of a small Christian publication. I sat down across from him, my hands shaking. I handed him the stack of stories I'd brought and prepared to be embarrassed.

But instead of saying, "These aren't good enough," he smiled and said, "These are terrific. Exactly what I've been looking for."

"Really?" I said. "Because I'm not a real writer, you know. I'm just a mom. I write at night and when I think no one knows, but I'm pretty sure my husband has known all along."

He chuckled. "A lot of us feel that way. That struggle to be a 'real' writer. But have you seen your name tag?"

That editor — who is now my friend — gave me such a gift that day. He let me in on a little secret: We all struggle with our identity sometimes.

I went home from the conference feeling different. I displayed my name tag above the desk where I write. It still felt like a lie, but I was determined to make it come true someday.

That first writers' conference was eight years ago. I've grown a lot since then. Now, if someone were to ask me how many times I've been published, I could answer, "Oh, hundreds of times, and you've even heard of some of the magazines."

My tag still hangs above my computer desk. I see it every day. My name is Diane and I am a writer.

It's not a lie. It never was.

Now, finally, I believe it. But not for the reasons you might think.

Becoming a writer — becoming anything, really — isn't about being successful. It's about deciding to become who you were born to be.

Believing the words on that name tag was the single most important thing I've ever done for my writing.

Seeing it every day changed my mindset. I went from thinking, "Maybe someday," to thinking, "Today is the day. I'm a writer, not because of any success I've had, but because I was born to do it."

Those words weren't written in the future tense. My name tag doesn't read, "I will be a writer." It says I already am.

I knew it when I was eight years old, writing secret stories in my closet. I knew it then, but it has taken me my whole life to really believe it.

We can do anything we set out to do. But only if we believe we can. My name tag is right. My name is Diane and I am a writer.

~Diane Stark

The Right
Kind of Control

It is not the mountain we conquer but ourselves.
~Edmund Hillary

y the end of my senior year of high school, I had it all. I was the ultimate well-rounded student. I excelled academically, participated on the swim team for three years, got in touch with my faith, and was ready to begin the next chapter of my life — college. I had received a major scholarship to the University of San Francisco — my dream come true. All of my hard work had paid off, and I couldn't have been prouder or more excited!

And so, I began the countdown to leaving for college. I was packed two weeks in advance, ready to start my new adventure. Finally the big day came, and I moved into my dorm. I cried as my family left. I was homesick immediately. I tried to dismiss it. After all this was what I wanted.

The first month away from home was the loneliest, most devastating time of my life. Each night I cried myself to sleep. I was confused. This empty feeling was foreign to me, and not knowing what else to do, I threw myself into my studies and started working. I quickly found myself occupied with two jobs and studying when I wasn't busy working.

Desperate to try and escape my depression, I forced myself to go to the gym. It helped me cope at first. I thought the better I looked and the more toned my body was, the happier I would be with my life.

Soon the exercise wasn't enough. I began to restrict my food intake. Restricting helped me cope — at first. It gave me a euphoric high that I cannot explain. It gave me control. Finally I was in control of my life. Though I had no control over particular events that were happening in my life, I did have control over how my body could look. After my menstrual cycle stopped, I finally went to see a doctor.

When I heard my weight read aloud by the nurse, I became obsessed. All I could think about was the number. I had to lose more weight. I continued restricting, and I lost more.

When I finally went home for Thanksgiving break, my mom was concerned. I looked awful.

I gathered all of my courage and finally confessed to my mom that I was suffering from an eating disorder. I think at that moment we were both relieved. I needed help, and even though I had gotten a 4.0 GPA my first semester of college, I had no choice but to take a break the following semester.

Even though I have had to steer away from my "perfect plan" this has been the wisest, bravest, and best decision I have ever made. This week will mark three months that I have been in recovery from my anorexia. From digging into my past abuse, to challenging my biggest fear of gaining weight, and learning to love myself, I have overcome so much.

I never would have thought that I would battle an eating disorder. But looking back and reflecting upon all I have learned, I am grateful for this struggle. For the first time in my life, I am taking care of myself. Each day that I follow my meal plan, or eat a croissant (as I cry the entire time), or choose to journal instead of count calories and meticulously plan small meals for myself, I know that I am conquering my eating disorder, and I am one step closer to freeing myself.

I am in a lighter place. I can finally see the sunshine again, and my body and mind are so much healthier. I am discovering my passions, including my love of writing. I never imagined myself revealing my secret to the world, but I am so much more courageous than I ever have been before.

~Vaneza Paredes

51

Polepole

*For every obstacle there is a solution. Persistence is the
key. The greatest mistake is giving up!*
~Dwight D. Eisenhower

"Polepole," he said to me in Swahili as I stared up into his weathered face. I was ready to collapse from exhaustion. It translated as "slowly," but took on more of a meaning like the old saying, "slow and steady wins the race." I nodded, repeating the word back to him. And then I took one more step in the dark, frigid night air of Mount Kilimanjaro.

I spent most of my life making cautious, predictable choices. Last fall I decided to change that and booked this trip to challenge myself in a way I'd never done before. Now here I was setting out at midnight on the fourth day of the climb, accompanied only by a guide named Moses. We were taking on the toughest part of Kili: the eighteen-hour summit hike. I had to keep a decent pace in order to make it to the top and come back down off the ice caps before the afternoon sun had a chance to melt the snow. That's when the avalanches happen. Although I wore a headlamp, its rays did not penetrate more than five feet. Besides the rocky ground, the only other things visible were the backs of Moses's scuffed-up Nikes a few steps ahead.

He had taken a sudden turn to the left. As I attempted to follow him, the rubble beneath my boots gave out. My feet slid an inch, then a few more, and I was sure that I would tumble down the mountainside at any moment. I panicked, hyperventilating in the oxygen-deficient air, the coldness of it scalding my lungs. I fell onto all fours and clutched the gravel.

Moses's hand shot into the glow of my headlamp. I grabbed onto it and managed to muster enough strength to rise and plant myself into the ground. He then led me to a more solid piece of earth. "You're tired. Eat something."

It was true. For the past hour I'd experienced gnawing hunger pains, but I was afraid to stay still and allow the bitter chill to creep further into my bones. I shook my head no.

Moses put his hand on my shoulder. "This is not a race, Rachel. You must take a break." I knew he was right.

I unzipped the outer pocket of my backpack and pulled out one of my energy bars. Taking a bite, I almost broke a tooth. It was frozen solid. I covered the end with the wrapping and tucked it inside my several layers of clothing. The water in my plastic bottle had also turned to ice, so I buried it deep alongside the bar and let the heat of my body warm them for a few minutes.

The winds surrounding us were merciless, howling in my ears and pecking away at my raw face. My nose became a running faucet that I couldn't shut off. I'd given up on wiping it. Staring up into the stars, I wondered how many more hours until I reached the top. I considered asking Moses, but he'd snuck a few yards away to smoke one of his hand-rolled cigarettes. Having grown up in these peaks, he was impervious to the altitude. When he returned, I stayed silent, fearing his answer would only discourage me.

For the next several hours I couldn't see anything but scree, hear anything but whipping air, and feel anything save for the cold and despair that had become a palpable weight on my chest. I felt lost somewhere in time and space, trapped in a numbing monotony that I was sure would go on forever. I'd done a lot of reading on Kilimanjaro prior to the trip, but nothing could have prepared me for this.

Why hadn't I picked something more feasible to take on? After I stumbled and fell onto my knees a second time, I realized I was not going to make it. Would that really be that shameful? Several hikers I'd met at the base camps had turned around during the summit ascent. People did it all the time.

"Wait. Stop!" I called out to Moses. When he looked back there was concern in his eyes. "Moses, I'm sorry but…" I trailed off, panting. So many thoughts raced through my head: the months I'd spent in preparation jogging several miles each day, my long flight across the Atlantic Ocean to Tanzania, our hike up the base of the mountain together the past four days. I didn't want to quit, but at the same time, I felt too weak to go on. As I debated how to express this to him, the line from an old church song popped into my head. It reminded me that when fear becomes overpowering I need to rely on God's strength to finish the course. From somewhere deep within, I felt a spark of hope ignite.

"I need a moment to rest," I finished, surprising myself.

For the next several hours, I kept those lyrics and other familiar hymns running through my head like a radio. Along with prayer, it helped pass the time, and before long we'd come to a clearing with a little sign in the center that read "Gillman's Point." I'd heard from a fellow hiker that this spot was about two-thirds of the way to the top. If Gillman himself had been there, I would've thrown my arms around him and kissed him! Instead poor Moses was the sole recipient of my sudden burst of energy. He must have thought me crazy. One minute I was laughing and bear-hugging him, and the next I had perched myself on a rock and begun to weep. "I know," he said. "You have the headache and the nausea. Drink some more water."

"No, I feel fine," I replied. Yes, I was freezing and short of breath, but we'd passed other hikers along the way who couldn't stop retching from altitude sickness. I knew how lucky I was. I smiled up at him through the tears. "I'm crying because I know I'll make it now."

As we pressed on, the sun appeared over the horizon, making the nearby mounds of ice sparkle. Rays of sunshine, warm and thick, dripped down like honey from a cloudless sky. It became much easier to push forward with all this surrounding beauty.

Soon I spotted another wooden sign off in the distance. As we approached it, I read aloud its simple words printed in English:

"Congratulations, you are now at Uhuru Peak, Tanzania. Africa's highest point. World's highest free-standing mountain." I drew in a deep breath of fresh, almost sweet air. I had made it.

Moses and I exchanged high-fives over mutual grins. As I walked up to the sign to take the obligatory picture, I wondered what the peak's name signified. "So what does *Uhuru* mean in Swahili?"

"Freedom."

I laughed. My shackles of fear and doubt had indeed fallen off. Knowing that God would be there to guide me through even the most difficult circumstances, I could now confidently embrace the rest of my life's journey. All I had to do was keep putting one foot in front of the other, *polepole*-style.

~Rachel E. Printy

52

Fly Like an Eagle

*When we are motivated by goals that have deep
meaning, by dreams that need completion, by pure
love that needs expressing, then we truly live life.*
~Greg Anderson

My husband Phil and I strolled along, hand in hand, running our bare feet through the pristine sand of a beach in Nassau, Bahamas. He described the landscape: the deep, blue waters of the ocean, the crystal clear, blue sky, and the lush greenery with gorgeous flowers in this fantastic paradise. Through Phil's voice I was not blind.

As we laughed and teased one another we approached a small straw hut with several brightly coloured parasails lined up in a row. Phil had me touch one and we both laughed uncontrollably until I said: "Yes, let's do it!"

I felt exhilarated. But then, my smile disappeared and negative thoughts filled my head. I thought all about the dangerous things that might happen. I pushed my husband away and would not discuss it any further.

We walked along the beach back to our hotel in silence. Then, I stopped and thought to myself that this was a once-in-a-lifetime opportunity and if I didn't take action right now, in this moment, to challenge myself and face my fears, I would regret it for the rest of my life!

Before I knew what had happened, I found myself in a small boat headed for a large, white, floating raft out somewhere in the deep blue waters of the ocean. We explained to the two gentlemen on the floating raft that I was "legally blind" and wanted to experience the adventure of parasailing! One of the gentlemen was quite nervous about this, but the other, who had a deep, calming voice, smiled and grasped me firmly as he strapped me into the beautiful kite. He carefully guided my fingers over the ropes and poles as he described the process and the instructions.

After a few moments of quiet contemplation, the kind gentleman took a deep breath and said, "Okay! This is what we are going to do! When you begin your descent, you will feel yourself coming down and as you get closer to the raft, I will shout out to you, and when you hear my voice, give me a signal that you hear me by giving me two thumbs up! When you are low enough and almost ready to touch down on the raft, I will give you a hard slap on the back of your leg. When you touch down on the raft, we will both grab you under your arms and will continue to run with you a few feet but will stop you before you run off of the other side of the raft." I listened very seriously to everything he said.

At this point I realized I was really going to do this! My body began to shake but it was too late to back out. I stood on the edge of the floating raft, locked into the beautiful kite and my heart began to pound like a jackhammer! The strong arm held onto me firmly. I heard the engine of the boat start. I could feel the curled rope beneath my toes leaving the raft. I took a deep breath and I felt a hard jerk of my body! I was up and gone!

It happened so quickly! Surprisingly, the wind was soft and welcoming. I flew higher and higher. I told myself I was an eagle and I was really flying! I took a few calming breaths, I allowed myself to relax. This was an amazing opportunity! Smiling, I began to enjoy the sound of silence! My hands were comfortably hanging onto the bar attached to the kite. I slowly loosened my grip and actually let go! I outstretched my arms and embraced the heavens! I was flying like an eagle! Huge tears began to roll down my face; not because I was afraid but because I was suspended in mid-air and feeling free and happy! As

I looked around at the deep, blue waters of the ocean and the crystal clear, blue sky (just like Phil had described it to me) I realized that there were no lines or barriers separating them from one another. I felt healed! I did not feel like a misfit blind girl trying to explain and fight my way through life.

I could put all those hurtful memories to rest. Throughout the years I had allowed my negative thinking to prevent me from taking control of my life, from seeing the strong, independent, and sassy woman who was confident and had finally found her true identity.

"I am not disabled! My disability is only one small part of the person I have developed into today!"

I felt my descent begin all too quickly, just like it began. I wiped the tears from my eyes and vowed that I would never again allow negative thinking to stop me from experiencing greatness! This experience was one of those "aha" moments that changed my life and gave me a new perspective.

~Lynn Fitzsimmons

53

To Love Living

Believe that life is worth living, and your belief will
help create the fact.
~Henry James

efore doctors put a word to it, the best ways to explain it were: "I just hate everything I used to love" or "I feel completely empty and I don't know why" or even "My heart just hurts." Then, in eighth grade, doctors put a word to it, and I stopped trying to explain it for a while.

In high school, depression ruled me. My emotions were like the month of March. One day, the sun would come out, and I would swear that spring was here; my painful, lonely winter was over. But soon after, the sky would go gray again, and my hope would shuffle off to put on a sweatshirt and sleep for a long time.

Every March, we ask each other, "Is this winter ever going to end?" By the time I was a sophomore, I was sure mine would not.

I hid it well. I'm funny, which helped. I was always laughing, telling jokes; people told me I was "the last person you'd expect to be depressed," which I took a strange pride in. I played field hockey; I was on student council; older kids and teachers liked me. I was named Class Clown in the yearbook.

I was glad that people knew that person, instead of the person I became when I was alone or with my closest friends. The real me was the person who cried when Rachel didn't get the solo in *Glee*, because she was really crying for herself. I became a person who didn't care about school, and eventually stopped caring about student council, and then field hockey, indifferent to the people she was disappointing. I became the person who went to therapy three times a week and lashed out viciously at her parents when they desperately wanted a family session, just to try to understand her a little bit better, just to try to help. I turned to alcohol, marijuana, and sex in an attempt to rid myself of this awful feeling. I was the person for whom the doctors couldn't find the right medicine, the person who felt completely empty and didn't know why, the person whose heart just hurt.

I couldn't figure out how to enjoy life. School trips to Washington, D.C. and Disney World were incredible, packed with wonderful experiences, but I had fun as if I were reading about a character in a book having fun. "This is great," I would think. "Look at me, what a life I have," but I could never quite feel the joy deep inside. On the outside, there was Disney World, and on the inside, there was a jail cell with no windows and an unknown sentence.

I made plans to commit suicide at least five times in high school. I certainly wanted to do it badly enough. When my friends begged me not to, I could see the pure anguish in their eyes and all I could think was, "How can they be so selfish? Asking me to endure this gruesome pain so they don't have to?" But the plans were mostly just a coping method: it was comforting knowing that any time I wanted to, I could get it to stop.

My first semester of college brought me lower. My beautifully constructed support system was now miles away. Despite being very social and adept at making friends in the past, a bout of depression hit right as I arrived, leaving me with no desire to meet anyone or even leave my room. I thought back to my high school reputation, the Steph most people had known, and thought, "How the mighty have fallen." For all the times I'd been sure it couldn't get any worse, it had. The plans to die suddenly became serious; they had research behind them — "most effective methods of suicide" Google searches — and they were near foolproof. I had real power to do it now.

When second semester began, I was at one of the lowest points I had ever been. I was so ashamed of what I felt and where I was.

Now that my friends had new lives, and my parents were enjoying an empty nest (or so I was convinced at the time), I could no longer ask for help, and I was embarrassed to still need it. I scolded myself every day: "At what point are you just going to get better? You must be doing something wrong. You can't keep expecting these people to save you."

On February 24th, I was in the middle of this self-hatred, when another voice popped into my head. It almost didn't sound like my own thoughts. "But Steph, why are you ashamed? You should be proud: you are still alive. You are still here, living and breathing and thinking. Think what you have felt and what you have wanted to do. How strong you must be to have gotten this far. Why aren't you celebrating?"

I sat up straighter. "Yeah…" I said to myself. "Why am I ashamed? Why am I embarrassed? I am proud. I'm here." I still felt desperately sad. My insides still felt like an endless winter, a windowless jail cell. My heart still hurt. But I picked up my phone and wrote a message on Twitter advocating better acceptance and honest communication about mental illness. I ended the note with, "I'm here, I'm finally healthy again, and no longer ashamed, so let's talk."

I don't think I really was healthy again at the time. But as soon as I posted, people started sharing my Tweet and responding with admiring and encouraging messages. The people who knew me as a clown… they liked me as a survivor too, an activist. I could be both. I didn't have to hide my struggle. Later, people reached out privately and told me how much it had meant to them in their own emotional and mental journeys.

"Now you can't let yourself die," I thought. "Your message would be lost. This is why you're still here. You have a purpose now; you have to stay."

So I did. And so I will.

I began posting more on Twitter, then other social media that reached more people. I spoke in a video for my high school's Suicide Prevention Week. Even more people contacted me then, telling me I was brave, that my message was important. I will continue to speak up, tell my story, and give help to others, until the stigma surrounding mental illness is abolished.

Today, I am healthy. Depression will always be in me; an illness does not just go away with positive thinking. I must monitor my emotions and take responsibility for my mental health, putting it above all else. But it was that kindness I finally gave myself, and pride I allowed myself, that ignited a spark in me and gave me a reason to love my life.

~Stephanie E. Sievers

54

Think Outside the Book

The mediocre teacher tells. The good teacher explains.
The superior teacher demonstrates. The great
teacher inspires.
~William A. Ward

What could a young, city born and bred, university-educated woman learn from a bunch of fifteen-year-olds who had never even seen the city?

It never occurred to me to ask myself this question as I took up my first teaching appointment in Moruga, a village in Trinidad that seems to have been forgotten by time. I would be teaching history and had spent the preceding weeks gathering additional books and making notes. I was well prepared and energized by my new independence and my honors degree as I swaggered into Moruga ready to make a difference.

Education, I knew, was the key to ending ignorance and poverty, and educate I would.

But Moruga had its own ideas that were very different from mine.

With the exception of about five children in a class of forty, school seemed to be the last place these students wanted to be. As I asked for volunteer readers for Chapter One — The Coming of the Europeans — the literacy level of many of the students alarmed me. My questions on what was read remained unanswered. What bothered me most was the way my students dragged themselves out of class at the end of the period. I had not been able to inspire them in those first forty minutes.

They say everything happens in life for a reason. My primary school days had been traumatic. I had hated school and never envisioned myself as a teacher, but now here I was teaching. I had told myself that I would be a different kind of teacher — the kind who inspires students to think and learn.

When I brought up my concerns in the staffroom some weeks later, many of the more experienced teachers gave me tips on getting the students to remember the key things so they would pass the exam, but I wanted to get those students excited, interested, involved — because I remembered how daunting and lonely and unkind school had once been to me. I remembered how I had thought of myself as a dunce because I got too terrified for spelling tests and got zeros. I remembered how I had feigned disinterest in school because my belief in teachers and education had been shattered — until my Literature teacher in secondary school had finally got me interested again. Now I wanted to be that kind of teacher.

The term crept to an end and my students' marks in the end of term exam horrified me. The older teachers said I was getting too attached. My husband said I was expecting too much. I questioned my decision to become a teacher and my ability to teach.

January brought the new school term. I focused on the inspiring teachers who had changed my life and the possibility of me being able to do the same. For the first time though, I admitted to myself I did not know how. My teachers had had something to work with — I was an avid reader and a good story writer — but what could I work with here? Many of my students were below the literacy level or were simply not interested.

A few weeks later a meeting with my principal made me run late for class. As I got closer to the classroom I heard laughter and drumming — my students obviously thought they had a free period! I entered the classroom and the drumming stopped. Some students standing at the front of the classroom scrambled to their desks.

"Good morning, Miss," they tried to sound happy to see me; their faces were animated but I knew this was not for me.

"What are you all doing?"

"Nothing, Miss."

They pulled out books and sat and waited, but that thing I had seen in their faces, that thing I had so hoped to bring with my teaching, that thing was slipping away now as they got ready for class.

"Nothing? You were doing something. What?"

There was quiet and I realized they thought I was angry. Eventually one of them said, "Oh gosh, Miss, just acting."

"Acting?"

More quiet. Guilty faces stared back at me.

I put my book on the desk and crossed my arms and faced the class.

"Columbus Day, Miss."

"Columbus Day? What is Columbus Day?"

"You know, the day Columbus reached Trinidad with his ships."

"Christopher Columbus?"

"Yes, Miss. Some of us will be in the Columbus Day play. Miss, every year in Moruga we put on a play on the beach about when Columbus came here with his ships and met the Amerindians."

"Wait. Wait, you mean the same Columbus in the history book? Christopher Columbus?"

"Yes, Miss."

"But… well, we did that chapter in the book. You didn't answer my questions." I felt my heart pounding hard. "So, you didn't realize that the play is the same thing as Chapter One in the history book?"

"No, Miss."

"Open the book, come, quick," I was excited now. "Okay, so who is taking part in the play?"

A few hands rose; all eyes questioned me.

"Okay, so come to the front, let's act out this play."

"Miss, you said to open the book. We're not going to read?"

"I will read, you will act and you will drum and you will see how the chapter and the play work together."

"You mean like a story?"

"Yes, exactly." My words rushed out, fast, in time with the beating of my heart.

"Move the chairs. Where are the drummers?"

The students stared at me as if I was crazy.

"Miss, for real?"

"Yes, for real!"

Had I hit upon something here? There was something I hadn't seen before — these faces — excited, smiling, alive. These faces were what I dreamed of!

One week later I gave the students the same questions on Columbus that few had passed the first time and this time more than half the class passed!

This experience informed my teaching and later my writing. I came to value the power of storytelling and its ability to educate. I came to recognize that books are enough for some students, but for others, life as they know it has little to do with what's in the book and unless they see a co-relation, they dismiss, even suspect, what's in the book.

Most of all I came to understand the circle of communication. Here I was, teaching history that was informed by the book, yet knowing nothing about the culture and life and history of this place and having to be informed by those who might be labeled as "ignorant" simply because they did not go by the book.

Education, I knew, was the key to ending ignorance and poverty, and educated I was at Moruga.

~Joanne Haynes

55

The Heart of the Matter

> *Anxiety is the rust of life, destroying its brightness and weakening its power. A childlike and abiding trust in Providence is its best preventive and remedy.*
> *~Author Unknown*

'll never forget the evening of July 28th, thirty days before my forty-fifth birthday. After dinner, my husband Dave and I went out for a walk around the block. Once home, I settled in to watch TV with Dave, hoping to take my mind off things that were troubling me.

Suddenly, excruciating pain pierced through my chest; I felt as though my ribs were being crushed. As the pain increased, I said to Dave, "Honey, I'm not feeling well. I have pain in my chest. I'm going to the bedroom to rest."

"Okay," Dave replied. "Let me know if there is anything I can do for you."

The pain intensified. I knew something was seriously wrong when my face grew clammy while I gasped desperately for air. Frightened, I shouted, "Dave, come here!"

Immediately, Dave rushed in. "What's the matter?"

"The pain is unbearable, and I can't breathe," I replied. "I have to go to the hospital."

"Should I call an ambulance?" Dave asked.

"We don't have time to wait," I responded. "I think I'm dying! You're going to have to drive me." Dave assisted me into the car. I later learned that was the wrong decision. You are always better off calling for an ambulance, since they can diagnose you, take your vitals, and start treating you right away as they race you to the hospital. Having someone drive you, you may get to the hospital a few minutes sooner than if you had waited for an ambulance, but you won't have received any lifesaving treatment along the way.

As we dashed through traffic, the pain intensified. When we drove over some railroad tracks, I felt as though a train had wheeled over my chest. As soon as we pulled up to the ER, an attendee rushed out and asked, "Do you need a wheelchair?"

"Yes," Dave yelled. "I think my wife is having a heart attack." As Dave wheeled me in, he hurried over to a nurse sitting at a desk and notified her of my condition. She quickly registered my name, fastened a name band around my wrist, and handed me two aspirins to take. She then rolled me in to the emergency room for evaluation.

Immediately, another nurse took a chest X-ray, drew blood, hooked me up to a heart monitor, and administered morphine for the pain. She then said, "Try not to be too nervous. The doctor will be in shortly to see you."

When the doctor entered, he looked surprised when he saw me, as though he was expecting someone else. "Mrs. Alpert, I looked over your test results, and they reveal that you had a heart attack. Is the pain lessening?"

"Yes, it is starting to ease up," I answered.

"That's good news; however, we'll be admitting you. In the morning, a cardiologist will perform exploratory surgery in your heart to find the blockage." As the doctor left, Dave and I glanced at each other in disbelief. We never imagined someone my age would have a heart attack, especially since I've always maintained my weight, exercised daily, and eaten a healthy diet, and my cholesterol was always within a healthy range. Perhaps that is why the ER doctor seemed so surprised when he saw me.

The following day, the heart specialist conducted further tests and found the blockage. "Mrs. Alpert, because of the size and location of the blocked artery, it's best that we leave it alone," he said. "Your heart was damaged. It will take time to recover; however, you should be fine once you recuperate." A few days later, he released me from the hospital to recover at home. Before leaving the hospital, he scheduled a follow-up visit to his office.

One thing that concerned me was why I had experienced a heart attack at such an early age. As I read about women and heart disease, I discovered that stress was a contributing factor. This information made me realize that the perpetual anxiety and stress I lived with probably produced havoc within my heart. I needed to change that in order to avoid another heart attack.

Although my heart recuperated, and I became physically well, I couldn't stop worrying about dying. I was alive, but my fear of a second heart attack was getting in the way of really living.

Then one morning, while bathing, I had a wakeup call! The New Year was approaching, and I asked myself a simple question: If you only had this upcoming year to live, what would you regret not accomplishing?" I didn't have to think about the answer; there were three books I wanted to write. My life had a purpose. Those fears of dying swirled down the drain with the bath water, replaced by happiness.

I finished getting ready for the day, rushed over to my computer and began writing. I could not stop!

As I sit here and write this story, I am almost fifty. It's a blessing to report that no second attack occurred, my three books have been published, and my stress has decreased dramatically since I learned how to say "no" without feeling guilty. Through this journey I've come to learn that yesterday is over, tomorrow is not guaranteed, and I should live in the present as happy as can be!

~Barbara Alpert

56

The Worst Dancer in Class

Dancing with the feet is one thing, but dancing with the heart is another.
~Author Unknown

W hen I was a teenager, my mother had a hard time finding me onstage at the dance recital. I was always in the back row, out of sight, out of mind. Sometimes the stage lights didn't even reach me, and I ended up dancing in the shadows. Sometimes the girls in front of me rendered me invisible. On the show recording I was usually visible in exactly three shots: when the camera panned across the stage at the beginning, middle and end.

Being in the back row is an interesting thing. Why are you there? The reason could be something as simple as the fact that your dance teacher just doesn't like you — as was my case for a few years — but it tends to trigger overthinking. Maybe you're a horrible dancer, you ponder. Maybe you're too large or too skinny or too tall or too short. The more your confidence crumbles, the more your dancing suffers, and the more likely you are to be thrown in the back row again. It's a vicious cycle.

It's interesting how this mindset can affect those who are otherwise confident. I have never been a shrinking violet, so to speak. I've been writing professionally since I was fifteen and I've been able to defend my work vociferously. The same has held true with my art, my philosophies on life, and my personal beliefs. With dance, however, I've had nothing but the back row mentality.

I didn't start out that way. As a kid, I was a fierce, enthusiastic and confident dancer. At eleven, though, puberty hit me hard, I gained weight, and I somehow became invisible. I still hopped through my recital routines with energy, but I was always placed in the back row. My teachers didn't remember my name half the time.

In high school, I found a ballet studio that seemed promising. What I forgot was that ballet was perhaps even more critical and demanding than other disciplines of dance. "You need to lose weight," my teacher snapped. "You don't need this — and this — and this." She poked at my hips and belly, which truthfully weren't that large. They were there, though, and in her dance school, their very presence was loathsome. Needless to say, I wasn't her star pupil. When they cast the *Nutcracker* one year, every single girl in my class was given a role except me. I could do the same moves they could, but I was still the girl from the back row who didn't have a "classical" physique, and I just didn't count. After I saw the *Nutcracker* cast list, I decided I'd had enough: I walked out of the studio and never returned.

Dance was still part of my life, though. I choreographed and performed in an off-off Broadway show during college. I took classes off and on at another school, and at my university. I volunteered as a puppeteer in the Village Halloween Parade and danced up Sixth Avenue in a dragon costume. I even ended up performing on Broadway for two nights when I was invited to be part of the singing chorus at a benefit show at the historic New Amsterdam Theatre, former home of the Ziegfeld Follies. All I could do was marvel at my luck at being on the same stage that had hosted Olive Thomas, Doris Eaton, Mary Eaton and scores of other talented performers.

Eventually, I decided to start performing in flash mobs. The first one I did ended up being a film shoot for a major theme park. Another dance was staged in a cemetery. We boogied to Buddy Holly music on a morning television show. While I had no interest in making it a career, I enjoyed my occasional projects.

I ended up doing a major network television show about flash mobs. On the first day of filming, the dance captains pulled the strongest dancers for featured spots. As I crossed the floor to audition, a woman deliberately stepped right in front of me. I had to stop moving to avoid crashing into her, which made me lose my place. The dance captain frowned and asked us to do the combination again. That time I danced well, and I was chosen. The woman who had tried to sabotage me was not.

The show kept inviting me back. More often than not, I was placed in the featured dancers' group. On one occasion, the choreographer handpicked me. When our last episode was filmed, she smiled and told me, "You've been getting better with every show. I've had my eye on you!" I was stunned. She had to look after hundreds of dancers at every single taping, and she was giving me a thumbs-up, even though I wasn't a lithe, slender ballerina. I was featured in two of the show's press photos and shown on camera in four of the five episodes I did.

There was only one problem: Despite all the fun I was having, I still believed in those teachers from adolescence instead of myself. Deep down, no matter what anyone said to me, I still thought that I was a horrible dancer.

At one performance, the director of the flash mob company, Staci, finally called me out on it, point blank. She told me, "You'd better not hide in the back row this time, if you know the dance. You're not doing anyone any favors back there!" The comment shocked me, but after a moment, I realized she was right. In most of the mobs I'd done, I'd automatically gone to the back. Nobody had placed me there; we picked our own spots. Staci had correctly pointed out that I was undermining myself.

I plucked up my courage and stopped hiding in the back. And the more I stayed in the front row, or in the middle, the more confidence I gained. I eventually reclaimed the fierce dancing spirit that I'd lost when I was eleven. It brought freedom and joy back to my performance.

I hope my old dance teachers have seen me on TV and wondered, "Wait, wasn't that girl in my class?" On the other hand, most of them weren't good at paying attention to the girls in the back row, so they may well have forgotten I ever existed. No matter. I'm the last person they ever would have tagged to do anything in dance as an adult. No, I'm not Pavlova or Baryshnikov, I am not a professional and I would never presume to be; and there's always room for improvement, but I'm the best Denise I can possibly be... and now, finally, I am able to look at my dancing and think that it's good.

In the end, two decades, a major network TV series and others' words couldn't convince me I was a good dancer. I had to discover that for myself.

~Denise Reich

Think Possible

Chapter 6

Rising to the Challenge

57

Time to Fly

If you were born without wings, do nothing to prevent
them from growing.
~Coco Chanel

had been depressed for months. My boyfriend had left me for another woman. I was recovering from anorexia. I had passed out in my apartment and had to move back in with my parents. I was slowly gaining weight but still felt uncomfortable in my own skin. I hated everything, but mostly myself. Something had to change.

I woke up one Sunday morning and slipped into my favorite superhero T-shirt and leggings. I had an appointment that day to try a new experience, hoping it would snap me out of my funk. My mom curled my hair and helped me put on my make-up. I looked in the mirror and saw the girl that I once was and knew I could be again. I put on goofy socks and a pair of ridiculous fuzzy boots, and got in the car.

We pulled up to the place and got out of the car. I stared up at the imposing structure before me, my stomach tightening and my breath catching in my throat. "You can do this," I said to myself. My mom walked around the car, grabbed my hand and said, "You can do this."

We let ourselves in through the closed gate and approached a woman sitting on a bench. "You here for the 10 o'clock?" she asked as she pulled her hair into a tight ponytail. I nodded, in awe of this beautiful, confident woman who exuded happiness and warmth. She handed me a form and I filled it out slowly. As I turned the waiver form in, the woman asked, "I'm J. You ready to fly today?"

Boy, was I ready. I had always been an adventurous person but I had somehow become more cautious since college. J put a harness around my waist and led me over to a group of people in similar gear. She had us stretch our legs and arms while instructing us on what we would be doing. A muscular older man walked over to us. "This is going to be a fantastic day for all of you. Trapeze is not only the most fun you've ever had, it is the best therapy you will ever need. If you're scared or hurting, you'll lose it all up there on that bar."

I started to feel hope.

After a test run on the ground and on a lower bar, we were all ready. I patiently waited my turn while my stomach did somersaults. Then I was next.

I reached a sweaty hand out to the ladder and hauled myself the twenty-five feet to the top platform. I grasped the post at the top and swung my leg around it to get to the other side. I chalked my hands. J called me over to the trapeze bar. My toes hung over the edge. My right arm stretched out toward the bar as J pulled it toward me with a long hook. It hit my hand.

"Listo! Ready! Hup!"

Hup means to jump. And jump I did. I swung out over the net, the wind blowing apart my carefully coiffed hair. "Legs up!" I swung my legs up and over the bar, then flung myself backwards, arching my back, hands toward the heavens. "Good. Now flip back. Good. Kick, back, kick, and somersault!"

I hit the net and made my way to the side and down the fifteen-foot ladder. I smiled at the man holding the rope and at my mom. "That was amazing! I've never felt anything like it in my life." The man looked at me and said, "Are you ready to try a catch?"

Was I? Was I ready to trust again? Was I going to let someone catch me after being dropped by my boyfriend?

I had to try it. I made my way up again and waited for the man to tell me he was ready.

"Hup!"

I reached out as far as I could. I felt his hands catch mine. I soared through the air, his strong hands and arms allowing me to feel the sensation of true flight. I had done it. I laughed hysterically as he told me to let go and fall. I lay in the net, still laughing but proud that I had taken a chance and trusted someone again.

That day changed everything for me. I laughed more. I felt more. I got healthy and realized that life is too precious to waste in a cocoon of depression and pain. Sometimes we hurt. Sometimes we're weak. But that doesn't mean we can't burst out of that cocoon and fly.

~Lauren H. Pottinger

58

The Pin

*I love to see a young girl go out and grab the
world by the lapels.*
~Maya Angelou

Ever since joining my high school's wrestling team, I
dreamed of pinning a boy. I knew that it was rather farfetched as I was smaller and weaker than the boys in my
weight class, who appeared to have been training for
wrestling ever since they were born. After being unable to compete
freshman year due to a serious concussion, I made it my mission to
pin a boy during my sophomore year, and every second I spent at
practice was another second I was closer to achieving my dream.

That victory would come sooner than I expected.

In early January, my team was invited to participate in a tournament at a local high school. Despite losing all my matches so far in
the season, I remember feeling rather optimistic that my dream would
come true as I packed my singlet and headgear into my duffel bag.

My first match in the tournament was over in two minutes. I was
near the edge of the ring, sprawling with my legs stretched out far
from my body. But in an instant the boy had hooked his arm around
my leg and toppled me over to my back, pinning me. I lost my second
match too.

By this point in the tournament, I was exhausted, both physically
and emotionally. I wanted to give up and go home. But then I gave
myself a lecture: "You don't practice two hours each day to go home,"

I thought, preparing for my third match. "You practice to succeed."

As I stepped onto the mat with my opponent, I took a moment to observe him. He was around my height and definitely stronger. Nervously, I shook his hand, starting the match.

We spent the first few seconds tugging and pulling on each other, snapping each other's heads down. Thinking I had the opportunity to shoot, I took a shot — lurching forward as I glided my knees across the mat and grasped his leg. Within an instant, he sprawled, kicking his legs back and dropping his weight on me. I struggled to hold onto his leg, feeling my fingers slipping as he continued to stretch his legs back and dig his hips into my neck. So instead of holding on, I decided to slide out from under him.

Quickly, I moved my right leg and slid out from under him. He fell on to the mat, and as he sprang back up, I heard cheers around the mat as the spectators realized that it was a girl who had slid out of a boy's grasp.

I felt my confidence growing. The second round had started. I started on my knees and had to scramble onto my feet. He made an attempt to lock me in his arms, and I successfully peeled myself away from him. We continued to pull and tug at each other's arms as we contemplated what to do next.

By the third round I was out of breath, and I began to fear I'd lose out of pure exhaustion. But as he made a grab for me, I managed to slip around him and wrap my arms around his torso, making a quick but sturdy butterfly grip.

I tried lifting him off the ground by bumping his hip with mine. He just teetered forward, too big for me to lift him. Instead, I turned my body in a corkscrew-like motion, twisting him to the ground as I landed on top of him. My heart hammered in my chest. I kept my knees off the ground as I continued to apply pressure by digging my hips into his broad back. I felt him flatten under me, and I continued to push harder as I gasped for air, completely aware of all the eyes staring at me.

As my coaches and teammates shouted words of encouragement, I shuffled around him to line up with his side. Quickly, he lifted up his arm so that his elbow made a bend as he started to get off the mat. Yet all those hours of practice flooded back to me in a split second and I fiercely hooked my arm into his and began to drive forward so that he, once lying on his stomach, was beginning to turn over onto his back.

"Stay off your knees!" I heard someone shout.

"Keep pushing!" another person roared.

The referee got down on the mat as I felt my opponent's shoulder touch the mat. I locked my feet in place, my legs shaking as I struggled to apply pressure by staying off my knees. I could feel him squirm under me, and the referee began the countdown to a pin.

The referee slapped the mat once.

I made my grasp around the boy tighter.

He slapped the mat again.

I looked up at the ceiling — "counting the ceiling tiles" as my coaches put it, so my chest would apply pressure to my opponent.

He slapped the mat again.

I could feel sweat dripping from my hair cap, my body almost crumbling from exhaustion.

The referee blew the whistle with a final slap, and the whole gymnasium erupted in cheers.

"I did it," I thought, pulling myself off my opponent. I was practically beaming as I realized what I had just done. "I pinned a boy!"

The referee grabbed my arm and lifted it in the air, signifying my victory.

I was a champion, and everyone on the bleachers could see it. And even though I didn't place in that tournament, I accomplished my personal goal. All the hours of sweat and exhaustion I had endured through practice had led up to that sweet moment of success. But my greatest victory that day was not my win, but my realization that by working hard, I could do anything I set my mind to, no matter how impossible it might seem.

~Madison Kurth

59

A Promise to a Friend

My best friend is the one who brings out the best in me.
~Henry Ford

She opened the door to let me in. I hardly recognized her. "Isn't it ironic? I have been trying to shed ten pounds all my life," she gasped for breath. "But not like this!"

Actually, she looked like she had lost twenty or thirty pounds. At 5 feet, 5 inches and 80 pounds, she was a shell of her former self. Radiation and chemo had not produced the desired results.

We talked about old times: the fun we used to have growing up in New York City, ice skating in Central Park, window-shopping on Fifth Avenue, and the sleepovers at the apartment she had lived in with her mom. We'd stay up late yakking about our hopes and dreams and boys, boys, boys, ignoring her mom's nagging to turn out the lights and go to sleep. When we got older we double-dated, sipping wine in trendy little New York clubs and dancing the night away. And we smoked.

Gracefully gesturing with a cigarette in my hand made me feel glamorous and grown-up. I emulated the actresses on the screen as I inhaled and exhaled in what I imagined to be a sophisticated manner.

But now Georgie had lung cancer. She spoke bravely about how she was going to beat this monster. There were new treatments she was going to try.

"My doctor says I will be dancing in six months," she said without conviction.

I had my doubts.

Before I left, she stopped me at the door.

She grasped me by the shoulders and wouldn't let go. It was surprising how much strength she had in that tiny frame.

"Eva, please listen," she pleaded, between coughs. "You've got to stop smoking."

"I will, Georgie," I replied half-heartedly.

"No! I mean it. When? Give me a date now!"

"Soon, Georgie. Soon."

She pressed a calendar into my right hand and still held on to my left.

"You have ten days. Mark them off on this, " she persevered, wheezing. "I will hound you, Eva." She was adamant.

"Okay, I will." I would have said anything by then.

She let me go only when she had extracted my promise.

We hugged as we said goodbye.

Walking through the parking lot to my car I happened to glance up at Georgie's window. What I saw shocked me! She sat there with a cigarette in her hand as smoke surrounded her once pretty face. She bore an expression of defeat and despair. Smoking didn't look so glamorous anymore.

Georgie was still smoking. She had given up on herself but she had not given up on me.

I called her daily to check on her. Sometimes it seemed as if she were checking up on me instead. She was always optimistic about herself but then she'd turn the conversation to me. Had I quit yet?

"Only a few more days, Eva," she'd remind me. "You promised."

I reluctantly hung her calendar on my fridge. I was going to humor her. I started marking the days off with an X.

"I'm working on it, Georgie."

Soon it became five days and then four. I had not intended to go through with it.

I had tried to kid myself. I had pretended I didn't see the yellowing of my complexion and teeth. I had looked past the accidental burns on my clothing and furniture and the foul odor of stale ashes that pervaded my house.

I had tried to kick the habit. I really had. I tried cold turkey, patches and cutting down. I even went for hypnosis. Nothing worked.

"Someday I will ditch this addiction for good," I kept telling myself. "But not yet."

On the tenth day, the phone rang. "It's Georgie," I thought, as I lit up a cigarette. I didn't want to hear her annoying reminder. I didn't answer.

Later that night I listened to my recorder. "We lost Georgie today," cried an unfamiliar voice.

My heart broke for my friend. She had lost her battle. Yet she had tried to save me and I had failed her.

It was Friday. I had the whole weekend ahead of me and I was on a mission. I went to bed and stayed there until Monday morning, getting up only when necessary.

I assumed the yoga corpse position. Flat on my back with my hands by my side, palms facing up in soft surrender, I would murmur, "I will not smoke today — for Georgie."

One day at a time I repeated these words. They worked. So I continued for a few more days and then a few more.

It wasn't easy but I did it.

Eventually my skin, eyes and teeth became brighter. My wellbeing returned. I was one of the lucky ones. I had fulfilled my promise to Georgie. I said I did it for her. But the truth is, I did it for myself, *because* of her. I wonder if she knew.

The vow made to a beloved friend held more power than any vow I had made to myself. That was twenty-five years ago. With the exception of one slip-up, I have not had a cigarette since — thanks to Georgie.

~Eva Carter

The Break Through

Martial arts is not about fighting; it's about
building character.
~Bo Bennett

I remember the moment that changed my life forever with a snap and a rush of endorphins and an overwhelming feeling of shock, joy, and amazement. I remember the smell of the wood, the sweat in my eyes, and the laughter that flowed from me right after it happened.

No, I'm not talking about the birth of my children (which, don't get me wrong, was amazing in and of itself) or of the moments that I treasure as milestone moments (getting married, buying a house, my kids' first days at school). This was a different kind of moment. This was a moment of self-discovery, empowerment, and truly a moment of strength.

The piece of 1x12 pine snapped because I kicked it. I broke a board. An actual piece of wood. With my foot. This was not magic, or some sort of special effect or a mysterious superpower that I was given….this was just me.

But I have gotten ahead of myself.

Let me return to the beginning. I am a "recovering" attorney whose idea of being in shape meant lifting coffee cups, not weights. When I first started training in Taekwon-Do, it was essentially by accident.

A friend of mine had convinced me to try a class because she loved it so much and so I agreed, rather tentatively, to try it… once.

But in that first class, I learned something so very simple and yet so compelling—how to get away from someone grabbing your arm.

It's not the kind of thing you learn in school or really anywhere else. But there's a mixture of physics and philosophy, technique and art, strength and perseverance that keeps you invested and interested. And yet, for a very long time, I didn't consider myself a martial artist. I was a dabbler, not serious about it at all. I enjoyed the classes, the camaraderie, the "me time" away from my family to focus on things other than the talk of dinosaurs and Cheerios that seemed to consume my other waking moments.

I loved it—the art and beauty of the patterns, with each move flowing seamlessly into the next; the exacting details of the technical aspects of each individual move and learning the angles and dimensions; the proper preparation and execution of the techniques. I loved it all—but I still doubted my abilities.

From the moment I stepped on the floor as a white belt, I was aware of how awkward I was physically. Being short and heavier than I wanted to be, and without natural flexibility, I looked at myself in the mirror in my white uniform and felt like a marshmallow. So, more often than not, when we practiced in front of the mirror, I would look away.

Patterns were my favorite. Learning the moves and the order and putting them in motion, I could get so focused on them that I was no longer thinking about how big my butt looked or how silly I felt. I was truly happy doing patterns. Some of the other aspects like learning to kick or jump or spar were less comfortable for me.

When I was kicking, I felt awkward. I didn't have the flexibility that many of the other students had, nor was I naturally athletic. And it took me much longer than everyone else to understand or replicate a move. But I was determined to get it. So I kept going back.

Eventually, despite my multiple mess-ups and clumsy feet, my instructors tested me for my first belt rank of high white belt (white with a yellow stripe) and I realized I was going to have to go out in front of people and do this. And I was, quite honestly, terrified. But by then I had grown a little thicker skin, a little more confident, and a little less worried about what everyone else was going to think. And so I showed up for my first test.

I wish I could tell you that that was the moment of my triumph. It wasn't. It was, in fact, a disaster.

I was so nervous I couldn't get my head wrapped around my left-side requirements at all. I messed up my patterns, flubbed some of the other testing elements, and barely managed to kick high enough to avoid a Chihuahua had one been standing in front of me. But my instructors reminded me that I had already earned my new belt with my hard work and dedication and that the purpose of the test was to demonstrate the skills already proven to them. And so they passed me anyway.

At every new rank, I found something impossible. Whether it was the kicks we suddenly had to start doing in the air (I asked for a crane and pulley system but to no avail) or the increasingly complex patterns, or other requirements. But over time, "I can't" turned into "How can I?" which then became "How will I?"

And then, one day, I showed up to class and the students were breaking boards. Real wooden boards. And I was convinced they were all insane. And boy was that "I can't" voice yelling again.

I watched, in astonishment, as student after student walked up to perfectly solid pieces of wood and broke them with their hands or their feet.

I was terrified. When I was given the opportunity to try, I chickened out. I didn't want to hurt myself… and I didn't see any way I wouldn't.

But my instructors were extremely patient. And kind. They invited me to come in and work individually with them and a few select students (there had to be someone there to hold the board). I refused their first offer, and the next one. But finally, I agreed to try.

I remember I couldn't stop trembling. Just looking at the board made me a little nauseated. But I listened to them when they told me that board breaking was more a mental challenge than a physical one. I suggested that they let me break one in my imagination, but they didn't buy that.

So I let them teach me how to line up to break that board. And the first time I went to kick it, I was so afraid that I missed and accidentally kicked someone's fingers (he was holding the board for me). I felt terrible but he encouraged me to try again. I literally told that doubting voice in my mind to "shut up!"

I focused on the positive. I thought about how far I had come and how much I improved and how at every step along the way, whether it was intentional or not, I had surprised myself. I told myself I deserved to believe that I was capable of doing amazing things. And then… suddenly that board looked a lot less intimidating. And I knew I could break it. And that it was going to be now.

I kicked with everything I had. And it worked. That board never stood a chance.

~Sharon Spungen

A New Stage in Life

*Don't simply retire from something; have
something to retire to.*
~Harry Emerson Fosdick

I was sixty and newly retired from my thirty-seven-year career as a probation officer for Los Angeles County. I was lost and didn't know what to do with myself. A friend told me about classes for seniors at a community program.

The following week, I entered the admissions office, found a stack of class schedules, and started flipping pages. I noticed a Scene Study class under the Theater Arts section. I just assumed that the students sat in their seats and went around the room with each one reading a line or two from a play before discussing and analyzing it. I'd always enjoyed plays and figured I could handle that, so I enrolled.

On the first day, I walked into a stereotypical classroom. Everyone else there seemed to know each other; they had obviously been taking the class for a while. I was the new kid on the block and felt intimidated. Soon after I found a seat, a man approached me.

"You want to read this with me?" he asked, holding out a few sheets of paper.

"Okay," I answered, not understanding what he meant.

He walked up to the front of the room and turned to see if I was following him.

"Come on," he said with a spark of irritation in his voice since I hadn't moved from my chair.

Oh my God! We were supposed to read standing in front of everybody?

I felt like running out, but how could I? During my career, I had worked with murderers, robbers, rapists and the like, the most feared members of society. Nevertheless, I had never conquered the agonizing stage fright that I had first felt when I had to give a book report in front of my class in grammar school.

Slowly, dragging it out as long as I could, I made my way up to the front of the class to join the man who had handed me the script. It was a scene from *Death of a Salesman*, an exceptionally complex play. I had never acted in my life or had any aspirations to do so.

I began to read my lines, not sure if any words would come out. After managing a few sentences in a croaking voice, a strange thing happened to me. I became so engrossed in the role that I completely forgot a roomful of strangers was watching me. When we were finished, everyone dutifully clapped. I looked up and realized where I was and that I was not Willy Loman's wife from the play. What a high. I had done it! I was hooked.

A few weeks later my mother died, and my usually outgoing, charismatic father was depressed and withdrawn.

"Come with me to my acting class, Daddy," I blurted out without even thinking about it. "You can just sit in the back of the room and you don't have to do anything."

It took some convincing, but I finally wore him down. We entered the classroom a few days later and sat in the last row. About midway through the class, the teacher called on my father to come up front and participate in an improv exercise with another student. I was concerned that he wouldn't want to do it, but he stood up and walked jauntily toward the front. While reading, he really seemed to be enjoying himself.

On the way home, Dad wanted to know what time I was picking him up the next week for our class. That began a magical journey for the next three years. We bonded more during those years than we had in the previous sixty.

I soon found that there wasn't any professional material available for an eighty-five-year-old man. I thought of trying to write something, but the only real writing I had ever done was as a probation officer composing reports for judges to assist them in sentencing criminal defendants. I had never done any creative writing. Nevertheless, I had to try.

I wrote humorous dad and daughter scenes where Dad was an irascible old man and Daughter was always tearing her hair out over his antics — not always so far from the truth. We performed our scenes in the acting class showcases twice a year before live audiences. We were the only senior father and daughter team ever in that class, and the audiences adored us.

I was starting to gain more confidence in myself, and my stage fright was slowly dissipating. I networked with other class members and learned that some were auditioning for real acting jobs. I wanted some of that; my thirst for acting was conquering the shy part of my nature.

I arrived at my first audition with much anxiety — another stage fright moment. However, my stronger side was determined and kept me from running out. I survived the experience, and after a few more awkward tries, I got better. I had professional headshots taken. I created a résumé, which was pretty sparse as I had only acted in class.

Soon, I booked my first paid acting job. It was a commercial, and I earned four hundred dollars. I couldn't believe it! Didn't they know I would have done it for free?

Eventually, I got an agent, went on even more auditions, and booked more jobs. I slowly started to feel like a real actress as my résumé began filling up. Of course, I shared it all with Dad, who was living in a nursing home by then. He was experiencing it vicariously through me. We loved to talk about acting whenever we could.

I have now appeared in numerous roles in commercials, television, film, theater, and print. I often work at UCLA Medical School portraying patients for student training. I have played such diverse roles as a granny rapper, a sexy senior, and a trash-talking gangster granny with a machine gun.

The story of my transition from retired probation officer to senior actress has been written about in *Time* magazine, the *Los Angeles Times*, and in a book by Marlo Thomas that profiles women who have reinvented themselves.

I wrote a memoir about my experience, which was published in 2013, entitled *Adventures with Dad: A Father and Daughter's Journey Through a Senior Acting Class.* I'm blogging now with the goal of helping baby boomers and seniors find joy, excitement, and satisfaction in their retirement. I also give public lectures to inspire them to find a passion as a motivation to change their lives just as I did.

~Lee Gale Gruen

Thoughts, Words, and Actions

By doing the work to love ourselves more, I believe we will love each other better.

~Laverne Cox

I sat across from my counselor Christina during my one-on-one session at the outpatient rehab. "You want me to do what?" I asked, incredulous. I had suffered from liver cirrhosis just two months before and had barely escaped alive. Determined to keep my newfound sobriety, I had checked myself into an outpatient rehab to learn about why I was an alcoholic and what demons from my past I could deal with. After spending seven years at the bottom of a vodka bottle, I was going to need all the help I could get.

"I want you to look in the mirror every morning and I want you to repeat your mantra for the day. I am going to give you these Post-its and every morning I want you to write something positive about yourself and say it in the mirror."

I hadn't looked in a mirror in years. Any time I was faced with one I averted my eyes and literally jumped out of the way. My eyes and skin were still yellowed by jaundice. My abdomen was immensely swollen from fluid and I endured daily questions about when I was due. My hair was falling out in clumps due to an iron deficiency, and I still couldn't climb stairs without running out of breath. I was crashing at my mother's house because I had nowhere else to go. I couldn't work.

I was broke. My limbs were so skinny they knocked together at night, waking me up with bruises. She wanted me to do what?

"So after you write it down on your Post-it note, I want you to paste it in your journal so you can see it throughout the day. I will be checking it next week." I started to grumble but she held up her hand. "Just try it. It's an experiment."

I left her office with a stack of Post-it notes. I had promised myself that I was going to try whatever they suggested.

The next morning I stared at my Post-It note, pen in hand. "You are important" came into my head and I jotted it down. Now for the hard part.

I peeked around my bathroom door. The mirror ran pretty much the length of the entire bathroom, so there really was no other option than to face it once you entered. I closed my eyes and walked in, laughing at myself for being so ridiculous, but also recognizing that my heart hurt. I felt so sad that I had come to the point that just looking in the mirror was such a burden. Did I really hate the sight of myself that much?

I forced myself to open my eyes. There I was, skinny limbs, jutting belly, bird bone wrists… I kept looking and told myself, "You… are important… You are im… portant… You are important. You are important. You are important!" By the end I was shouting at myself, shaking my fist at my reflection. I hadn't survived this far to give in to my fear! I needed to face myself.

I proudly posted my proclamation into my journal. I continued to do so every day that week.

I gained sober time, was put on a diuretic for the bloating and slowly began gaining muscle. The Post-it notes gathered in my book. "You are beautiful." "Look at how far you have come." "You are intelligent." "Your feelings are valid." Soon I was looking at my face in the mirror every morning without flinching.

Another part of rehab that filled in quite a bit of the puzzle was PTSD therapy with a local group that offered services for survivors of sexual abuse. All of a sudden I had a name for the terror that I felt, and an opportunity to take control of that fear. The counselor handed me a ball of clay. "I want you to sculpt your future. You're an artist, right?" she asked. I nodded my head. "You have as much control over your future as you have over this ball of clay. Shape it." I sculpted a tiny book for my novel, a Ph.D. graduation cap for my education goals, a small skull for my future shop, a plane for travel and a TV because one day I'd like to have my own travel show.

"Your thoughts become words, and your words become actions," she said, observing what we were creating. "Positive thoughts become positive words and your positive words will become positive actions." I had been talking to myself like I was a piece of trash for decades. No wonder I was where I was.

The next morning I said to myself in the mirror, "I love you. We are going to get back on our feet. We are going to get a job. We are going to find an apartment. I. Love. You." Those thoughts became words and pretty soon after landing a full-time job at a hotel, I got off the wrong stop on the bus. I huffed and lugged my bag off the bus. I still wasn't at full strength and was incredibly annoyed at myself for the added ten-minute walk. I started to curse myself and then stopped. That kind of thinking wasn't going to get me anywhere. Sometimes the best things are found when we get lost. I passed by the street next to the donut shop with all the lovely Victorian row houses, the last ones in Kansas City. I had always wanted to live there, but they never seemed to have a vacancy. Of course, this was the first time I saw a "For Rent" sign, and pretty soon I was living there and paying for it myself.

Actively practicing positive thinking continued to yield results for me. The crippling anxiety that I had lived with for years subsided. I had finally learned how to control the fear that seemed inescapable.

I have been sober for more than two years now, without a single relapse. I have recovered as much as a person can from liver cirrhosis and now lead a normal life, albeit with a lot of doctor checkups and a few prescriptions. And I will never be able to drink again.

That little flicker of optimism has turned into a full-blown lifestyle. Without it, I certainly would not still be here. People ask, "How do you stay so upbeat?" It's not easy. Sometimes I come home and want to sell all my things, live in a yurt in the desert, wear fancy hats and never speak to anyone again. That's okay. I let the emotion roll over me, but I don't let it control my behavior. After a good cry, it's back to planning mode. Happiness is a conscious choice, one that I make every single day. It's a choice that anyone can make. Make it.

~Monique Gabrielle Salazar

Milestone

I ran and ran and ran every day, and I acquired this
sense of determination, this sense of spirit that I would
never, never give up, no matter what else happened.
~Wilma Rudolph

riving to work one morning, I saw a common sight: runners. And, just like all the mornings before, that same little nagging thought jumped into my mind. "I wish that was me."

Only, for some reason, on this particular morning, the thought didn't come and go as quickly as it usually did. It lingered. I found myself not being able to shake it. At one point during the workday I turned to my co-worker and announced, "I think I'm going to start running."

"From what?" she asked.

Wow. Now there was the million-dollar question, wasn't it?

Here's what. I was stressed. My life was chaotic. I was searching for approval and recognition behind every face I saw — every face, that is, except my own. Suddenly, it was as if an epiphany fell out of the sky and landed in my life. It was time to be proud of myself for a change.

So, I started running. That was eight months ago. This past week I hit a new milestone. I ran six miles without stopping.

I'm not the fastest runner. Not at all. And, it was a treadmill run rather than an outside run (which people say is "easier," but I beg to differ). And I know I still have a long way to go before I'm fully ready for the half marathon that I have hesitantly, yet hopefully, signed up for. I know there are more advanced runners looking at my accomplishment with a knowing smile, remembering what it was like way back when they hit a little milestone like this.

But enough of that. Enough trying to downplay what I just did.

Because, let me tell you something. While yes, there may be more advanced runners watching me (while nevertheless cheering me on like I've won the lottery — because that's how we runners roll), there's also someone else watching me.

Last year's version of me.

Oh yeah. That girl was standing outside that gym with her hands cupped around her face looking through the window at me on that treadmill running six miles... and her jaw still hasn't come up off the ground. She's astounded. She would have never dreamed that this could be possible. She couldn't even run from the car to the front door of her house when it was raining outside. So, how on earth could she be looking at this girl who just ran six miles? Six miles! And yes, it took her an hour and four minutes to do it. But holy cow — she just ran for over an hour without stopping. Ran! For over an hour! Hello?

Oh, that chick is proud. Astounded, yes; flabbergasted, definitely; but oh so very proud.

And do you know who else is watching?

Next year's version of me. She's one of those advanced runners I mentioned before. She's watching me with that all-knowing little grin on her face, wishing that I know now what she's going to know then. She wishes I could see that I am working toward such amazing and awesome things that my little mind can't even comprehend them. She wishes that I could know that everything is going to be great — my runs, my life, my heart — all of it. She knows all of that and patiently smiles at me as she waits for me to catch up.

She knows that I've got this in the bag. That no matter how long it takes, I'm going to do whatever I need to do to succeed. She knows that I'm not going to let her down. I've made promises to her that she knows I fully intend to keep.

She knows that I'm going to make it.

Okay. Enough chatter. Time to get back to work.

There's someone in my future waiting for me to make her proud.

~Melissa Edmondson

A Place in the Class

"How does one become a butterfly?" she asked pensively.
"You must want to fly so much that you are willing to
give up being a caterpillar."
~Trina Paulus

"**A**ll these classes are filled," the girl on the other side of the registration counter tells me. I'd anxiously awaited as she, most likely a student herself, ran my course selections through the computer, the course selections I'd spent days working out and had approved by an administrator of the Returning Adult Program.

Now, I stare at her in disbelief. All the classes filled? How can that be? When I'd seen the announcement in the newspaper that the university was offering a special program designed to assist women wishing to return to college I'd wasted no time satisfying all the enrollment requirements. I'd provided all the required documentation and now I was submitting my course schedule well ahead of the published deadline.

"Are you sure?" I mumble. The girl only looks at me. Piteously, I think. I envy her. I envy her confidence. I envy the competent way she uses the computer. I envy the fact that she will likely never stand in a class registration line and be told she can't take the classes she wants to take.

She merely shrugs and nods.

I glance at all the other students milling about. Their nonchalance, their confidence, and their easy familiarity with one another make me feel more out of place than I already am. Why did I ever think I could do this? I want to argue with the girl. But I know she is only doing her job. She signals the next in line and a male student steps forward, unintentionally squeezing me out of line. I stand there a moment, dazed. Then I turn and whirl out of the building.

Once inside my car, I sit in a daze of befuddlement, disappointment mounting, unable to logically connect one thought to another. For more than an hour I stay that way as I watch swirls of dirt, pushed by gusts of intermittent wind, dance down the breezeway separating the parking garage from an adjacent building. I see all my dreams of continuing my education dance away with them.

I think of all the years I'd longed to return to school but couldn't because I worked swing shift in a dirty hot-in-summer, cold-in-winter factory to raise my sons. I think of all my dreams of one day getting a job I was passionate about, proud of, one from which I did not drag home tired to the bone from standing at the end of an assembly line all day. What a fool I'd been to think I could ever be brave enough to accomplish such a thing.

I'd always been a coward when it came to getting out of my comfort zone, trying new things. I let fear of the unknown keep me from doing things I wanted or needed to do in order to better my life. A constant flow of criticism from a mother who probably meant well but was influenced by her own less than nurturing upbringing may have caused those fears. I internalized her remarks as gospel, proclaimed them to be true. I learned a subtle self-censorship. I grew up afraid. I recall standing in front of my high school English class. The English teacher required that students not only write a term paper, but read it aloud in front of the class; our oral presentation would be part of our grade. When my turn came, I froze; as a result, for a term paper that would have earned me an A, I received a B. Years later, I fell into a bad marriage and stayed there longer than I should have because I wasn't brave enough to leave. Only when my husband tired of me and our sons and left of his own accord did I file for divorce.

And now, here I am, recently unemployed (the factory where I worked had closed its doors) and in my early forties. I'd read that there is no such thing as failure. You cannot fail; you can only produce results. What results had I achieved by attempting to return to school?

Another hour passes. As I continue my brooding, I watch processions of students troop out of the registration building. I find myself wishing I could go and be with them in their world, share, if only vicariously, in their times, but in the same instant I know that I never will.

Suddenly, something sparks inside me. If the education I had always longed for, had always dreamed about, was going to wash away, I would go down with the decks awash and the guns blazing.

I grab my schedule and march back to the registration building. There is a hallway just beyond the registration counter. I walk down it, not having a clue as to what I'm looking for. When I come to a door with "Registration Assistance" written on it, however, I gather my courage and knock. From behind the door a woman's voice hollers me in.

When I enter, the woman behind the desk raises an eyebrow. She looks slightly perturbed, but asks politely if she can help me. I straighten my shoulders. My little act of bravery might not be momentous to others — unlike a fireman I wasn't about to run into a burning building — but it's momentous for me.

I hand her my schedule and blurt out how I'd been told that all the classes I wish to take are filled. She looks at my schedule, then peers at me over the rim of her glasses. She holds still as a camera for a second, then, rising from her chair, says, "Come with me." I follow her back down the hall to the registration room where she walks brusquely to the head of the line. In a low motherly tone she explains to the girl something about a returning adult program… priority is to be given… She instructs the girl to adjust my schedule, beams a smile at her (and me), and disappears. The girl taps on her computer keys a moment, hands back my schedule, and tells me I'm all set.

I start to exit the building, then stop. There is one more thing I must do. I find my way back down the hallway to the Registration Assistance room and knock again. When, a woman's voice beckons me in, I open the door slightly and stick my head inside. "Thank you," I say. And then I leave, in order to go and be with the others.

~Barbara Weddle

Taking Aim at Excuses

The most powerful weapon on earth is
the human soul on fire.
~Ferdinand Foch

've always been an active person — I like doing stuff. But daily writing sessions and getting lost in a good book are necessary for maintaining balance in my life, too — sometimes I just need a little downtime to feed my inner-hermit self. Being a mother to two boys while working outside the home full-time keeps me busy, so I haven't had much chance to do those extracurricular activities. My family has always come first — their activities, their social life, their needs — and I wouldn't have it any other way. There will be time for my own interests later.

Over the years, however, I have contemplated different activities I would like to try when everyone leaves the nest someday. But I have a chronically finicky back so sticking to something safe like early-morning power walks for weight management, stress relief and overall wellbeing seemed like my best option.

But one dark morning during my walk I tripped and fell. I broke my arm, but that was the least of my worries. I had already had hernia surgery ten years before, and the fall all but destroyed my already compromised abdominal wall. I required two extensive hernia-repair surgeries over two years. This was no fun for a busy momma! Unfortunately, I was left with certain physical limitations. After the last surgery my doctor told me to live life to the fullest, but not to do things that would be overly strenuous for my abdominal muscles.

As I recovered from that last surgery, I wallowed in despair over all the things I would never get to do that I had wanted to try, like canoeing. But while wallowing is part of life sometimes, moderation is key. I dwelled so much on all the things I would never do that I lost perspective. I was still very healthy; I didn't have a disease and all my limbs were intact. Life really was not that bad, but still I wallowed.

I eventually got back on my feet and got on with things. Recovery was slow going, and two years later if I do too much I still get little "warnings" from various body parts. Yet I do what I can, when I can, how I can. I have always had a positive, move-forward attitude, and even though I got on with life, in the back of my mind I was still pining for lost experiences. I was so focused on what I couldn't do I didn't see what I could do was right in front of me all along.

My fourteen-year-old son, Matthew, excels in the sport of archery (target archery as opposed to bow hunting), and is involved with the Victoria Bowmen Archery Club. Over four years I have watched him work his way up from newbie to assistant coach to championship winner — truly commendable for a kid his age. I loved watching him and I had learned quite a bit about the sport. I had never tried his bow; archery was his thing and I didn't want to get in the way. And besides, his muscle strength far surpassed mine; his bow was too heavy and the string too taut for a muscle-lacking mother like me. I was sure my compromised body would never allow for such challenging equipment, anyway.

Excuses.

Other archery parents would often ask if I also did archery. I would chuckle and scoff, "Who me? I can't do that! Can you imagine?"

Yet the more times I brushed it off, the more I began to wonder. Could I? Did I dare? I'm not a sporty person; I'm a creative person. I was a dancer in my past life, now preferring hikes in the woods, early-morning walks, reading, writing and knitting (safer activities). My bad back, never mind my abdomen, would never allow me to do anything strenuous like pulling back a bowstring. Those bows can be tough.

However, the more I watched the more I wondered.

Then during one of my son's practices the coaches had a "fun day" and enthusiastically encouraged the typically sedentary parents to pick up a bow.

Before I knew what I was doing I was hopping around on the sidelines at the archery range. "Pick me! Pick *me!*"

Next thing I knew, I had a bow in my hand — one of the lighter ones, suitable for a newbie like me — and with the help of ever-patient Coach Bradley, I shot my first arrow.

And it hit the target.

I got 6 points out of a possible 10.

And then I shot another.

And another. And then another.

And that was it.

I loved it.

When time permitted, I would borrow a lighter bow from my son's archery club and practice on the closer, bigger targets while staying out of the way of the professionals. The more I did it, the more I realized I could do it. The following Christmas my family of three men pooled their money and bought me my own bow. It's taken some getting used to but I think I have found my thing. I am building up my arm muscles, and my stomach and back are adjusting without incident. I still watch my son's practices — he comes first — but I also go and shoot with him as well as attending my own "ladies only" shoot every few weeks with the Victoria Bowmen Archery Club.

I realize that not only will my body not suffer from this new adventure, but neither will my family — in fact, my husband has taken up the sport and my other son has tried it a few times as well! It's still too early to tell, but I think in some little way the sport has brought my family closer. I can practice at the same time as my son, but with everyone getting older and involved in their own things without me, I can now take a little time for myself — and that's okay, too.

I never imagined something like archery would be possible for me. I guess being faced with the concept of "limitations" propelled me forward. No more excuses, no more fears, and no more inhibitions. I just had to take aim and shoot — and find my way.

~Lisa McManus Lange

My Bike Tour Adventures

I have accepted fear as a part of life — specifically the
fear of change. I have gone ahead despite the pounding
in the heart that says: turn back.
~Erica Jon

When I was told that my maternal grandmother, Evelyn, was diagnosed with a brain tumor and had only six months to live I was devastated. When I was called only weeks later and told to fly to Illinois immediately to see her, I felt my world fall apart.

I spent her last days with her painting her nails, rubbing lotion into her skin and listening to her talk. She spoke of the power and importance of strong friendships, giving me advice that would change my life: "Be happy. That's all that matters."

After my grandmother died I felt empty. As a live-in nanny in New York, despite the fact that I loved the girls I cared for, I felt trapped. I felt like I couldn't do anything right or be who I truly wanted to be. My life revolved around materialism, paychecks, new clothes and drinking every weekend. I questioned how to be happy; I needed a change, but what? I discussed this many times with Kerry, my best friend. Many times I'd say, "I wish I could just bike off into the sunset!" One day, Kerry replied with, "Well, why don't you just do it?"

I began researching bike touring and realized that many people do it! I decided to get a bike and ride off into the sunset. In biking, I'd find happiness, I'd travel, and I'd be free. My grandma always encouraged us to travel. I was going to tour alone and I would find me. I knew it was going to be amazing.

Many of my friends were supportive. My family took some time to come around, but once they understood my reasons they became my champions as well. Some people would never understand and I had to accept that.

In February 2014, after eight months of planning, I sold everything, left my job, and flew to Austin, Texas — my starting point. I had my bicycle, dubbed Evelyn, and the supplies needed for my tour: tent, sleeping bag, foodstuffs, and clothing. In total, my bike plus supplies weighed 200 pounds.

Wheezing up the hills of Texas Hill Country, I questioned every day just what I had gotten myself into. I had definitely found adventure! I learned immediately to throw my plans by the wayside — there was no way I could plan how far I was going to go or where I was going to stay. Every day was different; I never knew what it would bring, whom I would meet, if I would be blown over or chased by dogs. At night I would hunt for a secret camping spot and if none were to be found I would ask farmers if I could camp on their land. When they heard my story most people were more than willing to go out of their way to help, like bringing me little snacks, buying me lunch or dinner and sharing their stories.

I found myself meeting people from all walks of life and connecting with souls I would never have interacted with otherwise. One man sold his horse sixty years ago to buy his wife's engagement ring. Another picked me up when I needed a ride because the winds were forty to fifty miles per hour. We spent a whole day at a museum, had lunch, and he turned out to be an accomplished gospel singer! I was given a Chinese lantern and made a wish as it floated into the night.

After leaving Lubbock, Texas, things were flat for a while... until central New Mexico, where I hit mountains for the first time. That was hard and brought new challenges, but I was still free. I was living my dream!

I biked alone for 1,983 miles through four states: Texas, New Mexico, Arizona and California. I saw miles of desert and fields. I camped behind abandoned schools and saw snow-capped mountains in the distance. I woke up to the sound of hail hitting my roof. I ate frozen Clif Bars and wore all my clothes at once to keep from shivering all night. I got sunburned when I ran out of sunscreen, learned not to lick my lips when they split from the wind, and cheered out loud whenever I went down a hill. I learned extreme budgeting and spent only five dollars a day — or less!

I sang every song on my iPod at the top of my lungs and called out cheerful hellos to cows in fields. Snuggled in my sleeping bag I watched the sunsets, followed by the moon shining calmly on me and more stars than I had ever seen in my life. I hiked in Redwoods, took an impromptu ride to Mexico and back with some friendly old men, and felt the power of the Pacific Ocean waves. I climbed mesas, camped in the desert heat listening to coyotes sing, slept in the woods with bears, saw wild horses run past my tent, rolled down mountains at forty miles per hour, swam in canals and befriended ducks, and biked away from a dangerous host one night.

I felt my grandmother's presence throughout much of my trip: certain situations could have gone much worse than they did and when, seemingly, miracles would happen, I knew my grandma had a hand in that. All the way from Texas I saw signs saying I wouldn't see Saguaro cacti because they're only found in the Phoenix area. Rolling down a canyon road and seeing my first Saguaro cactus on a cliff side a hundred feet over my head was unlike anything I'd experienced thus far. It was a feeling of accomplishment so profound that I sobbed on the side of the road. "Look how far I've traveled, Grandma. Look what I am doing. You are my inspiration and I do it in your memory!"

Upon arriving in San Francisco I realized I was down to $200. I needed to find work. I landed an incredible job in Arizona starting immediately. I flew to Phoenix to do work that I love. Every morning I wake up and see cacti and little quail families scurrying around together and mountains outside my window! Every night the sky looks like it's on fire. Again I see my grandmother's work. I love it here and am so happy!

In letting go of my power and plans, and opening myself up to all things new, I've found a way to bring joy into my life everywhere I go. It is so important to let yourself experience the things that make you happy. Don't compromise on things that don't bring you joy. When people warn you against doing something because it's "not done" or that so many dangerous things could happen, ask yourself: Will you feed the fear and let others' judgment keep you from living your life to the fullest? I feel like I can breathe again, and continue to learn who I am meant to be. My adventures are far from over.

~Maria Dorsey

Loving My Inner Child

You yourself, as much as anybody in the entire
universe, deserve your love and affection.
~Buddha

A friend brought clothes over to my house. "I was cleaning out my closet and thought you could use these clothes."

"Thanks," I said. After she left, I searched through the bag. The clothes were clean, but faded, and the wrong size for me. I kept a couple of shirts that kind of fit, and donated the rest.

It wasn't long before yet another friend came over. "I have too many clothes," she said. "I thought you might need them."

Again I gracefully accepted them. Again, most were too big, but I kept some more shirts.

A couple months later, another friend showed up. "I lost weight and had to buy a new wardrobe. I thought these might fit you."

"Thanks," I said. My reflection in the mirror showed I had gained some weight. Did my friend think I was fat?

My friends were good people. But why were they always giving me their used clothes? I looked in the mirror at my typical outfit of jeans and an old shirt. I rarely ever bought myself anything new.

My priority was always my four children. I would give up everything so they could have voice lessons, dance lessons and money for a school trip. But me — I was their mom. That was my identity. I was the one who sacrificed, who took care of everyone else but me.

On a typical day I would berate myself. "I am so ugly and fat. I can't do anything right. I am a big nothing." These words ran through my head in a constant, negative tape that would never stop playing.

"No one loves me. Life stinks. I never have enough money. No one cares." I was a victim in life. I was a martyr. I was the one who sacrificed for everyone else so that my children could succeed. That was my job, wasn't it? Isn't that what moms were supposed to do, put themselves last? Moms were the ones who took the smallest piece of meat at the table and ate the ruined egg for breakfast. Moms were the ones who cleaned up the messes in life. Moms were the ones who told their children they could do amazing things. It was wonderful to watch your family living their dreams. So why wasn't I happy?

Because of me, my children excelled. Because of my sacrifices, the household ran smoothly. Yet, why wasn't I content?

Why, when I vented to my friends about how much I sacrificed, did they suddenly go silent and have to hang up the phone to answer the door? One by one, people began to get too busy to listen to me complain. I was a victim in life, and I desperately craved attention and validation for my martyrdom. Didn't the Bible say to love others more than yourself?

Then one day it dawned on me. It didn't. The Bible said to love others *as* yourself. I realized this one day and it floored me when the sad truth was revealed. I loved my family a lot, but I didn't love me. I constantly berated myself and said horrible things to myself that I would never dream of saying to anyone else.

One day I looked at my reflection. I thought of the little girl inside me who once had dreams of her own. I never did anything for her, not even setting aside a few dollars to buy her a new outfit. The cruel things I said to her on a daily basis were appalling. I would never dream of giving her singing lessons or sending her to a good college. I had given up on this little girl a long time ago. She felt sad and unloved.

It was then I realized I could change things. I had the power to change my life completely. Nothing was stopping me except for my biggest obstacle — me. My children were grown and happy and didn't need my constant fussing over them anymore.

I started loving the little girl inside me as much as I loved my own children. I stopped saying mean things to her. I looked at my reflection and said all the inspiring and nice things to me that I had said to my own confident children.

I changed "You're ugly" into "You're beautiful." I changed "Nothing good ever happens to me" to "Great things happen to me." I changed "I never win anything" into "I am a winner." I changed "I never have enough money" to "I have more money than I could ever need." I changed "I can't" to "I can." In the beginning it felt forced and fake, but after a while, as I kept repeating these new affirmations to myself, it became easy.

Miracles began happening. I faced my fears and chased after my dreams. I allowed myself to further my education, to work at losing weight, to pursue my career goals, and to buy myself some new outfits, without guilt. Soon, I was managing money better and rebuilding my life. Whenever I reached out to do something for myself, I found the resources to do it. Obstacles disappeared. It was amazing.

I stopped complaining about life, and soon my friends didn't mind talking to me again. Some of them actually looked forward to my phone calls. One of my friends gave me the highest compliment. She said I inspired her. Some of my fondest dreams were realized. When I graduated college in my forties, my children were proud of me. My success inspired my daughters even more.

And then, one day, I noticed that people weren't offering me their hand-me-downs anymore. They asked me where I bought the pretty dress I was wearing. The little girl inside me smiled. I was finally taking care of her too.

~L.A. Strucke

Think
Possible

Getting on with Life

All Things Possible

To forgive is to set a prisoner free and
discover the prisoner was you.
~Author Unknown

was sitting on my front porch on a beautiful, warm spring day. My life was about to change in a radical and traumatic way. I was flanked by two homicide detectives who delivered unwelcome news in a matter-of-fact fashion. They informed me that my brother Dave had been killed by police to put an end to his shooting rampage at a shopping mall just a few minutes drive from my home.

Even though I wasn't completely surprised, I felt like I had been dropkicked to another planet. The officers were asking me questions and my brain didn't want to work. I asked them to give me a moment, closed my eyes, and simply prayed, "Lord, help me get through this." Then I opened my eyes and calmly gave them the answers they were seeking in order to piece together the awful story.

Dave's life had been coming unwound for several years. It included a job-related back injury, addiction to painkillers, alcoholism and subsequent job loss, along with the traumatic removal of our mother from the home he shared with her due to her advancing Alzheimer's disease. He began isolating himself, not paying bills and, at one point, essentially camping in his house after the utilities were shut off. Then he ran out of food and alcohol.

I tried to help him; I got him food and turned his utilities back on and drove him around for job interviews, all the while believing that he would spend his first paycheck on alcohol anyway. He got a job as a security guard at a store in the mall where he ultimately did the shooting. As I feared, his drinking resumed after the first paycheck. I tried to talk to him about it, but as soon as he realized where I was heading, he became explosively angry. This is when I became aware of just how mentally compromised and potentially dangerous he was.

I did all sorts of things in preparation, in case Dave reached out for the kind of help he really needed. I went to Al-Anon meetings, researched treatment centers, read books on how to help alcoholics recover and even talked with recovering alcoholics at my church.

I came to realize that I was safe with Dave only when he hadn't been drinking. For my own safety I had to stay away from him when there was any possibility he was under the influence of alcohol, as it turned him mean, menacing and volatile.

I started sleeping with my head at the foot of the bed, concerned that he might try to shoot me through my bedroom window. I reasoned, "better my feet than my head."

I was anticipating him acting out against me but certainly didn't foresee what he actually did. Even so, I knew immediately why he went to the mall, guns blazing; he was committing suicide by policeman's bullet.

I answered the officer's questions; they took all the information and left. And I was left with an avalanche of thoughts, emotions, confusion and work to do. David's disease had cost four lives, including his own. One thing I knew — somehow, someway it had to be possible for something good to come of this.

The next afternoon, I stood in front of my church in the shadow of the steel cross with my pastor, my daughter and son-in-law by my side. I was facing a huge bank of microphones and an equally huge group of reporters with cameras. I spoke of Dave's condition and I offered condolences and an apology; I knew that it would do little to ease the pain, but I felt compelled to do at least that.

The mother of a young woman killed that day was watching the press conference and, somehow, it started some healing in her. Several months later she called my pastor and requested a meeting with me. We met in the pastor's office, hugged, cried, talked and ended up going to the site of the shooting together. In an ocean of cars in the mall lot, the space where Carolee's daughter, Leslie, drew her last breath was empty. We moved into that place and stood there holding each other, crying.

Later, over coffee, I heard the same determined sentiment from Carolee that I had uttered. It had to be possible to make something good come of this.

Over the weeks following our meeting we experienced a comforting, growing friendship. We started brainstorming about what we could do but nothing really jelled right away. Then it started coming together. We began getting requests to speak about the power of forgiveness. We weren't at all sure this was possible for us at first. Surely God could find some other good to bring forth from the tragedy. Neither of us was experienced at public speaking, but God kept bringing forth the opportunities and we couldn't refuse to share our testimony. It started small, with just the two of us and a TV reporter and cameraman in the comfort of my home. Then it moved to speaking before various groups at my church, which Carolee had started attending with me. The size of the groups grew larger and so did our confidence. Then one day we were guests on a live radio show.

When the mother of a slain daughter and the sister of the killer stood together and spoke of the importance and power of forgiveness, it had an impact. In the process of sharing our pain and efforts to heal, Carolee and I grew to a place of peace and joy together.

In addition to speaking on healing and forgiveness with Carolee, I've been blessed with an additional opportunity to share about God's healing after trauma. I've been leading the grief recovery ministry at my church and at a residential rescue mission. I continue to see the turnaround God brings forth through the mourning of the loss and the forgiving. I get to see people moving back to a place of joy.

I have learned many "impossible" things are, indeed, possible.

~Kathryn D. Cagg

Good Things from Tragedy?

*Things turn out best for people who make the best out
of the way things turn out.*

~John Wooden

The phone rang at 10:30 that Sunday night, just as I was getting ready for bed. I glanced at the caller ID. KCPD — Kansas City Police Dept. I immediately thought of my daughter Leslie. The policeman identified himself and said he wanted to come see me. I asked several times, my heart pounding harder each time: "Is this about my daughter? Did something happen to Leslie?" He would not answer me. He only asked if I was alone and then told me to call someone to be with me and he would be there in twenty minutes.

I called my son Dwight, who lived just a few minutes away, and then I dressed and paced around, picking up and putting things away like it mattered, and going over and over in my mind the possible reasons for this visit. My heart was pounding and my head throbbing the entire time. There was only one thing it could be... Leslie was killed in a car accident. I was praying to God that I was wrong. This was a mother's worst nightmare. Dwight arrived and we sat holding hands while we waited for the police officer. He was as terrified as I was that something awful had happened to his younger sister.

Earlier that day, as I was busy packing for a move, I turned on the TV and saw there had been a shooting rampage at a Kansas City shopping mall. My first thought was of Leslie, my beautiful thirty-three-year-old daughter who lived near there. Like moms do, I wondered where she might be at the moment. I didn't dwell on the thought since I didn't think she would have been at that mall.

I watched as they told of a desperate man who had stolen a rifle from his neighbor after beating her to death, then stolen her car and set out to kill others in his apparent desire to have his own life ended. He pulled into the parking lot of the mall. He parked and got out of the car, then shot and killed a young man and a young woman who were still in their cars, shot out some store windows, and then went inside the mall. Several other people were injured and many were terrorized before a policeman arrived on the scene and killed him. This was a shocking, horrible event, especially since it was so close to home, but it was something I had certainly heard of before. I switched off the TV and went back to my packing.

When the detective sitting across from me in my living room asked if I had heard about the shootings at Ward Parkway Mall, I told him that I had. He said, "Your daughter was one of the victims." I didn't believe him. I asked, "Are you sure? What was her name?" They had to prove it to me. They had found my phone number in her cellphone under "Mom." There could be no doubt. Leslie was the young woman so brutally shot and killed that day. I remember I was gripping the arms of the chair I sat in and I collapsed back into the chair. I was too stunned to speak. I was barely capable of breathing. The detectives talked about what we should do the next day and then left. Just like that my whole life, and that of my family, was turned completely upside down, never to be the same again.

Dwight went home to his kids and I went to bed. I stared at the ceiling all night. I couldn't believe what had just happened. I couldn't pray. I couldn't even cry. But even then, I was already thinking, "Is it possible that anything good could come from the senseless murder of my child?" That would be my determined hope and desire from that day forward.

My older daughter, Audrey, flew in the next day from London where she was living at the time. Our family and friends, especially Leslie's friends, surrounded us and took care of everything. The celebration of Leslie's life was moving and perfect in the overflowing church. She was loved by every person who knew her and she had lived a full and exciting life in her short years on earth.

A couple of weeks later the awful tasks of sorting and moving Leslie's things and moving my belongings to my new home were over. With the funeral and confusion settling down, I was finally able to break through the fog I had been in. I cried and prayed and became more determined to find something good in the aftereffects of the destruction of my daughter's life. I decided to start by forgiving the man who had done this, if only for my own sake. I didn't want to live a life filled with anger and bitterness.

Right after the incident, I saw the sister of the shooter on a television newscast. She was standing in front of her church with her children, her pastor by her side, and a bank of microphones in front of her. Tears were streaming down her face as she expressed her sorrow for what her brother had done and sympathy for all the people whose lives had been so terribly affected that day. She was so sincere. I knew that I would need to meet her as soon as I felt ready. About three months later I contacted her pastor and asked if he thought Kathy would like to meet me.

Kathy was eager to meet me, too, so we soon got together in the pastor's office. We hugged each other and cried. I told her I had forgiven her brother for what he did. We felt an instant bond and talked for hours. We drove to the spot in the shopping center where the shooting had happened and hugged and cried some more. It was a huge step toward healing for both of us. We knew God expected forgiveness of us and had brought us together for that purpose.

Kathy and I were given opportunities to stand together and tell our story on television news in Kansas City, a radio program, and several groups at church. Kathy has since become the leader of a successful grief recovery group as well.

That Sunday night in April 2007, I could not imagine ever feeling whole again. My heart was broken. But though my life has changed so much, in some ways it is better. Many new friends are now part of my life. Old friendships are deeper and stronger. I have become a more loving and caring person. Our family now has a tighter bond because of our shared grief, and I have grown tremendously in my relationship with God. So, yes, some good things have come out of a devastating event.

As life goes on I'm sure there will be more trials but just as many possibilities for good.

~Carolee Noble

A Scar Is Born

Scars are just another kind of memory.
~M.L. Stedman, The Light Between Oceans

They followed me like a pack of wolves hunting for prey under the moonlight. As it turns out it wasn't nighttime and it wasn't a pack of wolves. It was just three kids who looked to be about seven years old. I was a kid myself and I had just turned twelve. These kids were practically stalking me in the bright sunshine of a brilliant June day. It was summer vacation and I was trying to enjoy a day at the swimming pool.

I wanted to splash with my friends, speed down the water slide and jump off the diving boards without any worries or hassles. The possibility of that happening was being hindered by these three kids who continued to follow me around. You may be asking yourself what was so interesting to them.

It seems these kids were enthralled by two large and rather gruesome scars that I had received courtesy of my heart surgeon at Nationwide Children's Hospital in Columbus, Ohio. The scars made a lower case letter T across my upper and lower chest. The scars were less than a year old so they were still various shades of purple, red and blue. They were jagged and long because back in those days surgeons had to be more invasive when they cut into you. The surgeons had not only saved my life, they had made me into a novelty

As the kids followed me and gawked and whispered, I felt like a circus sideshow. I was embarrassed and thought maybe I should go and put on a T-shirt. I didn't really want to wear a shirt at the swimming pool as it was fairly warm out and also once those shirts get wet they cling to you like plastic wrap clings to meat.

So I tried to lose the kids. A couple of times they lost track of me, but they always found me. It was useless. I had a fan club.

Finally, one of them got up the nerve to ask me, "What happened to you"? I could have told the truth and tried to explain the intricacies of open-heart surgery to three seven-year-olds. I could have told them it was none of their business and to leave me alone. But they would have walked away disappointed and I thought maybe I should make this scar thing a bit more interesting for them and myself.

So I blurted out something really outrageous. Something I knew would grab their attention. I told them that I had been attacked by a shark. This was just weeks after the movie *Jaws* had come out. Sharks were on the minds of everyone across America. To be a shark attack survivor sounded way cooler than to be a heart surgery survivor. The three kids agreed. Their jaws (no pun intended) dropped. One kid uttered, "Wow!" The other two looked at me like I was some type of superhero.

I proceeded to make up an entire story about how I was attacked on vacation, fought off the shark and had to be rushed to the hospital. I told them I barely survived and was on the news. I even capped off the story by telling them I had one of the shark's teeth on my dresser at home. The kids ate it up and told me how lucky and brave I was. Then I watched as they rushed over to their mothers and pointed to me and explained about my shark attack.

Until that day at the pool I had looked upon my scars as embarrassing. After all, when my family and friends first saw them they cringed. Scars are pretty ugly. You usually see them in horror movies or hospital dramas and your first reaction is to turn away. No one wishes for scars, but sometimes they are a fact of life. On that day I took lemons and made them into lemonade. To those three seven-year-olds, I went from freak show to superhero and it was great!

After that I used my scars in all types of situations. I got out of long distance running and strenuous activities in gym class by showing my scars to Physical Education teachers. I won bets by daring others to show a larger scar than mine. I asked girls if they wanted to see or touch my scars. Then I told them about all of the emotional and physical trauma I went through during my heart surgery and hospital stay. They ate it up and felt sorry for me. It created an immediate connection.

People have asked me if I would have my scars removed if it were possible. I think about it briefly and then I say "no." My scars are about survival. They are a reminder of how I fought a battle for life and won. They remind me of kids I met in the hospital who were not as lucky as me and who died. Though I knew some of these kids only briefly, I will remember them always and cherish our brief connection. The scars remind me of all the doctors and nurses who cared for me and how miraculous science and medicine can be.

Scars are a part of life. Some scars are physical and transparent; others are emotional and hidden. We all have scars of some sort. My scars are smaller now; they are faded and less gruesome. They do not attract as much attention but they remain. Some days after showering I look in the mirror and see those scars and think what life would have been like without them. Then I remember that it is because of them that I have life.

~David Warren

71

Turning Tragedy into Triumph

Breathe. Listen for my footfall in your heart. I am not
gone but merely walk within you.
~Nicholas Evans

t was the day after his funeral. I was sitting on a couch in a darkened living room that precisely mirrored my mood. Gloomily surveying the wreckage of what was once a beautiful life and paralyzed by the thought of facing the future without him, his words echoed within my grief-stricken heart: "Take our family's experience and use it for good by helping others."

All I could think was, "I can't even help myself or our daughter. How am I supposed to help anyone else?"

A bigger-than-life man who filled a room just by entering it, Mike and I were best friends for almost fifteen years before we married. Ours was not a conventional marriage. His work as an undercover narcotics investigator meant that he was often working more than he was home. However, we always took advantage of the time that we had together and had an enormous amount of fun — both as a couple and a family. We worked hard, we played hard, we chased our young daughter from one activity to another. In short, we absolutely loved the life that we had created.

Then in what seemed like the blink of an eye, the life that we had so carefully crafted came to a screeching halt when Mike was diagnosed with ALS (Lou Gehrig's disease). Although the doctor followed his heartbreaking diagnosis by gamely attempting optimism, we all knew what this devastating news meant: Mike was going to die and it was going to be sooner, rather than later.

Mike's illness progressed rapidly. Only one year after the symptoms first appeared, he lost the use of his arms and hands. Six months later, he was in a wheelchair. The disease then viciously attacked his respiratory system. Shortly thereafter, he required a feeding tube.

One evening, Mike and I were discussing the sort of things that no couple wants to discuss. One of his most emphatic wishes was that after he was gone he wanted me to "take our family's experience and use it for good by helping others."

I had no idea what he meant, let alone how to fulfill such a wish. How on earth could this experience — watching my husband die bit by bit — be used in any way for the "good" of anyone else?

Two months after our discussion, in the midst of what should have been a beautiful holiday season, Mike passed away peacefully at home, surrounded by his loved ones.

I quickly realized that while it was tempting, crawling into a metaphorical black hole was not the answer. A perpetual state of mourning was not what Mike wanted for us and it was not the behavior that I wished to model for my daughter. I wanted her to see that life could knock us down, but that we did not have to stay down. She needed to understand that while we could not control the circumstances that took her daddy away, we could control our reactions to those circumstances and actually design a life for ourselves. Most of all, I decided that remaining in mourning forever was not going to be my destiny.

My Healing Journey had begun.

My daughter went back to school and I returned to work, only to receive word that my father had been hospitalized. He was diagnosed with terminal liver cancer and died nine weeks later. In a time span of only four months, I had lost the two most important men in my life. The grief was so overwhelming, it felt insurmountable.

Deeply grieving but determined nonetheless, I again picked myself up and resumed my Healing Journey.

Time passed. I endured and survived the "firsts" that everyone faces after the death of a loved one — the first birthdays, anniversaries, holidays and so forth. I helped my daughter with her grieving and rebuilding processes. Later, I learned how to go out and enjoy myself on my own. I rebuilt my business to its former success. We moved into a new home. Slowly but surely, I was getting to know the post-tragedy woman I had become.

Five years after Mike passed away, I was marveling at how far we had come in our recovery. I found myself thinking about how little there was in the way of guidance or support for the bereaved. I had read many books on the subject of loss and, while they were terrific, none had provided any solid, practical advice. No one was answering questions about things like post-loss dating and love, handling financial and legal matters, helping a grieving child, coping with not-so-supportive people — and much more.

I grabbed a pen and began making notes. When I finished, I had written what eventually became the Table of Contents for my first book. But in the process, something even bigger had occurred. I had discovered my new purpose.

Another journey had just begun.

Of course, naysayers and negativity abounded. While confident in my skills as a writer and with the subject matter, I was still an unknown author who had chosen to write in one of the least popular genres in the marketplace. After all, who really wants to talk about grief and bereavement? However, rather than give in to the negativity, I remained focused on the millions of people sitting in darkened living rooms while surrounded by their own particular life wreckages, each convinced that they were alone in their misery. It was time to fulfill Mike's wish.

One year after scribbling notes onto a legal pad, I founded Widows Wear Stilettos. It was one of the first online support organizations of its kind and welcomed widows of all ages and walks of life. Three years later, *Widows Wear Stilettos* was published and two more books, *Happily Even After* and *When Bad Things Happen to Good Women*, have followed. I continue teaching those who have been touched by life-challenging situations to find their own triumph-after-tragedy paths to healing.

While tragedy will shape you, it does not have to define you. It remains my goal to help others in need on their healing journeys and teach as many as possible that there is indeed triumph after tragedy. While yours may not be the life that you originally anticipated, it is a life that you are entitled to lead in happiness, in abundance and most importantly, in peace.

"Take our family's experience and use it for good by helping others." I pray that I am doing just that… and I like to believe that somewhere, Mike is smiling.

~Carole Brody Fleet

72

Learning My Worth

Never be bullied into silence. Never allow yourself to be made a victim. Accept no one's definition of your life, but define yourself.
~Harvey Fierstein

I was pushed out of the car in my high school parking lot late on Monday morning. Crying, I stumbled my way into the building. I didn't have my things and my clothes were torn and bloodied. At this point, I was too relieved that the worst weekend of my life was over to feel embarrassed.

As I staggered in, I realized the main foyer was empty. My heart sank until I turned a corner and a teacher saw me. She looked horrified as she ran over to me. I collapsed into her arms and cried tears of joy and shame. At eighteen years old, I felt like a helpless child. How could I have let someone do this to me? Why me? I was so relieved that it was over but at the same time I was devastated because I knew this was the end of my relationship with my boyfriend.

I was brought into the principal's office while the police and my mother were called. My poor mother thought I had gone away for a nice weekend with my boyfriend. What she didn't know was that my phone was taken from me and I was locked in an attic where I couldn't call anyone and no one could hear my screams. When my mother and my favorite teacher arrived, I told them the entire story through choking sobs. I was so humiliated. I thought it was all my fault.

I was taken to the police station to file a report and request a restraining order, which was granted that day. These were the first steps into my new life, and I wasn't sure how I felt about it. I was at war with myself. I scolded myself for missing him.

After telling detectives the gruesome details of what happened that weekend, I never had to speak a word of it again. He went to jail and I was free of him. I spent months trying to heal from the pain that someone I loved so dearly could hurt me so much. I tried not to wonder how he was doing or how he was feeling. Did he regret what he did to me? Did he miss me?

A year later, I got a phone call from a blocked number.

"Hi, Shay, how are you?"

I froze. It was him. I hung up and regretted it instantly. All those months of wondering how he was and whether he missed me or regretted hurting me… I could've just found out and I had lost my chance. But the phone rang again. This time, I answered it and calmly talked to him. He told me how sorry he was and that he'd regretted his mistake ever since. He told me he was going to therapy and that he was a different person. He'd never hurt a fly now.

He asked to see me and apprehensively, I said yes. I was going to meet him at the park halfway between our two homes. When I hung up the phone, I was so excited. My inner conscience tried to yell at me, but my emotions took over and I ignored what I knew was right. I drove down to the park and I was literally shaking with excitement as I exited the car. I saw him sitting on the rock wall and he jumped down and began approaching when he saw me pull up.

As I reached him, I realized how ugly he was. He smiled at me with his stupid smile and I gave him a fake smile in return. He held his arms out for a hug and as I hugged him back, I wanted to throw up. I didn't miss this man. I hated this man for what he did to me. What had I been thinking?

I told him I needed to go and he forcefully grabbed my arm and said, "No, you don't." I turned and looked him directly in the eyes and said, "Don't you ever touch me again," and I yanked my arm from his grip and ran to my car. He stood in shock as I drove away. That day, I changed my phone number and I finally cut all ties with him.

In my mind, our relationship wasn't over until that very day. When I drove away and saw him in the rearview mirror, I realized who I really was. I had wasted a year missing a man who didn't care about me. Somehow, seeing his face made me realize I was worth a whole lot more as a person.

Six years have passed and in this time I've learned to forgive him. His poor actions were a result of his own personal suffering. Although I haven't spoken to him in all these years, I do hope that he's found a ray of hope within himself and never feels the need to hurt anyone again.

I have also learned to forgive myself for allowing the treatment that I endured in that relationship. In some crazy way that I'll never understand, I once thought I needed him. Now I know that all I need is to love and respect myself and to be surrounded by those who treat me as I deserve.

~Shaylene McPhee

73

A Message at Stake

Not everything that is faced can be changed, but
nothing can be changed until it is faced.
~James Baldwin

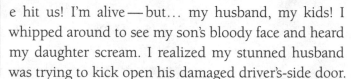

He hit us! I'm alive — but… my husband, my kids! I whipped around to see my son's bloody face and heard my daughter scream. I realized my stunned husband was trying to kick open his damaged driver's-side door. Outside, rain blurred the dark night. The driver whose SUV smashed into our compact car had stopped his vehicle across the road, and was running toward us.

Moments before, seeing headlights coming at us, I'd screamed, "Watch out!" My husband swung right, hoping to avert a head-on collision. But we were still hit, our car destroyed. We had no cellphone — this was 1997 — to call for help. The man who hit us claimed his cell had no reception in this remote area.

"Oh, God, send help," I prayed. Within minutes, several cars stopped. One couple offered to cram our two teens and me in the back seat and take us to the nearest hospital, thirty miles away. Another offered to take my husband.

The man who hit us provided his name and insurance, but insisted on staying with his disabled vehicle. In the dark confusion of that night, we could only think of our son, the worst injured. He took the brunt of the passenger-door impact, suffering glass cuts all over his face and the loss of his front teeth. He had just finished three years of expensive orthodontia and had a beautiful smile. Not now.

"Suspected alcohol involvement," state highway patrolmen told us hours later in the emergency room. "It's a miracle you survived," one added. When they arrived at the accident scene to arrange towing and investigate, the other driver was gone. But they said his disabled vehicle had a strong alcohol smell and was littered with discarded beer cans. A grocery bag contained a receipt indicating a beer purchase a few hours before the wreck. The wet snow beside his vehicle revealed a trail up an embankment, where more cans of the same brand were found. Going to his home address that night, they found nobody home.

It made sense. Why else would someone who caused a bad accident try to hide? Doing so enabled him to avoid a blood alcohol test. He was arrogant with investigators the next day. But the circumstantial evidence wasn't enough to charge him with a more serious crime.

"Why us?" I wondered, as a long night passed in the emergency room. The next day, my husband, his wounded left cheek swollen, drove a rental car the remaining 300 miles home. Being non-drinkers with good driving records hadn't spared us this terrible experience.

As word got out, friends brought food. Someone delivered a yellow potted chrysanthemum, the type of plant I often associated with funerals. In a moment of exhaustion, I plopped on the couch and gazed at the flowers. What was that piece of blue plastic deep inside? I pulled out a message stake to read, "It's a boy!"

I laughed — a much-needed laugh. At fifty, I had no plans to have another baby. Little did I realize that something better would be "birthed" of this traumatic experience.

One day, my habit of reading the Bible brought me to Proverbs 3, which talks about trusting God to make our paths straight. I found myself pausing at verses 25 and 26: "Be not afraid of sudden fear... for the Lord will be your confidence." I marked the date of the wreck in the margin. Somehow, I believed, the confidence lost by this "sudden fear" would return.

About five years later, I noticed a two-inch article in my newspaper about speakers needed for "drunk driver education panels." At their discretion, judges sentencing drivers convicted of "driving under the influence" could require offenders to attend meetings at which victims spoke. The hope was that meeting real victims, seeing photos and hearing of their anguish would help offenders say "no" the next time they were tempted to drink and drive. The greater goal was to cut the grim statistic of a thousand killed every month in the nation by impaired driving.

Although I had done public speaking, I wondered if I truly wanted to get involved in this. In the darkness and confusion on the night of the accident, I didn't even remember the face of the man who hit us. But his dishonest and evasive behavior left a wound in my heart. I cut out the article and finally called to volunteer. Within a month, I was facing a room full of people who shared the crime of "driving under the influence of alcohol or drugs." I was surprised by my nervousness as I spoke of our trauma and of the family he almost wiped out. By speaking to them, I was speaking my heart to the man who caused us pain.

I spoke a second month, a third, and continued for years. My story changed as the teens grew up, earned all A's in high school, were active in church, received amazing scholarships to college, graduated, and married. I reminded listeners that these accomplished young people could have had their lives ended that night. A few years later, our former neighbors lost their adult daughter, a talented violinist, to a wrong-way drunk driver on an interstate highway. I added her story to my talk, and then the tragedy of a prominent doctor in town, father of one of my daughter's classmates, killed by a drunk driver, just blocks from home. Other speakers had profoundly sad experiences. One older woman lost her son, hit one morning on his way to work. The panel's moderator had grown up with a legacy of alcohol abuse and impaired driving.

I hardly missed a month, even hobbling there with my broken ankle in a cast. Then, after a decade, I sensed "mission accomplished." The message of admonition had become the medium for my own healing. How many people did I reach? My best guess is more than 2,000. Sometimes, to my surprise, audiences applauded. Several people came up afterwards and hugged me, saying, "After hearing your story,

I'm never going to drink and drive again." One day, checking out at the grocery store, the clerk paused and remarked, "Thank you for speaking." Seeing my quizzical look, she added, "I was at the DUI panel. Two glasses of wine got me in trouble. I'll never do it again."

Leaving the store, I passed by the floral department with its prominent bank of yellow potted chrysanthemums. And I smiled, remembering that jaunty little blue "It's a boy!" message stake hidden in the foliage of our "sympathy" plant.

Ironically, one compelling reason to end this life chapter of speaking out against drunk driving was a baby boy, my first grandchild. When my daughter-in-law went back to work, he came to me for daycare, his crib set up in his dad's old bedroom. This was where his dad — my son — years earlier recovered from painful dental repair, suffered with shingles attributed to the stress of the wreck, and learned to play guitar as an emotional release.

We were hit, almost killed, but we lived. And I trust that, by using my painful experience to advocate sober driving, a few others are alive today, too.

~Jeanne Zornes

74

Finding Light Within Darkness

*Physical strength is measured by what we carry. Inner
strength is measured by what we can bear.*
~Author Unknown

The drive home from my therapist's office that July day in 2010 remains crystal clear. I had been attending sessions on a weekly basis for months. There were a number of things going on in my life, but my husband's rapidly declining mental health was priority one. Scott couldn't go on in his current condition any longer. He was hardly sleeping anymore, and would wake me numerous times during the night to discuss random, irrational concerns. My attempts to calm and rationalize his fears were futile. His anxiety consumed him, so he would pace the house for hours.

I spoke with Scott's parents during my ride home, and we all agreed that he needed inpatient care again. Thankfully I had a few hours before our son was to be picked up from school. I was hopeful that I could get Scott admitted to the hospital before Tyler came home.

I pulled into the driveway, and reflected with sadness on how quiet and closed up our home was on a warm summer day. Scott had long been avoiding socialization, so he would make it appear as if no one was home. The garage door was closed and for a brief moment I held out hope that he had ventured out. During those dark days I would look for any small sign that he was going to get better. As the garage door went up my hope vanished. His truck was there.

I walked into the house and noticed a piece of paper fluttering in the breeze. A handwritten note had been taped to the doorframe of the laundry room. My mind began to race when I realized the note was in Scott's handwriting. Scott rarely left me notes.

It read: "Please don't let Tyler go downstairs. I'm sorry. I love you both."

The words crushed my chest like a ton of bricks. I knew immediately that he had hurt himself. I stood in the back hallway stunned, my hands trembling. Denial took over and I began running from room to room screaming for him. I alternated yelling his name with screaming "No." How could this be happening? It had to be a dream.

When Scott didn't respond, and I had failed to find him on the main level of the house, I headed toward the basement door. My stomach was in knots as I started down the stairs. I only went down a few steps and stopped. My gut told me that whatever was down in that basement, I did not want or need to see it.

Adrenaline kicked in and I suddenly became calm and felt numb. I walked outside onto the driveway, and as I stood there in the beautiful summer sun, I called 911 for the first time in my life. It wasn't long before I heard sirens in the distance. As the sirens grew louder, the weight of the world became heavier and heavier.

Within a very short period of time my house and yard became a whirlwind of activity. Emergency vehicles, lights flashing, filled the road in front of my home. Emergency responders made multiple trips in and out of my house. Concerned neighbors walked over to see if I was okay as I wandered the front lawn in disbelief. My fears were eventually confirmed. Scott was dead and had been for hours. He had hung himself in our basement.

On that July day, at the age of thirty-five, I became a widow and the single mother of a five-year-old. I lost the man who I had known for seventeen years, thirteen of them as his wife. During the day I held my head high and stayed strong. I learned how to manage the finances, do small repairs around the house, and tend to our one-acre property. In the evenings, when my son was in bed, I allowed myself thirty minutes to break down. Sometimes I'd sit and cry uncontrollably. Other nights I was so angry I couldn't shed one tear. Most of the time I'd write in my journal as if I were speaking to my late husband. I'd share events of the day, funny stories, etc. It gave me a way to communicate with him despite the fact that he was gone.

Losing Scott in such a tragic way left me with so many unanswered questions. Early on I spent time trying to rationalize his actions and evaluate how I handled his struggle with depression. Eventually, I realized that suicide could not be rationalized. Mental illness is devastating. Everyone suffers. I now try to focus on the fact that Scott was a good man who loved his family. In a haze of sickness and despair he felt we would be better off if he wasn't around. He didn't mean to hurt us.

In the years that have gone by since Scott's passing my life has changed quite a bit. How could it not? We are all products of our life experiences. Those experiences mold us into the people we are and I am no longer the same person I was five years ago. In some ways I miss who I was, but I also embrace and love the person that I am now.

This challenge has shown me just how strong I can be, emotionally and intellectually. I have chosen to pursue dreams and goals that I had originally put aside for "when I'm older." I make a point to find something special to love each day. I have even found the courage to open my fragile heart and love again.

Life doesn't always play out the way that we might hope. What matters is how we approach and navigate the obstacles. The loss of my husband was a very dark period in my life, but I bumped, tripped and felt my way through. At the end of this journey I found light again. I bask in its beauty with a new appreciation of life and continue to grow every day.

~MaryAnn Austen

75

Infinite

The only way to live is to accept each minute as an
unrepeatable miracle, which is exactly what it is: a
miracle and unrepeatable.
~Storm Jameson

I knew I was in trouble when my internal dialogue shifted from "I promise you will be here tomorrow, keep going, keep breathing" to "I will forgive you if you let go, it's okay, let go." I listened to the mechanical pulse of the machine I was connected to. It was strong, steel, immortal. And I was decidedly not. I was cold like an empty vacuum, hollowed out. The doctor's face was no longer a face, but a road sign on my way from Here to There. I wanted to keep going, further and further into the white — where hearts don't stop working, because there are no hearts and everyone is safe at last.

"Let go, let go." I placed my temple on the cool metal bedrail, and I slept.

I woke up to a world of harsh color under florescent light and nurses calling me "a miracle." Specialists buzzed in and out of my room. One doctor misted up, tears running down to meet his thick black mustache. He said, "How are you still here? Do you understand how very special you are?" I stared back at him, confused. I was just a seventeen-year-old girl alone in the ICU. I didn't feel special. All I felt was broken.

There was something I didn't tell the doctor. I didn't tell anyone because I didn't trust anyone to understand. When my heart had stopped, what happened to me felt like something quite the opposite. I slumped in bed with Technicolor love rising from my chest like pop rocks and soda. Love wasn't an emotion; it was a physical force spilling out. I was lifted with gentle hands up, up toward the ceiling. Then there was no ceiling, there was no hurt, and I became a burst of colors dissolving into air.

That's all I remember. It had felt like a release. As time stretched on in the ICU, I sat under scratchy hospital blankets and thought. Many people live their lives afraid of dying, but I realized that is misplaced fear. Instead, we all should be afraid of not getting the chance to truly live.

I wasn't so great at walking once I finally went home. First, I stepped out onto my driveway, unsteady in the November breeze. My feet were planted hip-width apart and they might as well have been tree roots. Moving seemed impossible, but deeply necessary at the same time. My fingers stretched out into the wind and all I wanted to do was run with it — past the ordinary lawn clippings and mailboxes of my neighborhood. I wanted out in the most desperate way. But instead of running, I wobbled up the stairs to the four walls of my bedroom and cried rivers of tears. I thought I would never be wild and free again. But we human beings, in our limited sight, have a way of being wrong.

I was diagnosed with Addison's disease, a destructive and rare autoimmune disorder. My cells wage civil wars, fighting over nothing, fighting until my body is a nuclear holocaust. Organs, like villages, are flattened one by one. There is no cure. I don't know how long I have left, but let me tell you something — neither do you. And as for me, I refuse to live the remainder half-dead by settling. When I realized that, my life truly became the "miracle" the nurses were boasting about. What a strange design, that it took coming to absolute zero to realize how infinite I am. We all are. We hold inside ourselves a tiny infinity of love and joy — just waiting to pour out into the world.

I am twenty-four years old now and I have fit more adventures into the past seven years than many people will experience in their entire, long lives. I've been body slammed by Pacific waves on my surfboard. I tried to sneak chocolate croissants from France through customs. I learned how to blow glass into heart pendants in Venice. I fell in love with a boy with a rolling accent over an orange cardamom latte. And I never miss a morning run. Every sunrise, I lace my tennis shoes up and run toward the horizon. The gentle pink and orange light washes over my body, baptizing me for the coming day. I run because I can. I run in honor of everything I have overcome.

I want to touch-taste-feel-be everything. I want it all: the beautiful, the terrible, the art, the disaster, the sweet, the bloody bitter. Everything. I have become beauty. I have become brokenness. And I believe they are the same. The one outlier that sickness can never touch is the tenacity of the human spirit.

I am even grateful for my diagnosis. It has opened me in a way that is irrevocable. And it couldn't have happened any other way. Now, I will never settle for anything but the fullest life. I am living every day of this miracle in gratitude, awe, and adventure.

~Morgan Liphart

76

The Tree

It is difficult to realize how great a part of all that is cheerful and delightful in the recollections of our own life is associated with trees.

~Wilson Flagg

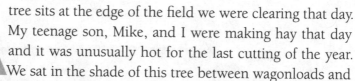

A tree sits at the edge of the field we were clearing that day. My teenage son, Mike, and I were making hay that day and it was unusually hot for the last cutting of the year. We sat in the shade of this tree between wagonloads and talked. We talked about everything and nothing, like we always did. We were comfortable with each other. There was none of that teenage animosity toward me; Mike was an easy kid, always had been.

Even though it was hot that day, there was a soft breeze blowing and the shade of the tree was deep and cool. The tree was in full leaf, green and full of life, a contented place to be. It was just like the lanky, 6'1" blond teenage boy sitting beside me: beautiful and full of life.

The next day, Mike was gone, killed in a car wreck, and I was shattered.

A couple of months after my son lost his life, I looked down the field and saw the tree standing there. Bare of its leaves, dark and barren, being pummeled by heavy, cold November winds. It looked like I felt, stripped of life. Something told me to take a picture of it. It was important. I was leaning heavily on my faith at that time and this period of time taught me to strengthen my spiritual ears. So of course I went and took the picture.

It was a typical cold, blustery November day. As I walked down the field dark gray clouds hung over me. Fast moving clouds were being pushed quickly across the sky and the wind was whipping against my face. It was nearly sunset when I walked through the field to stand in front of the tree. The tree appeared dead, although I knew it wasn't; it was just dormant, resting and protecting itself from the winter storms that were to come. The weather that day and the tree itself all combined to mimic the turbulence in my soul.

It was an eerie photograph, beautiful in its starkness; I framed it and hung it on my bedroom wall in an ornate frame my dad gave me. Often I would look at that picture and remember the last day I had with my son. In a strange way it gave me comfort to see the tree looking so forlorn. In reality the tree at the edge of the field went through its life cycle every season. But the one hanging on my wall was forever frozen in time. As I thought I might be.

But time moved on and without realizing it I did heal, to the extent that a mother can heal after something like that. Slowly, a desire for life began to return to me. Like the buds on a tree in springtime the promise of the green leaves of summer began to form. Time passed, joy and laughter crept back into me. Life has a way of bringing gifts that heal. Last summer I was playing in the back yard of my daughter's house with her children. We were painting at the picnic table in the shade when a still, small voice said, "Look where you are." I realized that we were under the shade of the same tree where Mike and I had spent our last day together. The tree was green and full of life, it had swings hanging from it and two toddlers and a beagle playing under it. Something told me to take a picture. And I did.

~Shari Bowes Deaven

Going the Distance

*It is not enough to take steps that may some day lead
to a goal; each step must be itself a goal and
a step likewise.*

~Johann Wolfgang von Goethe

When I awoke from a coma with a severe brain injury everything had changed. I had to learn to walk, talk, read and write, basically everything, all over again. Only this time everything was harder. Much harder. Nothing came easy. I found myself at the proverbial crossroads. Would I give up and accept my lot, or would I push on?

The choice may seem obvious when you see where I am today. I've been happily married for more than twenty-five years. I worked for twenty-three years in a factory and have now retired to pursue more fulfilling work as a caretaker for the Washington County Historic Courthouse. I have a wide circle of friends and an extensive list of awards and accolades. In a word, I have thrived.

When I was in the hospital I had no idea what brain injury recovery involved or how long it would take (essentially a lifetime). Had I foreseen what would be required I would have resisted. In fact, it was really about two years later, when I reached a plateau in my recovery, that I became clinically depressed. It was then that I realized I wasn't going to breeze through my recovery like a wunderkind and that I was going to be "brain injured" forever.

I didn't want to live a half life; I wanted to live a full life. From an overwhelming list of issues and deficits I chose the one that bothered me most, thinking that if I could at least do that, I could maybe keep going. For me, that big issue was walking and being in good shape. I had to have the energy to climb the mountains before me.

When I returned home from the hospital my wife would take me out for a walk. The first few times I couldn't even make it around the block. We'd get to the corner and turn up the block and by the next corner I'd be begging to go back. Bless her for her strength when I had so little. Over time we were able to make it to a nearby park that was about half a mile away. I started walking on my own. Before the year was out I would walk to the park and then walk the trails.

I worked out a one-mile loop on the trails and began walking laps. After a couple years I was walking five miles. This would take close to two hours, so in an effort to get done sooner I began running part of the way. Kind of a lope, really. My balance and partial paralysis made running difficult. I would run for a hundred steps and then walk for a hundred steps, alternating back and forth until I was too tired to run and then I would just walk the rest of the way.

I remembered a time when I was quite young and lived in Marine on St. Croix, Minnesota. There was a man in town who I would see on a regular basis running through town. I had heard that he could run ten miles. The nearest big town, Stillwater, was ten miles away. In my child's mind I imagined that if I could run to Stillwater, I could connect with the whole wide world.

Back in the present, I had gotten to the point where I was finally able to run a whole five-mile route. About this time I learned of a ten-mile race from Marine to Stillwater that was held during Stillwater's annual Lumberjack Days celebration. Here was something I could fix my attention on. From the deepest recesses of my memory I had this desire to run all the way from Marine to Stillwater. Could I do it? The distance had always seemed impossible to me because it was the dream of a five-year-old child. Revisited as an adult, although physically challenged, I thought it just might be possible.

I imagined just how cool it would be to add this chapter to my life's story. I started training with the goal of running ten miles. I began living my life as I would like to be able to remember it. This is always my primary motivation because it takes me out of the present, where things are real and tough, and gives me a future goal.

I kept at it and ten years later I entered the Lumberjack Days ten-mile race. The first time my exuberance worked against me and I started off at too fast a pace. Around mile six, as I slowed to a walk and cursed my bad judgment, my childhood hero, former Minnesota Viking and current Associate Justice for the Minnesota Supreme Court, Alan Page, came running by me and as he passed he said, "C'mon, you can do it!" That was all it took, I resumed running and was able to finish the race.

The following year I ran the race in ninety-two minutes. Although in his sixties at the time, Alan Page was still an amazing athlete who ran a strong race. In the picture of me crossing the finish line you can see Alan Page coming up fast right behind me.

It took me over ten years to accomplish, but what a story I have to tell!

~Michael Strand

Chapter 8

Think Possible

The Wonders of a Positive Attitude

How My Son Helped Me Stand in My Truth

The greatest enemy of any one of our truths may be the
rest of our truths.
~William James

thought I was a good mom. I made sure my kids were growing and learning. I made sure they had everything they needed for sustenance and for development. I was focused on their education. I had them involved in all kinds of sports and activities. I made sure they had their vaccines and went to the doctor when necessary. I fed them well.

I really thought I had the mom gig nailed.

And then my oldest child had the nerve to upend all of that and make me not only a better mom, but a better human being—a better me.

From the time he was born, he was what I lovingly referred to as persistent. As he got older, though, that persistence turned into what I not so lovingly thought of as downright stubbornness. I couldn't understand why he wouldn't listen to me. He demanded things be his way and never seemed to have any issue telling anyone in authority exactly what he thought. I've always admired that. He was "distracted" at school, and was labeled with having several learning disabilities, although his IQ testing was off the charts.

That should have been my first clue. You see, my son was born as a female. And he has had the strength and courage to stand in his own truth and be willing to transform into who he really is — a male. At two years old, he declared no more dresses. I didn't think too much of it, and still didn't when several years later we were shopping for school clothes and he complained that the girls' clothing was too "tight." He's always been irritated by things like tags in shirts, so I figured, no biggie — we can buy boys' jeans and pants. We continued to buy some girls' clothing that was looser fitting, but that, too, came to a stop.

He was also determined to have a short haircut. I mean really short. You know, boy short. I resisted at first, but then figured, it's his head — and he deserves to be comfortable.

I let him know that some people might wonder whether he was a boy or a girl, and we chatted about how he could handle it gracefully. He never seemed to mind that the questioning might happen and always handled it like a champ — respectfully, but firmly.

I'd get the occasional, "Oh, your son is so great!" and I'd quickly and politely correct the commentator, who, of course, would feel bad, and whom I would reassure: "Actually, she's quite the tomboy (I had no idea what else to call it at the time), and she likes it!"

After a few years, he asked me to stop correcting people. That was a tough one. But I did my best to comply and he was (mostly) gracious when I'd slip up and call him my daughter or use the feminine pronoun.

While I believe I've tried to nurture his independent spirit, there have been many times when getting him to do the things that society says are the norm — and therefore what I bought into for far too long — was torture... for both of us. About a year and a half ago, I decided enough was enough. I decided that what matters most is the relationship we have, not what society dictates is the right prescribed course for his life. One of the changes we made is I started un-schooling him.

It took years of back and forth frustration, therapists, different behavioral programs (aimed at changing him, of course, not me), issues with the schools, and finally desperation for me to realize it wasn't my son who needed changing. It was me. And my thought process. And my approach.

This child of mine has always displayed the most breathtaking charisma, determined sense of self, and old soul type of knowing. I've noticed, and often been told, he's wise beyond his years. About seven months ago, after doing research on his own, he sat me down and explained that he's never been comfortable in his body and he is transgender. He was ready to begin the FTM (female to male) transition. Tears immediately sprang to my eyes.

You know why?

Because this kid — at fourteen — has more bravery, more true-to-himself guts than most adults I've ever met. He's ready to face the world as who he is, no matter what. I'm just so damn proud of him I could jump out of my skin.

He's been seeing a gender identity therapist for the past six months, and will soon be heading into Boston to work with endocrinologists so he can begin to live even more on the outside as he feels on the inside.

When I decided that my relationship with my child was more important than anything society said I should or shouldn't be doing, our world began to change. It was then, too, that I realized it was my dysfunctional relationship with myself that had been holding me back. For far more years than I'd like to admit, I allowed fear to control my decision-making: fear of what would happen, fear of what wouldn't happen, fear of making a wrong move and ending up in the wrong place. I never allowed myself to just flow. To just be who I was and allow my life to unfold. I didn't trust myself enough, didn't love myself enough, and certainly didn't feel I was worthy enough. When things didn't work out as I planned, I would try to control everyone and everything around me. Which, of course, didn't work. I ended up frustrated, scared, and wondering how I could truly live the life I wanted to be living. I wanted to stop living by default, but had no idea what that even meant.

That is, until my son made me realize I could only truly control my actions and reactions or responses. I can't — and couldn't ever, really — control my child. And knowing what I know now, I don't want to. Ever. I want to allow my child to stand in his own truth, just the way he is. And honestly, it could be no other way. He is truer to himself than almost anyone I've ever met.

He has shown me how to exercise the freedom to stand in my own truth, too. I am becoming more of who I truly am because of his example. I have found a way to live honestly and unapologetically as me. I am pursuing avenues I would never have had the insight or the courage to traverse. Most importantly, because I have followed my child's example, I am able to help others stand in their truth as well.

Children are more than gifts and blessings... they are teachers. If we have the presence of mind to look for the lessons, our lives will become more fulfilled than we ever imagined possible.

~Melissa C. Harrison

79

Room 8

As we work to create light for others, we naturally light
our own way.
~Mary Anne Radmacher

When I was in seventh grade my study hall was extremely tedious and as much fun as getting shot with spitballs or having immense wads of papers hurled at your head. It was not for me.

I went to see my guidance counselor, Mrs. Greig. We discussed the various paths I could take to avoid study hall, from being a volunteer gym assistant to being an office helper.

I know that being a gym assistant sounds super exciting, but running three miles seems just as bad to me as feeling a spitball running down my neck. The option I chose to avoid study hall was helping out in an "artistic classroom."

The next day I wore a nasty old shirt to school so I wouldn't ruin a good one in art class. Along with that I wore stained pants with holes all over and shoes that had mud caked all over them. I looked as if I had been living on the street.

When seventh period rolled around Mrs. Greig took me to Room 8, the artistic classroom. When we got to the door, this gorgeous lady stood there. She was a little taller than average height, had beautiful soft brown hair, and was wearing a black dress. She did not look like she was dressed to lead an art class.

She said, "Hi! My name is Mrs. Magee. Welcome to Room 8, the autistic support classroom."

I said, "Don't you mean the artistic classroom?"

She smiled and replied, "Well they can be colorful sometimes, but I'm pretty sure I'm teaching a self-contained autistic support classroom. I know nothing about art."

I felt like a gargantuan idiot. Who else would get those two words messed up but me? I stood silently with my arms behind my back staring at the freshly waxed floors.

Mrs. Magee welcomed me with a warm smile. Then she introduced me to the students, who all rushed to greet me. I walked in and became their friend. I stayed until the bell rang.

When I got home, I bawled. I had always heard so many disagreeable things about that classroom. The students did not look like my classmates. They did not talk like my classmates either. The students talked in brief sentences. How could I help them? I doubted my abilities and myself.

I would have rather been a gym teacher's assistant than have that feeling. I thought about going back to study hall. My parents told me to give it one more day.

The next day I dragged my feet down the hallway as I reported for duty at Room 8. Mrs. Magee greeted me and then said, "If you have any questions about autism just ask."

That day I worked with a senior named Erika. She had long dark hair and a beautiful smile. I helped her with math, and that was the day something changed in me.

Maybe it was because she was like a child trapped inside an adult's body. Maybe it was because I saw that I was able to help her, or maybe it was because without knowing it, Erika captured my heart in an unexplainable way.

Whatever it was it changed my future.

I volunteered up until graduation day when I said goodbye in tears. These kids were my family. I took Roger's face in my hands. He was the most popular student in the class. He was crying too, but he smiled as he grabbed his backpack and walked out the door for summer vacation. "See you next year, Britt." I just waved goodbye; I couldn't explain to him that I would not be returning.

I glanced around the room and saw Chris, a game show fanatic, repeating questions from *Jeopardy!*. I smiled and tried to fight back the lump in my throat.

The last one in the room was Jarrett, the guy I took to the senior prom. I reminisced about the cheers we got walking down the aisle for the Grand March. We had linked arms as I whispered, "Left, right, left, step, step, step."

Quickly I snapped back to reality.

These were the faces I was afraid of when I started middle school.

My friends in Room 8 taught me more about myself than I would have ever learned without them. Room 8 brought me joy… and a career. I am going to be that teacher in the black dress. And I am going to tell the students who do not have disabilities about what makes the kids in Room 8 and all the other Room 8's out there special.

I cannot remember telephone numbers after hearing them once like Justin can.

I cannot get a crowd on its feet quicker than Roger can.

I cannot remember the exact questions and answers to a game show like Chris can.

I cannot take apart electronics and put them back together like Matt can.

I cannot solve as hard a math problem as Nate can.

I cannot love horses like Erika can.

I cannot remember every part of a car and what it entails like Robbie can.

I can, however, tell their story.

Our story.

~Brittany Autumn Austin

80

My Fairytale Life

There will be a time when you believe everything is
finished. That will be the beginning.
~Louis L'Amour

We were living a fairytale life, a life that included healthy kids, a messy house, and a happy marriage, when a suspicious bald spot about the size of a quarter appeared on the top of my four-year-old's head. The spot grew bigger and bigger along with our fears. We took Ian to a dermatologist who told us he had alopecia areata, a relatively common autoimmune condition. She gave us a topical cream and said his hair would grow back within six months. Only it didn't.

Over the course of a month the rest of Ian's hair fell out, and six months later his eyebrows and eyelashes vanished. I was angry. Why was this happening to my child? Before alopecia, Ian had a full head of red, curly hair, the kind that strangers admired and women coveted.

I wasn't prepared for this. I'd worried about many things as an overly imaginative mother, things like car accidents or cancer or house fires. I was ready for those things. I actually worked out in my head how I would handle them. Sometimes when I imagined too deeply, I would find myself crying at the thought. But I was ready.

I didn't know I needed to worry about my child's hair falling out, leaving him a bald preschooler. I wasn't prepared for this. What was I supposed to say to people? What would I say to Ian? How did

I explain the family picture in our Christmas card?

People said, "It's not life threatening." But it was in its own way. It was threatening the life I'd imagined for my son. I didn't want this to be happening. It was not acceptable. To me. To his siblings. To everyone who stared at him whenever we went out.

After extensive research and visits with doctors, we learned that not much is known about this disease. Alopecia areata affects millions of Americans. It doesn't discriminate by age, race, ethnic background, economic situation, or gender — anybody can get it. No one else in our extended family had ever had it. The most common cases involve only small amounts of hair loss (about the size of a quarter), which normally grows back, but a fraction of those affected develop alopecia areata universalis, which is loss of all the body's hair. So you could say that my son is very special (and you'd be right). Alopecia areata universalis has been around since biblical times, but research is pretty thin. Basically, no one knows what causes it and no one can cure it.

Prior to that December I had never heard of alopecia. I remember asking the dermatologist to write it down because I couldn't seem to remember the name, as if I was already trying to block it from our lives. It soon became all I thought about. Not an hour went by that I didn't worry about my precious child and his bald head. I tried not to talk about it so much because I knew the subject was growing tiresome for my friends. They denied it, but even I was sick of me and my sadness.

So I reached out to the only people I thought would understand my pain — other families with alopecia. People from all over the world responded to me through online message boards. There were others out there walking around with broken hearts like mine. And they were all connected to amazingly brave children who handled everything much better than their parents ever imagined. Knowing you are not alone is sometimes all it takes to regain your footing.

When Ian's diagnosis crashed into our near perfect lives, it taught me an important lesson. Everyone has a story. It's tempting to look at other people and think they've got no reason to be grumpy or difficult. It isn't until you've spent a year living with your pain exposed and your emotions fresh that you realize you don't have any clue what's going on in other people's lives and hearts.

Early in this adventure my mother-in-law said to me, "If that's the worst that happens to him, be grateful." At the time I wanted to smack her, but now I completely believe that with all my heart. Everyone has a handicap, a weakness. No one's perfect, and if Ian's weakness is that he simply doesn't have any hair, then Hallelujah.

Now when someone looks at me funny or is rude or disrespectful or even downright mean, I let it go. I don't know what's going on inside them. I don't know what kind of pain they're facing. So I can forgive their moodiness, their ill temper, their criticism. Instead of being hurt or angry, I simply wonder how tangled their life is and let it go. This has granted me a new kind of freedom in my own life.

When Ian was first diagnosed, people assumed he was a cancer patient. They were compassionate, kind, and gentle with him. I remember watching a complete stranger carefully spotting Ian as he climbed through the tunnels at a park, making sure he was safe. A security guard at Hershey Park gave Ian a giant chocolate bar and the ladies behind the fudge counter at the farm market always offered him a free piece of fudge. Once a waiter comped our entire check at Pizza Hut. In the beginning all I could do was nod thanks because every one of these encounters reduced me to tears. Now that I can talk about Ian's condition more comfortably, I still don't correct the kind strangers' assumptions. Another parent of a child with alopecia said, "Don't correct them. They feel good because they did something good for someone. Let them have that." So for the most part I don't say anything. I also don't say anything because my son doesn't realize why these people are so kind to him. He just thinks people are nice.

Imagine how kind our world would be if everyone treated everyone else as if they were terminally ill. No one would yell at anyone. No one would curse the slow driver in front of them or snap at the grumpy cashier or be rude to their waiter. We would go out of our way to help and be generous with our money, time, and words.

My life was never a fairy tale, but now I know that no one else's is either. So it's best to tread gently, granting others the benefit of the doubt, because I can never know what dragons they are facing.

~Cara Sue Achterberg

81

One Powerful Cookie

*Striving for excellence motivates you; striving for
perfection is demoralizing.*
~Harriet Braiker

"**W**hen are you going to realize you are slowly killing yourself?" My husband sat down on the bed. "Your standards are completely ridiculous, Denise. These gifts don't have to be perfect. The kids don't care."

I ignored him and kept on wrapping. It was true. I suspected I was the only one who had numerous "rules" for wrapping gifts. Each boy needed to have his own paper, and each gift had to be wrapped perfectly.

"Do you want me to wrap the toolboxes?" he persisted.

"Nope." I was in the zone and needed to get this done. There were numerous other holiday tasks that still needed my attention. I did not care how awkward the two giant toolboxes were. I was going to make them look as perfect as the rest of the gifts.

"What else can I do then? You can't do everything yourself. Do you want your blood pressure to keep creeping up because you have to have everything just the way you want it?"

I was exhausted, and fairly certain my blood pressure was, in fact, a little high. I had been feeling awful for months, experiencing anxiety, chest pains, and insomnia. The list went on. But I have three rowdy boys who are all home seven days a week and need tons of attention. I figured that stress went with the territory.

Carefully laying out the paper covered in robots, I placed a heavy toolbox in the middle. The paper ripped as I put it down, and I was forced to lift the unwieldy box off to start over again. Stubborn pride set in. "I don't need any help."

"Fine."

Billy was right. My standards were ridiculous. Everything from how clean I kept our house, to the numerous lists I made each week, to my grocery shopping rules. Our kitchen sink had to be dried out every time I used it, even if I would be turning on the water again in a minute. Every Sunday I made extensive to-do lists for everyone, and heaven forbid if they were not zealously followed. I suspect my entire family lived in fear of my standards.

I told myself I was just taking care of my family, but in reality, I knew my non-stop perfectionism was not doing us any good. My oldest son was clearly used to my ridiculous standards and just did his best to keep the peace by meeting them. My younger two were showing signs that Mom's standards were getting to them too.

"Cooper, make sure you put your books back where you got them," my six-year-old Caleb cautioned his four-year-old brother. "Mom puts the little books there and the construction books over there." He pointed to the different spots on the shelf. "Okay," the younger one agreed, blindly following his brother in adhering to their mom's craziness.

I knew I needed to change.

Two days after Christmas, my husband and I took our two older boys on a trip to Matamoros, Mexico. We were going to participate in an event known as the "Big Feed."

This entire operation could not have been more outside my comfort zone if I tried. I had no control over our schedule. We would be working in a field with strangers. It was dirty, there was no place to wash our hands, and to top it all off, a constant light rain had been falling for days, so we would be out in the mud the whole time.

Upon arriving at the facility, we sat down to orientation and listened to the director, Ben, give his standard speech about serving.

"We are not fair-weather Christians," he boomed in his deep voice, a gentle giant at well over six feet tall. "We won't complain. We won't stay inside because it's raining. And I have something that is going to guarantee all of you stay flexible, something formulated right here in our kitchen."

He passed out a small piece of cookie to each of us. "This is the Flexi-cookie." He instructed. "You eat this cookie and you are instantly flexible." He sounded so believable.

I listened to him talk about the problems we all have with flexibility. "I think it's a cookie problem," he stated to the room full of families. "When we go into Mexico these next two days, every time you start to complain, or maybe feel a little inflexible, we are going to gently remind you: 'Flexi, Flexi.' And then you are going to remember to be flexible. And if that doesn't work, I am going to keep a few extra cookies in my pocket for emergencies. Now let's eat this cookie together."

It tasted so ordinary, even slightly stale, but it worked in magical ways. I worked alongside my family for two long days in a muddy field. We passed out supplies and cooked for several thousand people, trudging through mud so thick our shoes quickly doubled in weight. I watched my oldest son skin raw chicken for five hours straight, with nowhere to wash his hands, and did not have a second thought as to the cleanliness of the operation. My middle son shared candy and played games with the other children all day in the rain, and I never once cleaned him up.

Late both evenings, I walked with my family across the International Bridge leading back into the United States in the dark; all of our clothes were caked with mud. And I thought about what happened when I made the choice to follow the cookie, when I chose to be flexible. Could I somehow package this Flexi-cookie and take it back home with me? The thought stayed with me on the three hundred-mile drive home.

And each morning since, I have prayed my new mantra during my morning devotions. "Flexi, Flexi." I mutter it throughout the day, reminding myself that I need to be less rigid. I cannot say I have completely conquered my crippling perfectionism, but I have made enough progress that the physical symptoms I was experiencing have diminished significantly.

And once in a while, on a really rough day, I sneak a cookie.

~Denise Valuk

82

Perspective

We can complain because rose bushes have thorns, or
rejoice because thorn bushes have roses.
~Abraham Lincoln

Six words changed my entire life: "Down syndrome is your best-case scenario." Those were the doctor's words at my twenty-week ultrasound. As we studied the monitor and watched the baby squirm and wiggle, the doctor pointed out the enlarged ventricles on the brain, the multiple defects in the formation of the heart, the lack of a nose bridge, the small limbs... Down syndrome was our best-case scenario because our first child's condition was most likely "incompatible with life."

An amniocentesis and three excruciatingly long days later, we received confirmation of the diagnosis. My prayers had been answered. It was only Down syndrome. It could have been so much worse.

It's amazing how perspective changes everything.

Our daughter Lily was born four months later. The doctors had done their best to prepare us for the worst. We expected her to be premature. She would be tiny and blue because of her heart defects, unable to breath on her own. I would not hold my child after giving birth to her. I would have to wait until the doctors examined her, hooked her up to the necessary medical equipment, saved her life. She would be taken immediately to the neonatal intensive care unit.

But Lily arrived two days before her due date. She was over eight pounds and bright pink. She not only breathed on her own, she screamed and cried like any other newborn. She was stable enough for the doctor to hold her up so I could see her. And after a swarm of specialists examined her and cleaned her up, the nurse handed her to me. I held my child within minutes of her birth, looked into her eyes for the first time and told her "I love you—and I'm so glad you're here." Under other circumstances I would have had hours to nuzzle my newborn, the opportunity to nurse her. I only had a moment, but it was more than I had expected.

Perspective.

Like other children, Lily entered kindergarten when she was five years old. She had already amazed us every day, proving that with patience, determination and courage, she could achieve almost anything. But when I imagined her in a classroom with twenty-four other children, none of whom had a disability, the thoughts brought only fear and grief. Would she make friends despite her social immaturity and unintelligible speech? Would she be avoided because she grinds her teeth? Would she be teased because of her odd behavior? Would the teachers be patient with her processing delays? Would she be part of the class or just a child who sat to the side and observed the "typical" children as they played and learned?

I spent days consumed by fear and worry, realizing that kindergarten was the start of the rest of her life. She would never be home all day with me again, under my protection and surrounded by my love.

And then I received an e-mail from a friend whose daughter was three and also has Down syndrome. Unlike Lily, Ashley's biggest challenges were not social or academic. She had battled leukemia every day for over a year. Her mother wrote about the sadness she felt because Ashley's hair was falling out for the second time. She thought they were past that stage. She'd been so excited when it had finally grown back. Suddenly, Lily in kindergarten was no longer a source of worry or fear. Relief and gratitude had returned. She wasn't spending her days in a hospital receiving chemo. She wasn't in bed at home too weak to go to school or play with friends. She only has Down syndrome. It could be so much worse.

Perspective.

As I dropped Lily off at school one day, I watched as she walked over to line up with the rest of her class. One girl noticed her and called out, "Hi, Lily!" Other children turned and yelled, "Lily! Lily's here!" A few others got out of line to rush over and hug her. All twenty-four children greeted my daughter as if she were their best friend. And through it all she beamed — responding and greeting each child by name.

I will continue to experience fear and grief throughout Lily's life. I will feel sadness every time she faces an obstacle that only exists because she has Down syndrome. I will worry that the day will come when other children don't race to greet her each morning. But I will also be forever grateful — for each challenge that allows her to grow and achieve great success, for each relationship that strengthens her character and accentuates her amazing personality, for the opportunity to be her mother and the recipient of her unconditional love.

If I focus on the gratitude, I can get through the fear. After all, it's just a matter of perspective.

~Nancy F. Goodfellow

Dancing

*Life isn't about waiting for the storm to pass... It's
about learning to dance in the rain.*
~Vivian Greene

My Uncle Bernie and Aunt Betty were curious to see my mother's new building—a seniors residence just around the corner from their condominium. Mom was scheduled to move the next week, but still had packing to do before she could vacate her apartment. Anxious about meeting the deadline set by the movers, she waved us out of the condo to continue packing in peace, encouraging us to take the afternoon off to explore what would soon be her new home.

Upon entering the gracious and spacious lobby, my uncle looked around in a disapproving fashion and said, "I've always disliked places like these. They're full of old people walking with canes and walkers, or confined to a wheelchair... and now I am one."

Uncle Bernie had been a strapping young man who served in India during World War II. Known always for his sweet demeanor and gentle ways, he had married Betty, a bubbly Brit and the love of his life, in 1953. While never blessed with children of their own, they were loved by their many nieces and nephews. Bernie and Betty went everywhere together and enjoyed an active and rewarding life. That is, until Bernie's arthritis moved into his spine in a most unwelcome fashion.

It had been a rough year. He had lost forty-five of his 159 pounds, had trouble swallowing, and suffered constant discomfort from his rapidly deteriorating arthritic condition, unable to walk without the help of a cane. He was worn out by the walk from the car to the lobby, so I suggested he sit in one of the handsome chairs in the lobby while my aunt and I looked around a bit.

Within moments after his settling in, the friendly voice of a woman standing hunched over a walker nearby called out, "Bernie! Betty! It's me… Kelly!"

Upon receiving a quick introduction, I was told that Kelly and her husband, Bill (who had materialized like an impish spirit behind my uncle's chair) had been my aunt and uncle's neighbors at their nearby condominium.

"So, Bernie… how are you doing?" Kelly queried with a broad smile and open heart.

"Horrible, just horrible," was my uncle's answer.

"Now Bernie," she chided, "nobody in this building is horrible. We're all doing great."

"So Bernie… are you moving in?" asked Bill.

"Oh no," Bernie replied. "My sister just bought an apartment here. This is my niece. We stopped by to see the place before Rose moves in next month."

"What floor will she be on?" Kelly asked.

"Nine," I piped up.

"Oh good; then she's not sick," Kelly said.

"I don't understand."

"We're on the second floor because we need more oversight through Assisted Care. Your mother is on an upper floor, which is reserved for Independent Living. We have our own dining room on two, and get three full meals a day — even in our apartments if need be. It's quite comprehensive. They take good care of us, monitoring our medications and so on."

"So, tell me about your mother," Bill said, abruptly changing the subject with a slight twinkle in his eye. "Can she dance?"

"Well, she's having a hard time walking right now, but she was 'The Queen of the Lindy Hop' in her earlier years," I said with a laugh.

"Aw… walking is hard, but dancing is easy!" Bill said, a thick shock of white hair emphasizing his sparkling blue eyes. "No problem. I'll get her up on the dance floor, you'll see!"

"I'm going to hold you to that promise," I chuckled, hoping that perhaps this light-hearted spirit might be able to shake her from her doldrums.

Looking at his watch, Bill turned back to my aunt and uncle. "Bernie, Betty— it's been great to see you again, but we need to get going. Kelly has to grab that bus or she'll miss her doctor's appointment," he said apologetically.

Acknowledging the need to depart with a small shrug, Kelly leaned over her walker to momentarily touch my uncle's hand.

"We'll see you soon, Bernie. When you come to visit your sister," she said gently. "Guess I've gotta go. My doctor has another round of chemotherapy planned for me as part of my post-operative treatment. I just had a mastectomy, you know."

Somewhat taken aback, my uncle nodded, the impact of her words rendering him temporarily speechless. We then bid fond adieus as Kelly maneuvered her walker in the direction of the lobby's front door to meet the waiting bus.

It was only at that moment that I could see Bill's full frame as he left his position behind my uncle's chair. This joyous, elfin sprite was gripping two metal canes tightly, one in each hand for support, the result, we learned later, of a recent stroke. Awkwardly throwing one leg in front of the other, he propelled himself forward to catch up with Kelly, who was approaching the shuttle bus.

I was dumbfounded as I watched his labored gait. Pausing for a brief moment, Bill looked back at me over one shoulder, and with a smile that simply melted my heart, reiterated the words that will forever ring through my soul.

"Like I said… walking is hard… but dancing is easy!"

~Sue Ross

Butterflies in February

Beautiful and graceful, varied and enchanting, small
but approachable, butterflies lead you to the sunny
side of life. And everyone deserves a little sunshine.
~Jeffrey Glassberg

t was the last day of the retreat, and we were all gathered in the lodge's main room for the closing ceremonies. It was the middle of February, cold and gray and muddy, and the younger kids were getting fidgety from a weekend spent inside the camp buildings. From seemingly nowhere, a confused butterfly fluttered through the room, awakened by the previous day's unseasonable warmth (which had disappeared as quickly as it had come) and the children chased it across the porch and out the lodge's front door. Laughing, the children rejoined the adults and we all formed a circle — each of the participants sharing something we had learned over the course of the weekend's workshops and sessions. One little girl, no more than seven or eight, was the last to speak. Bright eyed, with blond braids that made her look like a storybook Heidi, she said, "I learned that sometimes butterflies come out in February."

That was the thought that followed me home from that weekend in dreary February, and that was the thought that popped, unbidden, to mind several months later when I read in an e-mail from a dear friend that he had been diagnosed with aggressive brain cancer. Although he told me not to research the specifics of his type of cancer, I have never been one to do what I am told, and I went cold all over to learn that it had a six-month survival rate of only forty percent.

But then a little voice whispered inside my memory: "Sometimes butterflies come out in February."

He lived halfway across the country, so I began sending him cards in the mail — any card I could find that had butterflies on it. On every card I wrote that I knew he would beat this — that I had faith that he would — because if butterflies can come out in February, anything is possible. I probably sent hundreds of butterfly cards over the next year as he underwent treatments and surgeries and hospital stays.

That e-mail was more than ten years ago. At his last MRI, he was completely cancer free. In fact, he is the patient whose brain scans his doctor shows to other doctors, saying, "You're not going to believe this, but…"

He told me once that I kept him alive with my cards that first year. I said no, he was just too stubborn to die. But really? It was a cold winter day and a confused insect that helped us both.

Because sometimes butterflies really do come out in February.

~Dana L. Dickson

The Air Ball Queen

Every child comes with the message that God is not
yet discouraged of man.
~Rabindranath Tagore

Friday afternoon was our school-wide reading program finale in the gymnasium. The finale was a series of races and games. There were jump-rope relays, basketball relays, soccer relays, minute-to-win-it games, hula hoop contests, scoot-board races and a host of other challenges for my first graders. There were times when I was doubled over laughing so hard that I was crying because of balls escaping, jump ropes tangling, and all my first graders clapping and cheering each other on with abandon.

One of the harder games was a basketball shooting game. Each kid stood at a line and shot five baskets. This was a supremely hard task for first graders. That basket might as well have been in the clouds. One of my darling little girls — a teeny, tiny breath of a kid — was chosen for this game.

She was an adorable kid with curls that bounced each morning when she ran to me and wrapped her arms around my leg in a hug. When she got excited about something, her blue eyes opened wide and she flapped her arms. I'd seen her do this when reading her favorite books, when mastering particularly difficult math problems, when playing at recess, and especially when she painted.

She stood at the line, basketball in hand, with a serious expression on her face. She shot. Air ball. She scrunched up her face in concentration and shot again. Air ball. Her third and fourth shots arched through the air and again fell short.

I bet you're thinking this is one of those stories where she made the fifth and final shot and ran a victory lap around the gymnasium filled with kids who chanted her name and hoisted her up on their shoulders.

It isn't that kind of story.

Not one of her five shots even came close to the net.

Not a single one.

Back in the classroom, after the conclusion of the reading program finale, we gathered at the carpet to talk about all the fun we had.

My tiny air baller raised her hand to share, "Mrs. McCauley, I was nervous about that basketball game because I'd never played it before."

She paused and I waited, scripting in my mind words of encouragement or some sage advice about perseverance or something, anything to ease the sting of all those air balls.

She continued with her arms flapping in wild excitement. "I was nervous at first, but then I played the game and I was awesome at it!"

Wait, what?

She explained, "I'd never thrown a ball that high before. I threw it really high five times." She held up five proud fingers.

My face broke into a huge grin, mirroring the smile on her precious face.

How silly I was for thinking I needed to provide my "sage advice." As is so often the case, I found myself marveling at the unconventional wisdom of my students.

I can be so hard on myself when it comes to trying new things, so fearful, so unwilling to try lest I fail, or, worse yet, fail in public.

The next time I'm facing a new challenge, I'm going to remember her face, scrunched up in concentration. I'm going to remember her candor in admitting she was nervous. But most of all I'm going to remember her wild, flapping arms and the triumph on her face for throwing the basketball higher than she ever had before.

She didn't make any baskets that day, and for that I'm grateful, because if she had, I would've missed the lesson. She didn't score any points, but one thing is for sure, my little air ball queen was a winner.

~Alicia McCauley

I Can and I Am

If you want to test your memory, try to recall what you
were worrying about one year ago today.
~E. Joseph Cossman

My early twenties were rough. And I don't mean that in a "Woe is me, I was struggling to find direction" sort of way. I mean that I was housebound with a severe panic disorder that left me unable even to check the mailbox many days. Sounds were amplified, everything seemed too big, and my world closed in on me.

It all happened out of the blue right around the time of my college graduation. Before then, I was very social and adventurous. People were my thing. I always had friends around and I was a stage actress and singer — briefly professionally. My plan was to move with a friend of mine to Los Angeles and try for our big shot... and then the panic disorder derailed me.

I had to find a way to make a living without leaving my house because I could no longer perform. There had been too many close calls when I had panic attacks on the way to the theater. Professors had encouraged me to be a writer, so I figured I would give that my best shot. First screenplays and magazine articles, and eventually books. It took some time to earn a decent income, but I managed to build my credits quickly because I literally had nothing else in my life — I never went out, and at its worst, the panic disorder even robbed me of the ability to have friends come visit. They tried, but I wound up locked in the bathroom, shaking from head to toe.

Hope was in short supply. I didn't think I would ever get better, and I was running out of reasons to get out of bed. I sat at the computer nearly nonstop from the moment I got up until I went to bed. Often I didn't change out of pajamas (what was the point?) and I ate at my desk.

But after four years, something amazing happened: I got better. It was a gradual process that involved a patient boyfriend, a hearty dose of antidepressants, and small steps to get me back into the world again. There were little triumphs: sitting in a restaurant for the first time in years, getting my hair cut, bringing my cat to the vet. Then there was a monumental turning point for me: I went to a Counting Crows concert and had a great conversation with the young woman standing next to me. She was the first stranger I'd spoken to in years, and she saw me as a normal, healthy woman. She didn't see me as broken.

Getting better was so exciting and unexpected to me — I had figured that I would never leave the house again, let alone live a regular life. Within about a year, I was able to do most things again. I still had some panic attacks and there were some things that were still too scary for me, but overall, I was living again.

Through the worst of my agoraphobia, I had craved success stories… I wanted to hear from other people who'd been as low as I had and recovered, because I didn't really think it was possible. Now that I was recovering, I wanted to be that light for others, so I started writing about it.

One of the people who read my story was Jamie Blyth, who was then on the first season of *The Bachelorette* with Trista Rehn. He had gone on the show in part to challenge himself: He had social anxiety disorder and panic disorder, and he was trying to push his boundaries to get past it. After the show, he wrote to me to ask if I'd help him write a book about his experiences.

"Well, I've never written a book with anyone before, but if you're willing to take a chance on me, I'll take a chance on you," I said — and it worked. We sold his book to McGraw-Hill and I began the process of understanding Jamie's life story. It was pretty amazing. He had methodically put himself in situations that were more and more challenging to get past the anxiety. Among other things, he became a door-to-door salesman just to force himself to talk to people every day, and he flew to Sweden to join a basketball team without knowing a soul there. How brave!

Getting engrossed in his story and success was inspiring to me and made me dissect my own life. Here I was feeling pretty good and comfy about how far I'd come, but I'd hit a plateau. There were still things I was avoiding, and I had been okay with that. But Jamie lit the fire under me: "If he can go to Sweden by himself, I can fly to Florida with my family."

Truth was, I was terrified; it had been eight years since I'd been on an airplane. There was no escape if I did have a panic attack. No way to make them stop and put me safely on the ground again and let me go outside to breathe. But I used the power of positive thinking to get myself ready.

First, I had to combat my worries: What if I pass out? What if I have a heart attack? What if...?

I had to talk to myself: "You have never passed out from a panic attack before, and heart racing doesn't lead to heart attacks. You will be fine. You will feel so good when you arrive in Florida."

But what if I panic the whole flight?

"Then you will listen to music and talk to your sister and focus on your breathing, and it will be over before you know it. It will be worth it, and soon you'll be relaxing on a beautiful sandy beach."

But what if...?

And then I told myself, "I can and I am."

Those five words would become my mantra. No matter what fears cropped up in my mind, I would answer them with that: my shorthand version of "I can do it, and I am doing it." Over and over, drowning out any nervous chatter.

I'd like to tell you that I had a perfect flight, but that wouldn't be honest. I did have a panic attack part of the time and it was hard, but I kept thinking positive: "The hard part will be over soon, and I am so proud of myself for taking this risk."

I was right: the hard part ended as soon as we touched down, and

I had a terrific vacation. Taking that trip opened the door for what was to come next: I got a call inviting me to write a book with Celine Dion, and that meant I had to fly to Las Vegas several times to meet with her. I'm not sure I would have done it without having that "practice trip" under my belt, but I said yes even though I was still terrified. When the day came, I spent the whole morning bolstering myself with positive thoughts about how ready I was for this, how much Celine was going to like me, how wonderful this was for my career—and it became one of the best experiences of my life. She *did* like me, too!

Those flights—all of them—were perfect. It marked the final end of my panic disorder.

I don't have to think about panic attacks anymore. It's been seven years since I had even a minor one, and it's no longer part of my head-space. I'm a homeowner and a PTA mom; I've taught writing courses and made television appearances. Nobody who meets me now would ever know that I was once afraid to leave my front door. But what I've taken from that difficult time is my power to reclaim my thoughts from the grips of fear. Whenever I face a challenge now, I remember the power of those five words and how far I've come: I can and I am.

~Jenna Glatzer

Forgiveness and the Next-Door Neighbor

*We are all full of weakness and errors; let us mutually
pardon each other our follies.*

~Voltaire

The next-door neighbors were on their front porch waiting to welcome us on the day we moved into our first house, a small two-bedroom, gray house. They had three kids who were in high school. We were newly married and hoping to start a family.

We arrived in April and by May I was admiring the way the Mrs. next door planted an array of flowers that colorfully complimented their tidy brick bungalow. I enjoyed the picturesque beauty of her overflowing flower garden from spring until almost the fall. Through the years we worked on our handyman special of a house and my husband developed a green thumb, too, producing a bounty of blossoms that exploded with color in front of our little home.

Twenty-three years after we moved into our little A-frame we had the opportunity to tear it down and build a new one in its place. Unfortunately, with the new house came some unexpected problems — with the Mr. next door. Our friendly neighbor was not happy about our construction project.

When the Mr. became hostile and rude to us, we started to ignore him when we saw him outside. For so many years we lived happily just steps from him and now an invisible wall was put up that seemed unlikely to ever come down.

This went on for about eight years. Then one morning I looked out the window and realized that our neighbor was now an elderly man walking down his driveway with the help of a walker. It hit me just how much time had passed. He was now in the golden years of life and we had reached senior citizen status, too.

I suddenly found myself remembering those earlier years and I missed them. I remembered how our next-door neighbor loved dogs and always found time to pet our dog, Bingo, at the back gate. It wasn't unusual to see dog bones or other treats being passed from his hand to Bingo's mouth.

One evening Bingo got out of the back yard. Our family was heartbroken. We spent most of that night driving around the neighborhood but Bingo was gone. The next morning I woke to hearing my neighbor calling Bingo. I ran to the front window and saw my dog sitting in the front seat of our neighbor's car. He had resumed the search on his own and found our beloved Bingo.

Other memories came flooding back that morning. I recalled parties when we borrowed picnic tables and umbrellas from our neighbors and then gave them back along with coolers of leftover beer to say thanks.

I now stood looking out the window as the Mr. slowly shuffled to his seat in the yard. I missed those good old days and the easygoing neighborly relationship we had once shared.

I no longer felt anger in my heart. I didn't know what had caused our neighbor to turn so bitter toward us but in that moment I wanted to call a truce and I knew just what I had to do.

A little later that day I went into my back yard, peeked over the fence and said hello. The Mr. turned away from the baseball game he was watching on TV and returned the greeting.

I couldn't wait for my husband to come home to tell him that I had put an end to the long stretch of silence.

I was so relieved when he, too, agreed it was time.

My husband and I are enjoying our beautiful home. We have learned a valuable lesson. There's always hope when you can recall good memories, forgive the bad, and remember the good that is in all of us. Forgiveness is the fuel that frees you from the chains of someone else's actions.

~Kathy Whirity

The Birth of Courage

Courage is not the absence of fear, but rather the judgment that something else is more important than fear.
~Ambrose Redmoon

"'m sorry, but your baby has spina bifida." My husband and I sat stunned as the doctor told us the news. We were at my sixteen-week checkup and were thrilled that the ultrasound had revealed that we were having a baby girl. My routine blood work had come up abnormal a week ago, but the nurse had assured us that the results often came up false positive, and told us not to panic. So we didn't. I barely gave it a thought, truly believing that this kind of thing happened to other people, not me.

"What does that mean?" I managed to ask the doctor. I'd heard of spina bifida, but knew little about it.

She pulled out the ultrasound pictures and showed us the defect on our baby's spine. Simply put, she had a hole in her lower back, and the spinal nerves were exposed. The condition was anything but simple, however, as the damaged nerves led to varying degrees of paralysis, as well as neurological and urological dysfunction. There was no cure, just a lifetime of management.

I looked at the pictures with disbelief, and then with a growing sense of horror, as the doctor explained all the possible complications.

"You'll have to consider quality of life," she summed up gravely, intimating that our child was better off dead.

As the reality of the situation sunk in, I burst into tears and fell into my husband's arms. Why was this happening? There didn't seem to be any answer.

Over the next few weeks I researched spina bifida on the computer. My head spun with the complex list of problems the defect could bring: paralysis, hydrocephalus, bowel and bladder dysfunction, learning disabilities, as well as the need for catheters, orthopedic surgeries, braces, crutches, a lifetime of doctors and specialists, and on and on. It was all terrifying and overwhelming.

From the very beginning, our families offered their support and prayers, but inside me my doubt and fear grew to gigantic proportions. I was convinced I was the last person on earth qualified to take on such a responsibility. I'd never been exposed to disability, and knew little about dealing with it. Clearly the universe had made a mistake.

"I'm sorry," I whispered to my baby, rubbing my swelling belly. "I'm sorry this happened to you." I felt sorry not only for myself but for my child, who would have to live with this condition for the rest of her life.

It's difficult to untangle all the emotions I went through during that time. Denial, sorrow, rage, bargaining, I experienced them all, as if I were suffering through Elisabeth Kübler-Ross's stages of death. Only now, looking back, do I see that I was dealing with a death — the death of my old self. The one that fled from challenges of any kind. I'd spent my whole life avoiding it. I never left my hometown because I was afraid of the unfamiliar. I never pursued my passion for writing, because I didn't think I had what it took to succeed (or perhaps I was afraid of success). I had even put off motherhood until I was thirty-six years old, afraid of the commitment.

In fact, I felt I'd never really accomplished much in my life due to the fearful person that I was — except for this baby growing inside me. She represented all the challenges I'd never faced wrapped up in one tiny bundle. I felt her moving inside me, real, miraculous, fluttering with life. Already we were deeply in love with her.

The Wonders of a Positive Attitude |

I had never seriously considered termination, but I also hated the situation. I desperately wanted things to be different, but knew it wasn't going to change. After a few weeks of grueling self-assessment and conversations with my husband, I knew termination was not an option. We were going to have this baby. If I was going to mother this child with special needs, then that fearful person inside of me had to go. All we could do was love her and do our best. Maybe — just maybe — it was possible I could do this after all.

When Lilly Grace was born on February 8, 2009, I cried with joy. She stayed in the NICU for two weeks, and then we brought her home.

Those first few months were the hardest of my life, though it was mostly adjusting to motherhood rather than the birth defect itself that challenged me. Lilly had the same needs as any other baby. Feedings, diaper changes, and a willy-nilly sleep schedule taught me the true meaning of devotion.

Over time we grew accustomed to Lilly's many doctor appointments, though she is lucky in that her defect was low on her spine. That meant she had a good chance of walking, and she didn't need the orthopedic surgeries many kids with spina bifida had to endure. Neither did she need a shunt in her brain, which was a rare thing. When she took her first unassisted steps without a walker at three years old, our hearts sang.

We learned to catheterize her, got her through a tough spinal surgery, and braved the impossibly complicated maze of Boston to bring her to a great children's hospital. We've had to push the boundaries of our comfort zones in getting Lilly what she needs, and we've grown because of it.

Lilly is six years old now, a smart, vibrant, beautiful kindergartner who loves to read, enjoys arts and crafts, and appreciates the silliness of the Three Stooges. She endures her medical care with a strength and bravery that humbles me. She not only walks, but she runs, and she's determined to do the things other kids do. She brings such happiness to our lives and to the lives of others. We can't imagine life without her.

I still have dark days, days when I let sorrow or anger or worry get the better of me. In being Lilly's mom, I've found a strength inside me that I never knew was there. If I can do this, I can do anything. This new, braver me has even found the courage to commit to my passion, and I've been writing and submitting my work for publication on a regular basis.

Mostly, I've learned to view my child, who happens to have a disability, as she really is — not a tragedy, but a precious joy, the greatest gift of my life.

~Tina Williams

89

Deconstructing My Birthday

Plant flowers in others' gardens and your life becomes a bouquet!

~Author Unknown

"What do you want to do for your birthday?" my husband asked in an exasperated voice.

"I... I want... I don't know," I stuttered. "Something special."

"You want to go to that new restaurant?"

"No."

"Go out with friends?"

"No."

"What?"

"Something special, so I don't just feel old." Maybe I just needed to bite the bullet and get some hair dye or some new skin cream.

"Hmm." He disappeared into the garage. I've always thought garages were built just so men had a place to escape.

With no party in sight, I decided to use my positive thinking. How to celebrate? I couldn't think of any event that would improve my attitude toward my birthday. I had no idea what I truly wanted or needed. Christmas time had always been my favorite celebration. I loved to give gifts to family and friends. And that's when I realized it. If I loved giving gifts, then I could do that for my birthday! Why not?

This is how I came up with my annual Birthday Person.

In the months before my birthday, I think of all the people who have blessed me. I search for a small token — a gift. Then I plan what I want to say. After writing my first rough draft, I get a clean sheet of paper that doesn't have tearstains on it. And then I create the finished product and mail it with my gift. There have been many tears involved in writing notes to my Birthday Person, tears of joy, tears of healing — tears shared on the giving and the receiving end.

I chose my mom the first year. I was her eighth child. She gave me life and added a great deal of fun and love along the way. Next was my sister, Ouida. We shared everything. Best of all, she shared her faith with me and many others. She died a few years after I made her my Birthday Person.

I've chosen a Birthday Person or Persons each year: my sisters, brothers, daughters, youth directors, pastors, grandchildren, family and friends — all people who have changed my life in amazing ways. Some years it has been more difficult to choose a Birthday Person and several times I've selected a whole group — my Sunday school, Facebook friends and more. It has blessed me beyond any gift I could have received.

By changing my thinking from getting older to focusing on others, I have eliminated the fear of more wrinkles and gray hair. I'm amazed when glancing back over the copies of these letters to see many people on my list have now passed away — my mom, sisters, brothers and friends who changed my life. These were people who gave me so much, people who I could never thank enough— but at least I was able to thank them on my birthday.

Now I look forward to my birthday every year. Taking the time to say thank you not only makes me happy, it has changed my life.

My "Birthday Person" tradition has spread to many of my friends. The power of turning a potential negative into a positive, of saying thank you before it's too late, is more rejuvenating than any box of hair color or skin cream could ever be.

~Peggy Purser Freeman

Chapter
9

Think Possible

Recognizing Role Models

90

Broken Toys

*As we express our gratitude, we must never forget that
the highest appreciation is not to utter words, but to
live by them.*
~John F. Kennedy

His parents divorced when he was six and he grew up in an ugly part of town with a single, desperately invalid mother. They survived, barely, on welfare and food stamps, never owning a car or going on a vacation, seldom venturing more than a mile from their dilapidated, roach-infested, Section 8 apartment.

Two or three times a year he would sit in hospital waiting rooms through the night because his mother wasn't expected to live until morning.

He was ADHD before there was a term for it, and he hated school with a white-hot fury by the time he hit the fifth grade. He had few friends, he lied every chance he got, he would steal anything that wasn't nailed down, and he was familiar with the hard plastic back seats of a patrol car. The local storeowners knew him on sight, and he started carrying a hunting knife to school in the seventh grade.

By fifteen, he was on the second page of his rap sheet and was moving from a daily diet of pot and uppers to hard drugs. He was, in every sense of the words, destined to be a loser, a lost cause... a broken toy.

I was that kid.

There was a woman who lived in the same neighborhood; her name was Mardine. Her son John was my only friend at the time.

Mardine's life wasn't all that great either. Desperately poor, usually working two or more minimum wage jobs to raise her two boys, both with their own issues, she had a sometimes-working old pickup truck, and an often negative bank balance.

The first delivery pizza I ever tasted was in their tiny apartment. Mardine spent the better part of that week's grocery budget to order it for my fifteenth birthday. This woman had more than enough on her plate already without taking on someone else's problems.

But Mardine didn't see a broken toy. So, every week she offered to let me climb in the back of that old truck with her two sons and she drove us twenty miles to their church's Wednesday night youth meeting.

Every week she offered and every week I said no.

Then one day I said yes.

What happened that Wednesday night is the stuff of another story, but suffice it to say, my whole life changed.

The youth pastor was a man named Richie. He was loud, fun, and over-the-top crazy, and he became my idol the moment I met him. Like Mardine, Richie had plenty on his plate already — full-time pastoring, raising his own family, and running a large, rapidly growing youth ministry. Like any large group of youth, there's a "cream" that rises to the top, a small percentage of the obviously gifted and talented, and Richie certainly would have been justified to focus what little additional time and energy he had on those bright stars... in fact, some would say that was his responsibility.

There were national honor students already planning to attend major Bible colleges; it would have been almost negligent on his part to waste precious hours on one or two marginal kids when he could be mentoring future leaders.

But Richie didn't see a broken toy.

So he took me in... literally... giving me a room in his own home after my mother passed away. He got me a job at the church... and helped me keep it. He encouraged me, extolled me, worked me like a rented mule, chastised me, and bent me until I was sure I would break (but didn't). Most importantly, he never, ever, gave up on me (though I'm sure it was a temptation more than once.) He sent me to Nigeria, and to John Day, Oregon (of the two, I'd rather go back to Africa) where I learned two very different lessons in both success and failure.

The list of things I owe to Mardine and Richie is too long and too personal to list here. So, going back to my cream analogy, I'll focus on the one thing that rises to the top.

My deepest gratitude isn't about the feeding, and watering, and sometimes pruning that these two did in my life, the shelter they gave me, the jobs they helped me get, the education they encouraged me to pursue... though I will always be thankful to them for all of those things... but the debt that I can never fully repay, only pay forward, is that somehow, in those hours and days and years I spent watching them minister to myself and others, carefully cleaning, and patching and sanding rough edges, I gradually began to see people the way *they* saw them.

Because now, these thirty years later, when I'm helping to feed the homeless, or volunteering to teach life-skills to a room full of foster care kids, discarded and often abused, some of them drug babies and already a couple of pages into their own rap sheets, kids who I'm just trying to teach how to slice a tomato without cutting off a finger... I don't see broken toys, either.

I see beautiful kids who have been beaten down by their circumstances. I see what Mardine saw, what Richie saw.

And if one of these kids, even just one of them, learns to see that in others as well... then it's all worth it.

Because there are no broken toys.

~Perry P. Perkins

91

Adrenaline Rush

*Obstacles don't have to stop you. If you run into a wall,
don't turn around and give up. Figure out how to climb
it, go through it, or work around it.*

~Michael Jordan

The runway rushes past and gradually falls away. A roar fills my ears as the engine works to thrust the Beech Bonanza upwards and forward.

Tom, the pilot, gradually adjusts the controls until the plane flattens out at two thousand feet. The view through my window takes in the town and airport below. Beyond lies a patchwork of glittering silver and green; reflections from the numerous areas flooded by heavy rain over the last month.

I look over to my brother seated beside me and we share a grin. We both love flying. This joy ride is an unexpected bonus for both of us.

"We're up. Woohoo!" I call out.

"Lovin' it!" Dave responds, grinning with a thumbs-up gesture.

It's a perfect day for flying. As I take in the view and the three men in the plane with me, I find myself laughing. I am the only able-bodied person aboard.

"Wrong terminology," I tell myself. "I'm the only person in the plane with legs that work." Not that it makes any difference in this instance. These guys are all perfectly "able." The pilot is a fully qualified commercial pilot. If I hadn't watched each one haul himself out of a wheelchair and up the wings of the plane, I would be none the wiser.

Like all the planes sitting in front of the hangar we have just left, the Beech aircraft has been converted to hand controls, making the usual foot pedals unnecessary. It is the Wheelies with Wings annual Fly-in and the goal of the day is to give disabled people a flight. Wheelies Fly-ins involve pilots with planes flying into a designated location, then providing joy rides or training to those who don't have a plane. Many of the pilots are unable to use their legs. The passengers, "wanna be" pilots like my brother, generally have some flying training behind them but are not fully certified. All are restricted by life in a wheelchair or some other impairment of normal body movement. One pilot is an amputee. In the air, they enjoy freedom.

Dave took up a scholarship with Wheelies and after successfully passing his first flying course, signed up to try for his pilot's license. This annual event provides an opportunity for some free hours at the controls of his favourite bright yellow Foxbat trainer.

Most of my life has been spent watching my brother struggle with the debilitating results of contracting poliomyelitis as a baby. As a child, his legs were encased in metal and leather calipers; he endured night plasters, doctor's appointments, and my mother carrying out physiotherapy at home. He had to fight off kids at school with his crutches. It was all a normal part of our lives growing up.

I never consider Dave disabled. There is little in life he hasn't done or tried to do. For my younger brother and me, Dave is just "big brother" and we tease him about a soon to be celebrated significant birthday.

To say that Dave is my inspiration to get out and explore new possibilities might be stretching things. It is a matter of not allowing him to show me up rather than being inspired. In light of his consistent positivity, I have no excuses.

The sudden realisation that I am sitting in a plane, 2,000 feet above the earth, with three men unable to use their lower limbs for one reason or another gives me a jolt however. Completing a final circuit of the airfield, Tom adjusts airspeed, flaps, and altitude, bringing us down perfectly and on time for a sausage sizzle luncheon.

After lunch, my sister-in-law and I sit watching the activities from chairs set in the shade of the hangar. Dave has gone flying in the

Foxbat with his instructor. A happy but tired man will head back to the hotel for the night.

An airport security guard wanders across and slouches against the wall nearby.

"What happened to the guy out there? Do you know?" he mumbles through his chewing gum.

I glance across to where Tom's wife helps him from his wheelchair into their car.

"Gliding accident," I reply. "Glider got caught in the tow rope and plummeted straight to the ground. The impact severed Tom's spinal cord. He's fortunate to be alive. The amazing thing is that he chose to go back into the air."

I look across at the guard.

"With an engine in front of him this time," I grin. "Do you want to ask one of them to take you for a spin? I know they are up for it."

~Heather Reid-Bell

92

A Life Lesson in Courage

It was times like these when I thought my father, who hated guns and had never been to any wars, was the bravest man who ever lived.
~Harper Lee, To Kill a Mockingbird

I was sixteen years old when my brilliant, undefeatable father was diagnosed with multiple myeloma. At that time, it was considered a rare form of bone cancer that caused bones to become very brittle and easily broken. He was in the hospital for months, semi conscious. His discouraged doctor told my mother that we needed to get his affairs in order because he would probably live for fewer than six months. As I slumped on the chair beside her in the doctor's office in a state of shock, my mom graciously thanked him for the information but asked that he not tell my father that he had only a few months to live.

I adored my father and could not imagine a world without this kind and thoughtful man, with his twinkling blue eyes, always ready to help with advice or a hug. My father was still in the hospital when prom time came. My date and I went to the hospital first to show my dad how grown-up we looked. From his hospital bed, he charged my prom date with being certain that I was home by midnight.

Mom was a teacher and the life lessons she taught my two younger brothers and me as we were growing up were not the usual adolescent-oriented life skills. She set out on a courageous campaign to help my father fight for his life and we readily enlisted. Dad came home from the hospital, though he was wheelchair-bound for the remainder of his life due to the frailty of his bones. He opted to use a push wheelchair, rather than the easier motor powered type, because he wished to keep at least part of his body strong. His doctor assured him that he would be able to build strength in the muscles of his arms, though he would tire more easily.

Mom's determination and grit helped him be present at every possible school and scouting event in which my two younger brothers and I were involved throughout our school years. He proudly attended each of our high school and college graduations, though his eyes often glazed over with the effort and his physical suffering. When Mom had to be away for the day, teaching at her school, we learned to give the Dad pain tolerance shots prescribed by his doctor. She taught us how by having us practice on whole oranges and grapefruits. Both she and my father made sure they had time for each of us whenever we needed their attention, no matter how exhausted or how much discomfort either of them were in. They strove to ensure that the three of us had as normal a life as possible, despite the illness, agony and often depression that surrounded us.

Both of my parents had dreamed of traveling their whole lives. Even though my father was ill, nothing deterred my mother from arranging trips for the two of them all over the U.S., including Hawaii, and Europe. They refused help from nurses or companions on any of these excursions. Armed with letters to regional specialists from my father's physicians, Mom's tiny 5'2" frame could be seen pushing Dad in his wheelchair up and down hills, across cobblestoned streets, off and on buses, trains and airplanes. These were not luxury tours they joined. The two of them rented cars and used public transportation to go wherever their wanderlust took them. From Pearl Harbor to Stonehenge and many places in between, they roamed the world with love, laughter and courage.

When I announced my engagement a few years into my father's illness, I hoped to see him coaxing his wheelchair down the aisle between the rows of brightly glowing flowers we were planning in our back garden. I chose to get married and have the reception at home so that my dad could rest in his room if necessary.

The day of my wedding, I stood erect in the ecru lace wedding dress my mother had sewn for me, ready to take my dad's hand as a family friend pushed the wheelchair. Then I heard a collective gasp from our 300 closest family and friends in attendance. When I turned toward my father's wheelchair, I found him standing next to me offering his arm to walk me down the grass-covered aisle. My handsome groom's eyes glistened as he watched us make our way slowly toward him.

We made it to the end of that long walk, and my father insisted on standing throughout the ceremony. After a brief rest in his wheelchair, this astonishing man once again stood and asked me to dance. As I accepted through a haze of tears, I could feel what it was costing him in pain and energy.

My brave, diligent mom stood there, delight radiating throughout her whole being as she watched her only daughter and beloved husband dance to the "Tennessee Waltz."

It was due to my mom, and her determination to help my father succeed, that the idea of him walking down the aisle with me was born. While I dreamily mulled over wedding showers and parties, she had been driving my father to the beach, over an hour away from our home, several days a week for three months before the wedding. Once parked, he walked in the sand with her support. They spent an hour or more each trip so that he could build up his leg muscles enough to support him for what had to be a torturous long walk down the winding grassy path with his only daughter. It was a secret that my mother kept until after my father had gone.

It was not the only secret that she kept. My father lived ten years longer than the timeframe the physician specialists had predicted. He never knew that they had predicted a life span of only six months. My mother lived many years longer, never remarrying. When her beautiful grandchildren came along, she never tired of telling them how much their grandfather would have loved them. She traveled the world by herself or occasionally with friends or family members well into her eighties, riding elephants in Thailand, spending nights in pyramids in Egypt, joining a cooking school in France. At her death, as we were preparing for her memorial service, we counted almost 300 foreign stamps in her well-thumbed passports. She carried her indefatigable courage into her own final illness, assuring me that we would be visiting Africa as soon as she "felt a little better."

Life without my parents left me feeling orphaned, though I was an older adult myself when Mom departed. Our family was so strong, so loving and so cohesive that it left us all a little adrift. Mom and Dad taught us to face whatever life may bring with extraordinary courage and compassion.

~Donia Moore

93

Life on the Monkey Bars

Getting over a painful experience is much like crossing
monkey bars. You have to let go at some point
in order to move forward.
~Author Unknown

I was sitting on the landing at the top of the stairs, my heart pounding. I didn't know how I was going to make the next rent payment and the bills were piling up. I was ready to give up, but then I thought about the little girl sleeping soundly in the room next to me. I couldn't leave her. Not now. Not ever. I thought about her own spirit and a memory came back to me.

"Don't let go Mommy, hang on tight," yelled my daughter as I hoisted her on my shoulders to help her travel through the bars one by one. After the third round through the course, I felt a sudden numbing pain in my neck, so I decided it was finally time to teach my little five-year-old how to use the monkey bars on her own.

"No Mommy, no, I'm scared," she cried.

"You're scared because you don't know how to fall," I told her. Her little forehead wrinkled and her tiny brows came together in the way they always did when she thought Mommy was off her rocker just a little bit.

I continued, "If you learn how to fall, then you'll realize it wasn't so bad, so you won't be so scared to go through it. Look, let me show you." I jumped up on one of the bars and felt all of my 175 pounds pulling me towards the ground. I didn't realize how much more difficult it was to hang on with all the weight I was carrying, but I made an attempt to demonstrate. My fingers slipped off the bar, and I landed on my feet with a slight crouch to maintain my balance, arms extended in front of me.

"Let me try!" she shrilled with the eagerness of a five-year-old.

"You're smaller than I am, so I'm gonna keep my arms out in case you need to grab them on the way down," I assured her.

"No, Mommy! I want to do it on my own," she said with a pout, crossing her arms and stamping her foot.

She climbed the rungs and reached for the first bar. "Go ahead," I prompted, "throw your heart into it and your body will follow."

"I'm gonna fall... I'm gonna... Mommy... hold me!" she cried. I wanted to run to her, but I didn't move a muscle. I could feel the piercing stares of a group of mommies who were watching.

"You can do it. Let go if you have to and try to land on your feet."

Her hand slipped and she landed with a thud. She looked at me as if waiting to see what I was going to say. I heard some of the moms gasp and could only guess that their stares had now turned into glares. My thoughts raced: Was I a bad mother for letting her do that? Did they think it was child abuse? Was I going to be reported to CPS? Would they feel the same if she were a boy?

"Great job!" I cheered. "Was it that bad?"

"No, Mommy," she said with excitement as she dusted the wood chips off her backside.

"That's fantastic, sweetheart," I said. "And now that you know how to fall and pick yourself up, get back up again and start moving forward by swinging from one arm to the other. You just have to keep going."

"Okay, Mommy, but go away this time and let me try it on my own."

I resisted the urge to help once more and she swung herself with great fervor, her little hands moved from one bar to the next. She made it halfway when she called out, "Look, Mom! Look! Watch me... I'm gonna fall."

She beamed and I ran to her and swung her around.

"I did it! I did it!" she cried.

"You sure did, sweetheart! I'm so proud of you! You showed so much courage."

The memory was just what I needed. I stopped crying, got up from that landing at the top of the stairs and went to bed. Life hadn't turned out the way I planned. I had thrown my whole heart into a marriage that left me questioning my own self-worth and abilities. I had to embrace the challenge that life had given me, allow myself to fall, dust myself off, get back on that bar and keep going.

Tomorrow would be another day to try again... to put one hand in front of the other and keep moving forward.

~Jax Cortez

94

A Double Victory

The only thing that ever sat its way to
success was a hen.
~Sarah Brown

"Hi Sam," I said when I spotted him in the pack of first-graders walking down the hallway at his elementary school.

"Are you here to see me?" he asked in his usual monotone voice.

"Yep, it's Thursday, and I always come here to see you on Thursdays," I said. "I'm sitting at our usual table, and I brought my bag of fun activities."

He nodded. "I'll go in the classroom and get my pencil."

I'd already been in his classroom and spoken to his teacher. Mrs. Smith was just as concerned about Sam as I was. He was one of those "at-risk" kids, and that's why I volunteered to work with him each Thursday.

Sam was in first grade for the second time, and he was still hopelessly behind his classmates. I didn't know a lot about his home life, but one look at him made it clear that it wasn't ideal. He spoke quietly and without expression. In the eight months I'd been working with him, I'd seen him smile only once.

It was clear that the world had handed this little boy a tough lot in life, and I was determined to make it a little bit better.

Sam returned with his pencil. "Can I look in your bag?" he asked without looking at me.

"Yes, but Mrs. Smith wants us to work on your spelling words first."

"I hate spelling. Can't we just play a game?"

"You know the routine, Sam. You practice your spelling words, take your practice test, and then you can see what's in my bag."

"But I can't do it. I'm not good at spelling."

"Come on, Sam, you can do this," I said. I spotted the poster on the wall across the hall. In huge letters, it said, "You never know what you can do until you try." Underneath the poster, Mrs. Smith had hung up her students' exceptional papers. Many of them were spelling tests. And not once had one of those tests belonged to Sam.

I'd made it my goal that by the end of the year, Sam's spelling test would be good enough to go in the hallway. But it was May and we were running out of time.

I pointed at the poster and said, "What does that say?"

He recited it, rather than reading it. This was a weekly thing.

"You never know what you can do until you try," he said without conviction.

"That means that you're capable of a lot more than you think you are," I said. "You can do this. You just have to believe in yourself."

Sam rolled his eyes. He'd heard it all before. But still, he picked up his pencil and started writing the words.

The next morning, I received my Friday e-mail update from Mrs. Smith. "Sam missed seven on his spelling test," it read. He'd missed seven words out of ten.

Not good enough for the hallway.

The following Thursday morning, I received an e-mail from a writers' group I belong to. A magazine I'd always wanted to write for was seeking submissions for a special issue. A friend in the group encouraged me to submit something.

"Oh, I'm sure they're looking for writers with a lot more experience than I've got," I wrote back.

"So you're not even going to try?" she asked.

I really didn't see the point.

An hour later, I was helping Sam with his spelling words. When he insisted he couldn't do it, I pointed at the poster.

"What does that poster say?" I asked him.

"You never know what you can do until you try," he recited.

"That means that you can't give up, Sam," I said. "I know it's hard, but you can do it if you just keep on trying. You might surprise yourself."

And then I realized what I was saying. I was expecting an eight-year-old to do something that I myself wasn't willing to do.

I felt like a fraud.

Sam sighed. "Can I go to the bathroom before I write my spelling words?"

"Of course." As soon as Sam left the table, I reached into my purse for my cellphone. Before I lost my nerve, I sent an e-mail to my entire writers' group, promising to submit a story to that magazine.

I knew my story wouldn't be good enough to be published, but as I looked at the poster, I realized I needed to follow my own advice.

When Sam returned to the table, we worked on his spelling words. And that night, I worked on my story.

Two weeks later, I walked into Sam's school. As soon as he saw me, he pointed at the poster in the hallway. "Notice anything?" he said.

Sam's spelling test. Posted in the hallway with only three wrong. He smiled a little and said, "You told me I could do it."

"And you did," I said. "Sam, I am so proud of you." I wanted to hug him, but I wasn't sure how he'd feel about that, so I lifted my hand for a high five.

He smacked my hand and smiled a real smile. "You never know what you can do until you try," he said.

The next morning, I received an e-mail informing me that the story I'd written had been accepted for publication. My writing was going to be printed in a magazine I'd always dreamed of writing for.

And I knew that I had Sam to thank.

~Diane Stark

95

It Doesn't Hurt to Smile

Before you put on a frown, make absolutely sure there
are no smiles available.
~Jim Beggs

The last time my eighty-three-year-old mother-in-law visited, I asked how she was feeling. It's a valid question. She has, after all, had two knee replacements, a metal rod inserted in her femur, and a liver transplant. Pins hold her wrist together, and arthritis is settling into her bones so thoroughly she can no longer roll the dough to make her famous cinnamon crisps. She moves slowly and with precision to avoid another fall.

But she hasn't stopped moving. In fact, she and my father-in-law attended their first Jimmy Buffet concert this summer... where they sat on the lawn. Here's the thing about my in-laws: They never say no to an invitation or a new adventure. If they can make it work, they're willing to try just about anything. When we need them to come stay with the kids, we have to get on their calendars far in advance.

They inspire us daily.

When asked how she was feeling, my mother-in-law responded without an ounce of self-pity: "Well, most everything hurts every day. Some days are better than others. But you know what I've discovered? It doesn't hurt one bit to smile. So that's what I've decided to do... smile at everyone I see. I may not be able to do all the things I used to do, but I can at least brighten someone's day."

It is such simple wisdom, and such a profound shift.

Moving the focus from what we don't have, from what we've lost, from how we've been burdened to what we can offer others is the difference between living in the dark and radiating light. And illumination, of course, makes traveling so much easier for us and for others.

The key to a life worth living, I think, is to change perspective...

From inward to outward
From giving up to giving back
From self-consciousness to global awareness
From closing our minds to opening our hearts
From "No, thanks" to "Yes, let's!"
From judgment to acceptance
From self-importance to humility
From things to people
From indifference to love

You don't have to cuddle babies in a faraway orphanage or underwrite the expense of a much-needed surgery. It's not necessary to start a foundation that supports victims of domestic abuse or to ride your bike across the country while raising money for undernourished children. Of course, if you have the time and the means and are able-bodied to do those things, then by all means... Go! Do them! Ride like the wind! Start something important! Write giant checks!

But my point is this: Sometimes change arrives in a brown-papered package much smaller and less dramatic than the one with the glitter and the shiny pink bow. Sometimes change looks uncannily similar to everyday kindness and empathy. Sometimes change begins with letting a driver merge in front of you, with holding the door for a mother juggling an armful of groceries, with graciously acknowledging the curmudgeonly store cashier (even though he's much more comfortable mumbling and frowning than accepting a word of encouragement), with tipping your server extravagantly, with giving a hungry stranger something to soothe the rumble in his belly.

In chaos theory, the butterfly effect maintains that the smallest breeze from a butterfly's wing can change the path of a hurricane halfway across the world.

Imagine, then, the possibilities that exist within a single smile. Mamaw knows.

~Katrina Anne Willis

Finding Strength in Love

You have to be brave with your life so that others can
be brave with theirs.
~Katherine Center, The Gifts of Imperfection

My mother was my hero when I was a child. She was tiny in stature, but I looked up to her in so many ways. She was beautiful. It wasn't just the dusting of freckles across her button nose, or the curls that I loved to brush that smelled like powder when I kissed the top of her head. It wasn't just her shining blue eyes or the contagious smile that spread wide across her face that she bestowed upon everyone with whom she came in contact. She always called me "babe" and held my hand in the car. I never felt as special as when I got to spend time alone with her, without my brothers.

My mother is the kindest person I know. She is humble to a fault, and she has lived her life taking care of those she loves, even when she needs to find a way to take care of herself.

I don't know how old I was when I first realized that my mother was ill. Nobody came out and told me she had bipolar disorder, but I started to notice her mood swings. By then, she was single, working multiple jobs, and our trailer home was in shambles. My older brother was in charge of us more and more, and my special one-on-one time with my mom dwindled as she struggled to keep us afloat. But she made time to read to all of us, huddled on a mattress in the living room where she slept. Her voice made everything seem okay.

One morning, I woke up to find she had painted our entire kitchen pink. Another time, during an argument between her and us kids, she passed out. We panicked as she lay on the floor, and not sure what to do. I slapped her across the face to wake her up. Her symptoms seemed to be escalating, and I knew no way to help.

Sometime after, we left our tiny farm and moved into a small house "in town." A friend of hers lived next door and helped to parent us while my mother started to work on getting better. She started college and seemed more stable and attentive. But with the move, the confusion of her illness, and the onset of teenage hormones, I was left angry and I lashed out at my mother with hurtful words and actions. We fought often, and I struggled with my own depression in silence, not wanting to admit that I might be ill in the same way as she. But though my mother had so much on her plate, she put me in counseling, showed up at my school for meetings and made sure my brother and I got fitted with the braces we needed.

On "Take Your Daughter to Work" day she allowed me to attend classes by her side. I sat quietly, proud to be included in this new world my mother had bravely entered to reclaim a life of her creation. I never had the ability to tell her what this meant to me.

When I was nineteen, I found myself single and pregnant. My mother moved 2,500 miles to be near me and help me raise my son. And though I had accepted this journey of single motherhood thinking I would be on my own, I knew I was capable because of how much my mother believed in me. Because of my mother's love, I was never once alone. She stood behind me through a series of misguided choices and failed relationships. She encouraged me to pursue a path of personal growth and to find my place in the world. Because of her example, I have monitored my mental health closely and learned to seek help without shame or apology.

A few years ago, my mother decided she wanted to train to be a Mental Health Peer Counselor. With the help of a close friend, she mapped out a plan to achieve this goal. She ventured out of town despite her social anxiety to attend courses. I was never more proud. More recently, she earned her college degree, the first in our family to graduate from college. It took her twenty years.

I will never forget when my mother told me she had become part of NAMI, the National Alliance of Mental Health. I felt joy in my heart that she had found a place where she could positively influence the course of others who faced challenges such as hers. The woman who once avoided crowds at all costs called me to ask for assistance setting up for a benefit concert, saying that she was the volunteer coordinator for the event. I enlisted my son to help take down chairs after the show. We enjoyed the concert and my mom even danced with my son for a bit. I smiled inside, overcome with emotion and thinking about how far she had come. When they called the members of the committee up to the stage for introductions, I was shocked to hear that my mother was Vice President. I had no idea.

I never knew all the struggles my mother faced as I was growing up. But I know it took courage and strength for her to power through her illness. She fought fiercely and chose to be the author of her own adventure. This is why my mother will forever be a hero to me.

~Holly Wilkinson

The Matriarch

*A woman is the full circle. Within her is the power to
create, nurture and transform.*
~Diane Mariechild

Young men who attempt to date one of my three beautiful
daughters must first make it past my mother alive. We call
her The Matriarch.

At first glance, she doesn't appear that intimidating. She's
short and pale, and her red hair is never the same shade two months
running. Nevertheless, she interviews the trembling novitiate with her
blue eyes narrowed and a pitiless smile barely curving her lips.

"So, Daniel… what makes you worthy of our Rachel? How do
you plan to earn a living? What do you love best about her? Just what
makes you think you deserve her?" If she's in a generous mood that
day, she might let the unfortunate beau off with a mere forty-five
minute grilling.

My mother's frightening feminine force has apparently passed
on to her daughters and granddaughters, if we are to believe the men
in the family. Recently, a young husband was heard quietly coaching
a newcomer, whose wide eyes looked as though he'd accidentally
stumbled upon a tribe of Amazon warriors preparing for the hunt:
"Concentrate on the mother. The power flows from there."

Let me hasten to explain that my mother has a noble purpose,
greater than toying with the fragile egos of young suitors, amusing
as that may be. She takes her role as tribal elder seriously. Over her

seventy years, she has learned the value of prudence, primarily by making mistakes. She considers it her sacred duty to impart hard-won wisdom to those she loves, hoping to save them from wrong turns they might otherwise take in life. And so she stands guard at life's crossroads, posing hard questions intended to make her loved ones pause and think before proceeding.

My mother wasn't always a sphinx-lady swathed in bright, flamboyant clothing. Back in the early sixties, she was a small town teenager "in trouble." Friends turned their backs on her, and her new mother-in-law did everything she could to assure that the terrified girl would never forget her shame.

Life as an eighteen-year-old mother is never easy. But my mom had to face it without help or mercy. I didn't realize until I was grown that Mom had suffered from depression for most of my childhood, although it didn't surprise me when she admitted it. Having now raised my own four kids as a single mother, with my mom always nearby to help and support, I appreciate even more the strength she exerted just to get through each day on her own with her four young children.

"The only thing that kept me from killing myself," she confided to me once, "was knowing that you kids would be brought up by your grandmother if I wasn't there."

"Do you wish your life had taken a different turn back then?" I asked. "Do you ever wish you'd gone to Paris like you wanted to, instead of getting married and having kids so young?"

She answered without a moment's hesitation. "Never. I could have made lots of different choices at any time. You kids are the best thing I ever did. Anything more that I do in my life is just frosting on the cake."

I used to think Mom was easily distracted. No sooner would she get a degree or start a new job than she'd be looking at the requirements for the next one. In addition to her eclectic studies and many jobs, she owned and operated a plethora of businesses, made beautiful art, wrote a couple of books, got her real estate license, and filled her home with a gallery of interesting finds from estate sales and nature. Her hair got redder, her clothes got brighter, and she kept blooming in surprising new directions.

"The world is just such an interesting place!" she enthused. "With so much to learn and do and see, who could be content with just one life? I'm determined to cram as many as I can into this one."

Mom's stubborn refusal to bow down to circumstance was the example I needed. My own marriage was singularly unfortunate. My husband's ability to squirm out of his responsibility to our children and simultaneously cause us to live in fear and poverty was truly impressive… to most people. My mother was not impressed.

Late one night, at a time when I had packed up my kids in a panic and run home to Mom, looking for a refuge, my husband showed up. He immediately began browbeating me, convincing me that all of our difficulties were my fault, and that I needed to get back home where I belonged. At the time, I was too emotionally confused and physically weakened to protect myself. My mother heard the harangue from her room and descended the stairs like a night-gowned Valkyrie, red hair shooting out from her head like righteous flames. She ordered him from her house, backed him out of the door, and slammed it in his face, warning him not to come back. We had considerably less trouble with him after that.

I understand her ferocity better now, having grown children of my own. I can hardly imagine the pain she must have felt, watching me suffer through unwise life decisions, unable to fix them the way she did when I was little. What she could do, however, was be present, and be a proper, rollicking grandma to her grandchildren, even though she had a full life and interesting work of her own to tend to. Like everything else, my mother did her grandmothering with flair.

For years, my kids spent Fridays with Grandma Cindy while I worked. I would come to collect them at the end of the day, invariably finding them pink-cheeked and flecked with fabric paint from the sweatshirts they'd been decorating with fabulous designs, or their clothes blotched with homemade play-dough. One day, I found them out on the back porch, plastering multi-colored handprints on white, plastic chairs. More often than not, however, they would all be cuddled up together on the big, comfy couch, stuffing their faces with cookies, blowing bubbles, and watching cartoons — Mom, too.

With Grandma nearby, my kids learned that they were safe and loved, and maybe the world wasn't such a scary place, after all. In her own unpredictable way, she's still teaching them. Just recently, I came home from work to find my three grown daughters and my mother dressed in flowing gowns, boots, and floppy hats, having a tea party. Mom clutched a wizard's staff.

"Oh, good! You're just in time for tea!"

The manner in which my mother has lived her life is a great example to the rest of us: "Never stop learning; never stop reinventing yourself; don't be afraid to try something new; never give up; be loyal to the ones you love; for heaven's sake, color outside of the lines; and always… always do all things with passion."

~Rhonda Brunea

Words Behind Bars

A great vision is always birthed from a great burden.
~Dave Ferguson

I just mailed out another letter to a prisoner — the fourth letter I've sent this week. Three years ago I didn't think twice about the men and women behind bars.

Then, my coach and mentor, whom I have known well for thirty-five years, was arrested and imprisoned. My husband Jamie and I were thrown into the world of prison families. The shock was unbelievable. It's an invisible, silent community. Nobody talks about it. Families bear the burden alone.

Jamie and I knew that we would stay beside him, believing in him. He had walked faithfully with us for three decades; we would walk with him. We started writing letters. As a pastor, Jamie began to visit Coach at the county prison. I wanted to send him something that would brighten his heart in the midst of this dark, cold place. I pulled out my photo of daisies and used Photoshop to add Philippians 4:13 across it. "I can do all things through Christ who strengthens me." I printed the 4x6 photo with a white edge, tucked it in my letter and sent it.

Coach's next letter expressed how deeply my photo touched his heart. I created another verse-photo; then another, and eventually we started referring to them as WORDpictures. Other inmates began requesting them. They hung the WORDpictures on the walls of their cells with toothpaste. They sent them to their family and friends, because now

Recognizing Role Models | 373

they had a gift to give their loved ones. Prior to going to court, one inmate said, "This one went to court with me last time, and it's going with me again tomorrow," referring to the Joshua 1:9 WORDpicture I had made: "Be strong and courageous." The next week we opened a letter and out fell five beautiful toilet paper roses that were made by an inmate. This man created art and beauty from the one thing he had. I designed a WORDpicture from those perfectly sculpted flowers that he made without a hint of tape or glue, added the verse, "I have loved you with an everlasting love," and sent the WORDpicture back. Coach couldn't even open a letter from us without inmates standing around him asking for WORDpictures as soon as he pulled them from the envelope.

A bigger story was beginning to unfold. The words in Hebrews 13:3 were now jumping off the page at me: "Continue to remember those in prison as if you were together with them in prison." Continue? I just started! How had I missed that for all these years? I had never once considered a prisoner as anything more than… a prisoner.

Within the year Jamie, Coach and I began a ministry that we named Bound Together. We had the people in our church each adopt a prisoner and send him a Christmas card and a book. Our initial twenty-six men grew to more than 120 men and women, who now also receive a card on their birthdays and a letter each month. Coach is a vital part of the program.

Over 3,000 WORDpictures are currently behind bars. God escorts them right through prison security, razor wire, and steel and into the hands of these inmates who are hungry for Him. It's humbling to watch God work through these little photos! Timothy hit it right on the mark when he said, "God's Word is not chained" (2 Timothy 2:9). This morning we received two letters from prisoners thanking us for WORDpictures, and one letter asking, "How can I get more?" I sat down, wrote a letter, included a few WORDpictures, and walked it to the mailbox. Friends are beginning to send us stamps to help with the multiple letters we send per week.

Sometimes things come into our lives unexpectedly that change us forever. Prison has changed me. Prison has changed Jamie. It changes all the families that it touches. We are just ordinary people who waste time and give time, who spend time and take time, but never in a million years did we think that anyone we knew would do time.

I am beginning to understand how after spending years in prison, the Biblical character Joseph could say, "God meant it for good." Coach agrees. His exact words as we finished our recent visit were, "There are more positives to this journey than negatives."

He said it three times. For my benefit. He's still coaching.

~Julie Overholser

The Mints

*If you are planning for a year, sow rice; if you are
planning for a decade, plant trees; if you are planning
for a lifetime, educate people.*
~Chinese Proverb

enny's eyes were filled with tears when she approached my
desk. I reached for the tissue box with my left hand and an
extra chair with my right.

"What's wrong, Jenny?" I asked as she sobbed. I motioned
for Jenny to sit down next to my desk in the back of the room.

"I didn't do my homework." Her tiny brown frame slunk into the
chair. She began to unfold a note from her grandmother that read:

Dear Teacher:
*Please excuse Jenny from her homework last night. We are having a
family emergency. Her mother's cancer has spread and she went into surgery
last night. Jenny will complete her homework tonight. Please call if you have
any questions. Thank you for understanding.*
Sincerely,
Cindy

I slowly ran my fingers along the edge of the cookie tin that sat
next to the tissue box on my desk. "Here you go, Jenny. Take one of
each of these," I whispered.

She stared at the mints in the tin for a second. "No thank you," she whispered back. I placed one of the mint Lifesavers in front of her as I adjusted my desk chair so that it was about the same height as hers.

"Jenny, have I ever told you the story about my great-grandmother and the mints?" She shook her head no.

"Well, when I was four, I visited my great-grandmother's house. She had crystal candy dishes full of mints and I always wanted some." Jenny's sobbing began to subside and she opened the mint and placed it on her tongue.

"We called my grandmother Big Mama." Jenny chuckled. "Where Big Mama was from in Texas, all great-grandmothers are called Big Mama. The name shows she is the mother of all the mothers in the family and is to be respected through the generations by all family members.

"Big Mama asked me to go outside and play. I ran right to the eucalyptus tree and danced around the tree until I tripped on one of its roots and fell on a pile of twigs. I cried. I limped back to Big Mama's door with a bloody knee. She grabbed a towel and wiped my leg. She told me to get a mint, put it in my mouth, and go sit in the family room to watch *Perry Mason* with her.

"I limped into the room sobbing with the mint floating around in my mouth. When her show had finished I asked, 'Can I have a bandage for my leg?'

"'They are in the cabinet in the bathroom, Sugar Baby.' I bolted to the bathroom and grabbed one and placed it on my leg. I sat back in the family room next to Big Mama and thanked her.

"'Does your leg feel better?'

"'Yes,' I said with a smile on my face.

"When I was eight, ten, and fourteen years old, the same thing happened. 'You children will never learn,' she said, shaking her head. 'Go in there and get a mint and go sit down and watch television.' I volleyed that mint around in my mouth while we watched *Perry Mason* each time.

"At eighteen, I was too old to run around, but still felt like Big Mama could protect me from hurt and pain. I had tears in my eyes when I got to her door and rang the bell. 'What's wrong?' she said.

"'The doctor told me today that I have cancer and I may die.' I fell into her arms for a moment. Seemingly unfazed by my news, she pushed me away slightly and, as usual, stated, 'Grab a mint and come into the family room and watch *Perry Mason* with me.' She slowly moved into the family room while I brooded.

"'What is this stupid mint going to do?' I went into the family room and threw myself onto the couch and folded my arms while sobbing. I couldn't see the television and I couldn't think straight. I just knew I was angry and wanted to be anywhere but watching *Perry Mason*. I wanted someone to hold me while I cried. I felt like a big baby.

"I crunched the mint and swallowed it in a single gulp. 'Why do you always tell me to grab a mint? Did you hear me when I said the doctor told me I have cancer? I am going to die! Don't you care?'

"Big Mama picked up the old remote control and clicked off the television. She looked at me with soft and serious eyes. 'Do you feel better now?'

"'No, I don't feel better. I am going to die!' I yelled and cried tears that seemed to sting like each shard of the mint I chewed up that scratched its way down my throat.

"'Sugar Baby,' she explained, 'I always ask you to get a mint when you are hurting, because the pain goes away when you focus on something else. I worked like a dog for demanding people for years and never complained. I would simply pop a mint in my mouth and turn on the radio and in fifteen minutes, I could get back to work. Each time you fell down as a child, I asked you to do the same thing, and you were happy because the mint and *Perry Mason* helped to take the thought of the pain away.'

"My eyes began to water again.

"'Do you think you are the first person a doctor has told is going to die from cancer? Do you think you are the first person to worry? Well child I will tell you, I am no doctor, but I know most people die before death from worrying about dying. They get so caught up in it that they forget to live. I want better for you. I tell you to put a mint in your mouth so you can stop worrying. Ain't no need in doing that so hush, Sugar Baby,' she commanded as she kissed me gently on my forehead and turned on the TV again.

"I have survived cancer three other times since then. Whenever I felt scared, I popped a mint in my mouth."

"Here," I motioned with the tin of mints. "Take one for each of your family members. Tell them that if they just have a mint, it can be a real lifesaver for everyone. Assure them that your family will be okay as long as they do not worry themselves to death by forgetting to live while they are alive."

"Have a great day everyone," I announced as the bell rang. Jenny gave me a hug, quickly ran to her desk, grabbed her backpack, and ran to her next class.

My eyes began to water. I popped in a mint and was able to stop the tears.

~Christopher Davis

Astronauts and Olympians

My father gave me the greatest gift anyone could give
another person, he believed in me.
~Author Unknown

When I was eight I was diagnosed with asthma. The doctor was very intense about the diagnosis and I was given photocopied pages and stern lectures from the imposing, gray-haired man about all the things I would no longer enjoy in life. He told me that I could no longer have stuffed animals and that I couldn't have any rugs — that all the floors had to be able to be cleaned very easily. Even a throw rug was dangerous, as it might not get washed as often as it should. He told me that my mattress would have to be wrapped in plastic. Most devastating, he told me that I would have to give away my dog and that I could never be around animals again.

I clutched my new asthma inhaler as I left his office, shocked. I had just been told that the life that I knew was over and that all the things I loved best were to be taken from me. Even going outside would have to be approached with caution for fear that allergies could be triggered and that could, he declared, kill me.

I spent about a month being depressed. I did my chores and I read my books, but the desire to live life had been snuffed out of me. I took my asthma inhaler everywhere I went and that blue puffer grew huge in my mind.

My dad was concerned about the changes in me. I didn't see how worried he was for me at the time; I was too worried that every breath I took might be my last. My mom read over the sheets of warnings with me regularly and scolded me; she was the one who put the plastic on my mattress and took away my stuffed animals.

When my dad took me out for ice cream I was worried that he was going to tell me that they had found a home for my dog at last and that would be the end of her too. I was on the brink of tears as I ate my banana split but I was trying hard to be brave. He put a magazine on the table. It was open to a picture of a woman running so fast the camera had blurred the picture.

I looked up at him as he pointed at the picture with his calloused, working man's finger. "Do you see her, sweetheart? She won a medal in the Olympics and you know what? She had asthma; she had it real bad."

Suddenly the picture took on new meaning. This woman was a freak like me. She had to have her mattress wrapped up. She had clutched her blue puffer when she slept but she had run... she had run like the wind.

"Honey, you can worry about what the doctor said, or you can listen to me. You were living and running and playing with your puppy and all that ever happened was a little wheeze or two. You can do anything you want."

My gaze darted back to his eyes from the picture. "Anything?"

He nodded earnestly, "Anything at all. You can run in the Olympics and you can win the gold; you can be an astronaut and go into space. You and I are the same that way. You put your mind to it and there is absolutely nothing too hard for you."

The spell had been broken. I knew from his eyes that he was telling me the truth. I knew from the picture in front of me that he had sought out proof.

From that day onward, his words rang in my head. I have survived many hardships, accomplished many things and I have always set my sights higher. I didn't want to run in the Olympics and I didn't really want to go to the moon, but it was the knowledge that I could that made me strong in other ways. My dog lived to an old age and the plastic came off my bed. My stuffed animals were returned without comment and I didn't die.

Over the years I had a few asthma attacks that were bad enough to put me in the hospital, but they didn't scare me. I would overcome it. It wasn't just being positive, it was also being certain and having someone believe in me, believe I could be an astronaut or an Olympian. My father's positive attitude changed my life and it has propelled me ever since.

~Virginia Carraway Stark

The Wall

*I believe people are in our lives for a reason. We're
here to learn from each other.*
~Gillian Anderson

As a camp instructor, I was privileged to meet many amazing people. Several were extraordinary children who remain in my heart and memory. Although our mission was to make an impact on them, they were often the ones making an impact on me. As Rogers and Hammerstein so aptly stated in *The King and I*, "If you become a teacher, by your pupils you'll be taught."

One child in particular stands out. Emily came to camp one spring with her class on a one-week field trip. It looked like a normal group of preteen kids, but one of the group leaders pulled our staff aside to tell us about Emily, who had Down syndrome. Although I had friends with Down syndrome, I had never worked on a professional level with someone who had it. As her instructor for part of the week, I would need to understand more about Emily. Knowing this, I paid close attention to the instructions we were given.

As the adults began to discuss her, I sensed an emphasis more on the handicap than on the child. I have no doubt that the adults there meant well. As they spoke about Emily, though, there was a lot about what she could or couldn't do and nothing about who she was. I found this slightly disturbing, but told myself that I was being overly sensitive and brushed the thought aside.

Each child who attended the camp was special. As instructors, we tried to breathe something positive into every child's life. For me, however, there was always one child each week who stood out from the crowd. It was almost as if someone was shining a spotlight on a particular boy or girl. Although I always made a real effort to have an impact on each child, I found myself focusing on what a co-worker laughingly called my "projects." I poured much of my time, energy, and heart into each one.

That week, it was Emily. She drew my attention like a magnet. I tried to dismiss it, telling myself that I didn't have enough experience with Down syndrome children to help her. I felt that I had nothing to offer; I even searched the group for another special child. What business did I have, thinking that I could do something for her that trained professionals couldn't? My eyes, though, kept wandering back to that one little girl, standing apart from the rest.

As the week progressed, I saw how separated she was from her classmates. Even though she participated in activities, Emily was often on the sidelines. At times, the others might look around and notice her attempts to keep up. However, I realized that most felt she was holding them back. I heard them say things such as, "We have to wait for Emily," or "She's such a slowpoke! Why does she have to be in our crew?" When they said those things, I could see Emily trying to keep up. Her body just wouldn't cooperate. It was heartbreaking.

That week, I was scheduled to teach two classes. I began with my signature class, Orienteering. I would do five rotations of it, one for each crew. Then, on Wednesday after lunch, I would switch over to a class that I didn't often get the opportunity to lead. I would be facilitating as each crew took a turn on the camp's climbing wall, Goliath. It was a session I enjoyed leading on those rare occasions; I witnessed amazing things when kids got on that wall and climbed.

The week progressed, and the sessions with Goliath began. Each of the children set a climbing goal. Several achieved it; some surpassed it. There were a few who needed a little more encouragement, and there were those who surprised themselves when they scurried right up the wall. The smile when they accomplished their goal was a reward in itself.

There were always a few who froze on the wall. For some reason, they got only so far and stopped. Then, I would step in with needed encouragement. "Can you take just one more step?' I would ask. "Can you do one more?" Sometimes, the child would take that step and end up making it to the top. Other times, they would take the step and then ask to come down. There were also times when the child just couldn't go higher, so I belayed that child to the ground. I made certain to congratulate them no matter how high they climbed.

That Thursday, Emily's crew rotated into their session with Goliath. I gave my talk about setting a goal and then segued right into the safety rules. The kids eagerly strapped on harnesses. Within minutes, I had my first climber on the wall. I noticed that, yet again, Emily was hanging on the sidelines. No one had even considered her when harnesses were being distributed.

Her crewmates were surprised to see her step forward. Several started whispering about wasting time. Emily was undeterred. When I handed her the harness and helmet, she immediately put them on.

One of the adults walked up. "Just attach her to the rope and let her put her foot on the wall. She won't climb," she told me. "She can't do it."

As I secured her to the belay rope, she reached out and rested her hand on Goliath. She craned her neck, looking up to the top. Her crewmates tightened the slack; she bit her lip. Her hands went up, her left foot lifted… and slipped.

When it hit the ground, the murmuring started. "She can't do it. Why are we wasting time?" I watched Emily's face crumple at their words. Her arms came down to her side.

That's when it happened. Emily squared her shoulders; she studied the wall. Her hands came up; her left leg rose. Straining her trembling arms, she hoisted herself. Her body inched up the wall, and her feet left the ground.

At first, there was utter silence. Then, her crewmates began to cheer. By the time her leg lifted again, they were even louder. When she rose up the wall, they were roaring.

Emily only took two steps. There were many who made it further.

However, for the rest of that week, all her classmates were talking about her climb. Through a single act, she went from outcast to superhero.

I don't know what became of Emily. I have not seen her since, but she taught me a valuable lesson. When I feel like quitting, I remember how she conquered that wall and did what everyone thought impossible. I pull myself together and try again. And Emily, wherever you are, thank you for teaching me what faith, grit, and a little encouragement can do.

~Jennifer Lautermilch

Meet Our Contributors

Cara Sue Achterberg lives on a hillside farm in south central Pennsylvania with her family and way too many animals. She's written two books: *Live Intentionally: 65 Challenges for a Healthier, Happier Life* and a novel entitled *I'm Not Her*. Learn more at www.CaraWrites.com.

Steven Alexander is the founder and creative director of the video game studio Infamous Quests. When not writing, designing and programming, he spends time playing guitar and relaxing with his wife and two Boston Terriers.

Barbara Alpert is a wife, mother and grandmother living on the west coast of Florida. She has written books for children and adults along with her latest, *The Games We Play With God*. She is active in her church, serves as a women's small group leader, and is a devotional writer. E-mail Barbara at Arisemydaughter@aol.com.

Shantell Antoinette has earned her bachelor's degree in Communications from a private HBCU located in Charlotte, NC. She is mother to a high school honors student and a middle school student with autism. Life has been difficult, and singing and writing have been constant companions pushing her beyond her circumstances.

MaryAnn Austen received her Bachelor of Business Administration degree from the University of Wisconsin–Milwaukee. She has one son and two stepdaughters. MaryAnn enjoys traveling, reading and entertaining. She plans to write humorous fiction and inspirational books related to depression and loss. E-mail her at ssneuhaus@yahoo.com.

Brittany Autumn Austin is a passionate advocate for individuals with autism. She volunteered in a self-contained classroom for six years in high school and went on to major in Special Education, with honors. She is driven by her hopes, dreams, and family. E-mail Brittany at Baustin@mail.niagara.edu.

Rose Barbour is an addictions advocate and blogger. Always standing beside her and cheering her on is her husband and best friend, their three wonderful children and their beautiful granddaughter who is a constant reminder of all that is good in the world. Read her blog at shadowsinpei.blogspot.ca.

Having successfully launched four children into their own lives and completed a B.S. degree, **Rhonda Brunea** is reinventing herself in Orkney, Scotland, where she is rediscovering her love of writing and the healing magic of stories.

Sally Burbank has practiced medicine in Nashville for twenty-five years. Her new book, *Patients I Will Never Forget*, is a collection of hilarious and inspiring stories about her most memorable patients. Available on Amazon or her website at sallywillardburbank.com. Learn more at www.patientswewillneverforget.wordpress.com.

Kathryn Cagg leads grief recovery groups as a result of her personal experience with grief and finds it to be a great joy to walk with others through the profound journey of healing and discovery of God's leading. She also enjoys hosting a Transformative Language Arts group, home decorating, antiquing, family and friends.

Kathe Campbell lives her dream on a Montana mountain with her mammoth donkeys, a Keeshond, and a few kitties. Three children, eleven grands and many greats round out her herd. She is a prolific writer on Alzheimer's, and her stories are found on many e-zines.

Lorraine Cannistra is an author, speaker, blogger, wheelchair dancer and proud partner to her service dog, Leah. She enjoys using her writing to challenge negative perceptions some may have about those with disabilities. Follow her blog *Health on Wheels* at healthonwheels.wordpress.com. Learn more at lorrainecannistra.com.

Eva Carter is married to Larry, who's made her a "wicked" stepmother of three, grandmother of five and a great-grandmother of one. She's worked in finance and taught aerobics. She enjoys playing with her kitten, Ollie, yoga, dance classes and writing. The kitten and the writing are her passions. E-mail her at evacarter@sbcglobal.net.

Erika Chody lives in Austin, TX with her husband and a house full of pets. Erika teaches 7th and 8th grade English as a Second Language and is working on completing her master's degree in Reading Education at Texas State University.

Vidal Cisneros Jr. has two beautiful daughters. He is a contributor to *The Huffington Post* and The Good Men Project. Vidal speaks to audiences about the power of gratitude, and he is releasing his first book on his inspirational journey from brokenness to fulfillment. For inquiries, e-mail him at info@VidalCisnerosJr.com.

Robin Conte is a freelance writer and mother of four, including twins. Her humor column, "Robin's Nest," appears in the *Reporter Newspapers* in Atlanta. A Wake Forest University graduate with a master's degree in Education from Emory, she is writing a book about her family's three years in Germany. E-mail her at robinjm@earthlink.net.

Writing to inspire emotion is **Patrick Coomer's** specialty. Currently a bus operator in Portland, OR, Patrick draws from a unique perspective to write pieces that caress the soul.

Jax Cortez is a former schoolteacher with a master's degree in Education turned freelance writer, blogger, and indie author. She is happily married to her crime-fighting husband and adores her rambunctious little girl. She enjoys writing stories of empowerment and practicing the self-defense system of Krav Maga.

Barbara Davey is Director of Community Relations at Crane's Mill, a retirement community in West Caldwell, NJ. She received her bachelor's and master's degrees from Seton Hall University and is an adjunct professor at Caldwell University, where she teaches business writing. E-mail her at BarbaraADavey@aol.com.

Christine Davis is a published novelist with her award-winning series *Takers*, available on Amazon (under Chris Davis). She's currently working on two new book series and a television pilot screenplay, and has written several feature screenplays. Christine resides in Honolulu, HI.

Christopher Davis is a poet, teacher, and photographer. He holds a B.A. degree in English and in Pan-African Studies, and M.A. and Ed.S. degrees in Education. He has written thousands of poems about life. He is the author of a book of poetry entitled *Only, If: A Book of Poetry Volume 1*, which is available for download at the Apple iBooks store.

Shari Bowes Deaven lives with her husband Glenn on their family farm in Pennsylvania. They are blessed to watch their grandchildren grow up on the farm as five generations before them have done. Shari's writing is neither a hobby nor a profession, it is simply how she processes the events in her life.

Dana L. Dickson has been married for a really long time to an awesome guy, and is the mother of two incredible children. She is a voracious reader, and has a bit of an obsession with Halloween.

Maria Dorsey grew up in Urbana, IL before moving to Massapequa, NY in 2009. After finishing her bike tour, she moved to and now lives in San Leandro, CA. She spends her time painting her favorite landscapes from her trip, growing and talking to her wildflowers, singing, playing her guitar and petting every dog she sees.

Robin Martin Duttmann is an award-winning children's picture book author. Her book *Zoo on the Moon* was recently selected for the Primary Science curriculum in 147 countries through theiblibrary.com. She is also a Children's Literary Teacher for the Windsor International Writers' Conference. E-mail her at booga338@hotmail.com.

Melissa Edmondson, a wife, mother, and paralegal by profession, is proud to be appearing in her fourth *Chicken Soup for the Soul* book. She has also appeared in *Reflections on the New River* and has published her own book of essays, entitled *Lessons Abound*. Visit her website at www.missyspublicjunk.wordpress.com.

Peris DeVohn Edwards received his bachelor's degree in Social Work from Miami University in 2010. He is a firefighter and his favorite hobbies are reading, writing and traveling. He plans on writing inspirational books to inspire people to become all they can be. He also substitute teaches part-time for Toledo Public Schools.

Sydna Elrod is a Navy "brat" and proud of it. She has some college credits but considers her life experience to be of more value. She loves people, making new friends, reading mysteries, and going to Baltimore Ravens games. She also loves reading and understanding the Bible.

Lynn Fitzsimmons was born legally blind and for most of her life struggled to break through her fears to achieve and succeed. Today she is a professional speaker, best-selling author, and mentor/coach helping people to transform their lives to live a happy, prosperous, grateful, and joyful lifestyle. E-mail her at lynn@stepoutforsuccess.ca.

Carole Brody Fleet is a multiple award-winning author and media contributor, appearing on numerous television and radio programs and in national and international publications. Ms. Fleet resides with her family in Southern California.

James Foltz graduated from Penn State, and like many English degree graduates, he is writing the "Great American Novel." He enjoys "date nights" with his wonderful wife and playing "wrestle-house" with his two young boys while trying to avoid serious injury. His book *All the Past We Leave Behind* will be available in 2015.

Karen Frazier is a freelance writer and author. Her books cover multiple topics, including spirituality, health and nutrition, and cooking. She is married and has a college-age son, teenaged stepson, four dogs, and a cat. She lives in the Pacific Northwest with her husband.

Peggy Purser Freeman is the author of *The Coldest Day in Texas*, *Swept Back to a Texas Future*, *Cruisin' Thru Life: Dip Street and Other Miracles*, and *Spy Cam One*. Her experience as a magazine editor, student writing workshop teacher and her many published works in magazines across Texas inspire readers. Learn more at PeggyPurserFreeman.com.

Jenna Glatzer is the bestselling author or ghostwriter of more than twenty-five books. She is Celine Dion's authorized biographer and the author of a Marilyn Monroe biography authorized by her estate. Jenna has the most wonderful eight-year-old daughter. Learn more at www.jennaglatzer.com.

Nancy Goodfellow is a writer and mother in Naperville, IL. Since her daughter was born with Down syndrome, she has served as a support parent and public speaker for the National Association for Down Syndrome. She is currently writing children's books that encourage friendships with individuals with special needs.

Lee Gale Gruen became an actress, author, public speaker, and blogger in her senior years. She lives in Los Angeles, CA, and has two children and three grandchildren. Her published résumé includes a memoir, articles, personal essays, and an ongoing blog. Read more at AdventuresWithDadTheBook.com or LeeGaleGruen.wordpress.com.

Jen Gulka grew up in Toronto, ON. She currently resides in Saskatoon, SK, where she relocated (for love!) to find some peace and open air. Her passions include inspiring people through her website/blog at rainydayhappiness.com, traveling, writing, spending time with family, yoga, swimming, archery, and living in the moment.

Melissa C. Harrison holds a B.A. degree in English and Sociology and an M.S. degree in Psychology with a specialty in Leadership Development and Coaching. Melissa is a former educator and is now an Inspiration Specialist/Personal Coach. Learn more at www.melissacatherineharrison. com. E-mail her at melissacatherineharrison@gmail.com.

Janet Hartman sailed away from New Jersey in 2000 to follow the sun along the East Coast for six years. While afloat, she left software consulting to pursue her never-forgotten dream of writing. Since then, her work has appeared in a variety of anthologies, magazines, newspapers, and e-zines. Learn more at JanetHartman.net.

Joanne Haynes was a finalist in the 2002 Commonwealth Short Story contest and won the Derek Walcott/TTW Prize in 2005. In 2012 she received a Lifetime Literary Award. Recently she has delved into filmmaking. She marries her creativity and devotion to education through Pepperpot Productions. Learn more at www.pepperpot.org.

Linda Garrett Hicks lives in Middle Tennessee with her husband of forty years. She manages their family-owned herb store, staffed by their two children. Writing is Linda's number one pastime. Her works have appeared in various magazines; and *Through the Storms*, a book of poems, released in 2012. Learn more at lindagarretthicks.com.

Darrell Horwitz began writing at an early age, sharing his views on sports in the opinion column of the *Chicago Sun-Times*. His love of sports and writing has lasted a lifetime. He is currently working on a self-help book and resides in Chicago, IL, where he hosts a sports radio show. E-mail him at darrellhorwitz@gmail.com.

Ariffa Hosein received a Bachelor of Social Work degree from Ryerson University and Certificate in Human Resource Management from Sheridan College in Ontario, Canada. She enjoys reading and writing with her three children and husband. She has written her first novel and is working on her second. Ariffa is a recovering chocoholic.

Deborah J. is a performing artist from Maryland. She has delivered vocal performances for audiences across the East Coast, but her passion is the written word. In 2005, she graduated with honors from the University of Maryland Eastern Shore and worked for several news stations before deciding to pursue her writing career.

A past contributor to the *Chicken Soup for the Soul* series, **Alice Klies** is president of Northern Arizona's Word Weavers International writing group. She is currently writing a memoir. Her passion for writing is only surpassed by her love for her family and Golden Retriever dogs. E-mail her at alice.klies@gmail.com.

Susan Kocian is a native Texan, born and raised in Central Texas. She completed her education there and worked for a large corporation for over twenty-six years. She is a mom to a wonderful son, a birth-mom, and a dog owner. She enjoys traveling and flea markets. She has written a screenplay and is working on a novel.

Madison Kurth is a senior in high school. She plays varsity soccer and wrestles for her school. Madison has a strong fascination with biology and hopes to have a career in the medical field.

Lisa McManus Lange is a writer and archer in Victoria, BC. When she's not aiming her bow on the range of the Victoria Bowmen Archery

Club, she writes for her blog and for kids and teens. This is her eighth Chicken Soup for the Soul story. Learn more about Lisa at www.lisamcmanuslange.blogspot.com or email her at lisamc2010@yahoo.ca.

Jennifer Lautermilch received her Bachelor of Arts degree from Goshen College in 2002. She is a freelance writer living in Northeast Ohio. She enjoys nature, cooking, reading, and spending time with her friends and family.

Morgan Liphart is an emerging author from the heartland of Illinois. She strives to provide a fresh and compelling perspective on the human experience through her work. In the past few years, she appeared in literary journals across the country, such as *Magnolia* and *Bluestem*. E-mail her at morganliphart@gmail.com.

Katherine Magnoli is a thirty-one-year-old author of a children's book series entitled *The Adventures of KatGirl*. Her stories about a superhero in a wheelchair who helps kids who are being bullied both educates and entertains children about the topics of disability and acceptance.

Alicia McCauley is a first grade teacher, a teacher consultant for the Northern California Writing Project, and is the Founder and President of Vigilante Kindness — a non-profit that provides educational opportunities for children in developing countries. She is happily married to her high school sweetheart.

Shaylene McPhee received her Bachelor of Science degree, with honors, from Post University in 2015. She has a daughter who she loves spending time with. Her hobbies include writing, reading, crocheting and painting. Now that she has completed school, she plans to dedicate more time to writing inspirational works.

Cathy Mogus is a freelance writer, inspirational speaker, and author of *Dare to Dance Again: Steps from the Psalms When Life Trips You Up*. She has been published in the *Chicken Soup for the Soul* series, *Guideposts*, and many other publications. She resides in Richmond, BC. E-mail her at acmogus@shaw.ca.

Donia Moore is a freelance writer in Southern California. As a "rusty pilot" who hasn't flown in a while, she loves aviation and writes articles for several general aviation publications on a regular basis. Favorite weekend breaks are spent kayaking with her dog in summer and snowshoeing in winter.

D.J. Morhart is an avid roller derby player with Saskatoon Roller Derby League, and a student at the University of Saskatchewan. When she isn't holed up with her novel-in-progress, she's outside enjoying the frequently horrible Saskatchewan weather with her dog.

When **Gail Molsbee Morris** isn't chasing after God's heart, she chases rare birds across America. She can be reached through her nature blog *God Girl Gail* at godgirlgail.com or Twitter @godgirlgail.

Annie Nason is currently a junior in college. She has been a guest blogger for *Teen Cerebral Palsy* at TeenCerebralPalsy.com since 2012. "Three Simple Words" is her first published piece, and truly a dream come true! Annie would like to thank her family and friends for all their support and encouragement. She is incredibly grateful for this opportunity!

Carolee Noble was born and raised in Kansas. She lived a normal life raising her kids and enjoying her grandchildren. After the death of two of her daughters and a grandson she learned the importance of making the most of every moment. Carolee wants her legacy to be the knowledge that life can be fulfilling despite trials and tragedy.

Joyce Oglesby is a motivational, inspirational and generational speaker, author and radio talk show host of the *Just Ask Joyce* show. She is a pastor's wife and entrepreneur in the legal industry having owned the largest court reporting firm in Atlanta, GA and southern Indiana. Learn more at www.justaskjoyce.com.

Peggy Omarzu lives in a household comprised of four dogs, three cats, a guinea pig and an untold number of fish. She divides her time between working for a large non-profit agency, animal rescue and shelters, and veterinary medicine. Peggy writes stories about the animals and their people that have crossed her path while following these pursuits.

Julie Overholser is a photographer who started the now growing Bound Together ministry. She continually creates new WORDpictures as well as greeting cards specifically intended to encourage prisoners. Julie, Jamie, and their four children live in Northeastern Pennsylvania. Her cards are available at www.wordpictures.com.

Laura Padgett is an award-winning author who received her M.A. degree in Storytelling, with honors, from Regis University in Denver in 2009. She loves writing, dancing and traveling with her husband, Keith. Her first book *Dolores, Like the River*, about beauty and purpose in aging, was published in 2013 by WestBow Press.

Vaneza Paredes is currently attending Pasadena City College where she is learning something new every day. She lives in sunny Los Angeles, CA with her mom and sister. Vaneza loves reading and journaling, and plans on getting a degree in Psychology, so she can one day help young beautiful women love themselves.

Suzanne Peppers is passionate about life and writing. She is a mother of two married sons, Nani to three "littles," and celebrates forty years of marriage to Cliff, a pastor. Ministry follows long careers in media and law enforcement for the Peppers, who live in the Sierra Nevada foothills.

Novelist, blogger, and award-winning food writer, **Perry P. Perkins** is the CEO/Executive Chef of MY KITCHEN Outreach program. Perry has written for hundreds of magazines, and his inspirational stories have been included in many *Chicken Soup for the Soul* books. Learn more at www.joinmykitchen.com.

Debra Perleberg received her Bachelor of Arts degree in Communication from The University of Akron. She is married, has three children, and lives in Central Florida. She is a writer, public speaker and cheerleader of dreams. Her passion is to recognize the potential in others and draw it out. E-mail her at debra@underthepalmtrees.com.

Lauren Pottinger earned her Bachelor of Arts degree in Theater from the University of Central Florida after traveling with Up with People for a year. She is an avid performer, improvising and singing all over South Florida where she lives with her dog, Kevin. She is the creator and writer of a web comic called "PMS Adventures."

Rachel Printy's story "Polepole" is dedicated to her family and friends Caitlin Brazelton, Paola Buitron, and John Harbin, who continue to inspire her by running with endurance the race God has set before them. She also had her story "Sucia" published earlier this year in *Reed Magazine* issue #68. E-mail her at printyr@gmail.com.

Denise Reich is an Italian-born, New York City–raised freelance writer, dancer, photographer and world traveler. She has danced for *The Doctors*, *Mobbed*, *Good Day LA* and the Disney Channel, and recently "played the Palace" in Downtown Los Angeles. Her wonderful childhood dance teachers were Bridget, Chrissy and Mary.

A mother of two girls and grandmother to one grandson, **Heather Reid-Bell** lives in Perth, Australia. She loves bush walking, gardening and all manner of books.

Robin L. Reynolds is a working class hero, diehard fan of Howard Stern, and author of *Dear Jalen* at DearJalen.com. Now that class assignments are behind her, she enjoys traveling, listening to classic rock music and playing with her dogs Samson (German Shepherd), Delilah (rescue), Sadie (Vizsla), Sable (Vizsla), and Sasha (rescue).

It is rumored that the first word **Sue Ross** uttered gave her such satisfaction that she said it twice, "Author! Author!" Finding stories in everything she does, Sue revels in language that lifts and inspires. With a B.A. degree in English, she is completing her first novel, *Golanski's Treasures*. E-mail her at kidangel@me.com.

Monique Gabrielle Salazar holds a degree in Political Science and is an active member of the Kansas City arts community. She owns a suit accessories business that provides unique and one-of-a-kind stylish pieces. She enjoys making music, performing, painting, sculpting and above all, writing. E-mail her at mgswrites@gmail.com.

Stephanie E. Sievers is a nineteen-year-old from New Jersey who currently attends the University of Delaware as an English major. She hopes to use her experiences to become an activist for mental health acceptance, as well as to use her love of writing to become a novelist.

Laura Snell, her husband Dave and their dog Gus Gusterson live in Wasaga Beach, ON, where they operate their web development firm GBSelect.com. Her son Ryan lives in Melbourne, Australia. E-mail her at laura@gbselect.com.

Sharon "Fluffy" Spungen is a third degree black belt and one of the proud owners of Big Dog Taekwon-Do. She is a "recovering" attorney, helps run a dental office, tutors for the LSAT and writes résumés, but considers her most important job being mom to two amazing boys and wife to the most patient man on the planet.

Diane Stark is a frequent contributor to the *Chicken Soup for the Soul* series. She is a wife and mother of five and loves to write about the important things in life: her family and her faith. E-mail her at DianeStark19@yahoo.com.

Virginia Carraway Stark has written several novels, screenplays and many poems and short stories. She has been nominated for an Aurora Award and received an honourable mention at the Cannes Film Festival. She lives in Fraser Lake, BC with her husband and her animal children.

Mike Strand worked for twenty-four years in a factory after suffering a severe brain injury in a motor vehicle accident. He has won several volunteer awards for his work within the brain injury community. He retired from his factory job in 2012 and went back to school, earning his B.A. degree, with honors, in English.

L.A. Strucke is a writer from New Jersey and a graduate of Rowan University. Her stories appear in several *Chicken Soup for the Soul* books, *Guideposts* and other publications. She seeks to inspire others through writing. Her four children: Bill, Michelle, Ann and Krista, are her inspiration. Learn more at www.lastrucke.com.

Annmarie B. Tait resides in Conshohocken, PA with her husband Joe Beck. Annmarie is published in several *Chicken Soup for the Soul* books, *Reminisce* magazine, *The Patchwork Path*, and many other anthologies. She also enjoys cooking, crocheting, and singing Irish and American folk songs. E-mail her at irishbloom@aol.com.

Tsgoyna Tanzman is a speaker, author and life coach, and a frequent contributor to the *Chicken Soup for the Soul* series. A master of reinvention, she coaches people to discover, reveal and revel in their highest purposes. She knows the first step to enlightenment is to lighten up! Brainy and funny — her humorous essays appear in More.com.

Gina Tate is a stay-at-home mom of three. She enjoys cooking, learning new healthy recipes, sipping coffee with friends, and being active with her kids. Gina graduated from Bible college at Faith School of Theology in Charleston, ME and enjoys teaching from the Bible to kids, teens, and adults.

Tensie J. Taylor is from Louisburg, NC. She graduated from NC State University in 2009 with a B.A. in Communication and from the University of Southern California in 2014 with a master's in Education. Tensie is the manager of the USC Black Alumni Association in Los Angeles and is a red carpet host for an online network.

Annie Thibodeaux has two stories in the *Chicken Soup for the Soul* series. She lives with her husband, four children, new puppy, and one cat in San Antonio, TX. Annie enjoys working out, reading, and volunteering for non-profit organizations. This is dedicated to the amazing man she was lucky enough to marry.

Mandy Traut received a Master of Arts in Psychology, with honors, from Antioch University in 2006. After years in the counseling field, she became a passionate freelance writer. Mandy lives with her family-of-choice in San Jose. She loves going to retreats, musicals, and socials. Mandy aims to publish stories that inspire.

Lynne Turner has a Journalism degree from Ryerson University in Toronto, ON and spent nearly forty years as a reporter, then editor and manager of the *Mount Forest Confederate* newspaper. She enjoys reading, writing, walking, cooking and spending time with her friends and family.

Denise Valuk lives and writes from San Antonio, TX, while home-schooling her three boys. Her writing experiences include *Guideposts*, *Mysterious Ways* and *Chicken Soup for the Soul: Touched by an Angel*. Denise spends her free time hiking through Texas with her boys. Contact her through her website at www.denisevaluk.com.

David Warren has appeared in multiple *Chicken Soup for the Soul* books and also published a children's book titled *Mealtime Guests*. He is a regular contributor to *Dayton Parent* magazine. When not writing, David is Vice President for Lutz Americas. He lives in Kettering, OH with his wife Angela and daughter Marissa.

Barbara Weddle began writing after her four sons were grown. Her articles and essays have appeared in over 300 publications. Originally from the South, Barbara, retired, now lives in northern Wisconsin. In addition to writing, she enjoys traveling to see her grandchildren, photography and road travel.

K.L. Werle received a Bachelor of Arts in Political Science from LaGrange College and a Master of Public Administration from Columbus State University, both in Georgia. She enjoys traveling, reading, and is currently working on a fantasy series. She resides in Louisiana with her husband and their two German Shepherds.

Michael Whary is a sixteen-year-old from Ohio. He is an Eagle Scout, an honoree in ROTC and active in Marching and Jazz Band. He is on track to graduate with honors, and plans to attend college for business. Michael has produced an autism awareness video at www.youtube.com/watch?v=86MXGIDG7UM.

Kathy Whirity is a syndicated newspaper columnist who shares her sentimental musings on family life. Kathy is the author of *Life is a Kaleidoscope*, a compilation of reader's favorite columns. E-mail her at Kathywhirity@yahoo.com or learn more at www.kathywhirity.com.

Holly Wilkinson, her children, and her mother all live in the beautiful Pacific Northwest. She likes coffee, music, and rain, and writes short stories, blurbs and poetry on her *Woman at the Well* blog at womanatthewell-womanatthewell.blogspot.com. She continues to be inspired by the amazing strength of the woman who raised her.

Tina Williams lives in western Massachusetts with her husband Jeremy and beautiful daughter Lilly. When she's not working in a toy store she's writing stories, reading books, or watching movies.

Katrina Anne Willis is happily married to her high school sweetheart and is the mother of four teenagers. An author and essayist, Katrina was named a BlogHer 2015 Voice of the Year. Her first novel, *Parting Gifts*, will be published by She Writes Press in April 2016. E-mail her at katrina_willis@me.com.

A love of books set **Tammy Zaluzney** on a path to write from an early age, but a series of coincidences and mishaps changed her life's path. She ended up enjoying and sometimes cursing a long career in animal welfare. Thirty years later she is now writing about the compelling stories that shaped the course of her life.

Jeanne Zornes, of Washington State, is a speaker and author of seven books and hundreds of articles. She's contributed to several titles in the *Chicken Soup for the Soul* series. Jeanne writes an inspirational weekly blog titled *Jeanne Zornes* at jeannezornes.blogspot.com.

Meet Amy Newmark

Amy Newmark was a writer, speaker, Wall Street analyst and business executive in the worlds of finance and telecommunications for thirty years. Today she is publisher, editor-in-chief and coauthor of the *Chicken Soup for the Soul* book series. By curating and editing inspirational true stories from ordinary people who have had extraordinary experiences, Amy has kept the twenty-two-year-old Chicken Soup for the Soul brand fresh and relevant, and still part of the social zeitgeist.

Amy graduated *magna cum laude* from Harvard University where she majored in Portuguese and minored in French. She wrote her thesis about popular, spoken-word poetry in Brazil, which involved traveling throughout Brazil and meeting with poets and writers to collect their stories. She is delighted to have come full circle in her writing career — from collecting poetry "from the people" in Brazil as a twenty-year-old to, three decades later, collecting stories and poems "from the people" for Chicken Soup for the Soul.

Amy has a national syndicated newspaper column and is a frequent radio and TV guest, passing along the real-life lessons and useful tips she has picked up from reading and editing thousands of Chicken Soup for the Soul stories.

She and her husband are the proud parents of four grown children and in her limited spare time, Amy enjoys visiting them, hiking, and reading books that she did not have to edit.

Follow her on Twitter @amynewmark and @chickensoupsoul.